Scarman and After

*Essays reflecting on Lord Scarman's Report,
the riots and their aftermath*

Related Titles of Interest

BOUZA, A. V.
Police Administration: Organization and Performance

FOSTER, C. R.
Comparative Public Policy and Citizen Participation

HOWITT, D.
The Mass Media and Social Problems

MILES, I., and IRVINE, J.
The Poverty of Progress

WHITE FRANKLIN, A.
Family Matters

WIAI
Job Strategies for Urban Youth

Scarman and After

*Essays reflecting on Lord Scarman's Report,
the riots and their aftermath*

Edited by

JOHN BENYON

with an epilogue by
LORD SCARMAN

PERGAMON PRESS

OXFORD · NEW YORK · TORONTO · SYDNEY · PARIS · FRANKFURT

U.K.	Pergamon Press Ltd., Headington Hill Hall, Oxford OX3 0BW, England
U.S.A.	Pergamon Press Inc., Maxwell House, Fairview Park, Elmsford, New York 10523, U.S.A.
CANADA	Pergamon Press Canada Ltd., Suite 104, 150 Consumers Rd., Willowdale, Ontario M2J 1P9, Canada
AUSTRALIA	Pergamon Press (Aust.) Pty. Ltd., P.O. Box 544, Potts Point, N.S.W. 2011, Australia
FRANCE	Pergamon Press SARL, 24 rue des Ecoles, 75240 Paris, Cedex 05, France
FEDERAL REPUBLIC OF GERMANY	Pergamon Press GmbH, Hammerweg 6, D-6242 Kronberg-Taunus, Federal Republic of Germany

First edition 1984

Library of Congress Cataloging in Publication Data

Main entry under title:
Scarman and after.
Papers presented at a conference organized May, 1982 by the Continuing Education Unit, Dept of Adult Education, University of Leicester, with additional new papers.
Bibliography: p.
Includes index.
1. Scarman, Leslie George, Sir, 1911–   —Congresses.
2. Riots—England—London—Congresses. 3. Public relations—England—London—Police—Congresses.
4. Youth, Black—Employment—England—London—Congresses. 5. London (England)—Social policy—Congresses. 6. Brixton (London, England)—Social conditions—Congresses. I. Benyon, J. A. (John A.)
II. University of Leicester. Continuing Education Unit.
HV6485.G7S32   1983   303.6´23´0942165   83-13206

British Library Cataloguing in Publication Data

Scarman and after: essays reflecting on Lord Scarman's Report, the riots and their aftermath.
1. Brixton (London, England)—Riot, 1981 (April)—Congresses 2. London (England)—Riot, 1981 (April)—Congresses
I. Benyon, John
942.1´65   DA685.B8/
ISBN 0-08-030217-3 (Hardcover)
ISBN 0-08-030218-1 (Flexicover)

The essays in this book reflect the views of individual authors and not necessarily those of the organizations with which they are connected, or those of the editor or publisher

Printed and bound in Great Britain by William Clowes Limited, Beccles and London

TO MY MOTHER AND FATHER
LOUIE AND DON BENYON,
WITH LOVE

The use of force alone is temporary. It may subdue for a moment,
but it does not remove the necessity of subduing again.

(EDMUND BURKE, 22 March 1775)

Preface

Although two of the principal functions of the state are the regulation of conflict and the maintenance of order in society, public tranquillity is far from assured. English history reveals many instances of civil tumult of which the most sanguinary, at least during the last two hundred years, were the Gordon Riots. The ferocity of this turmoil in June 1780 is vividly described in Christopher Hibbert's *King Mob* in which he estimates that the riots led to the deaths of not less than 850 people. It is no wonder that the prospect of violent civil discord is greeted with alarm and consternation:

> Civil dissension is a viperous worm
> That gnaws the bowels of the commonwealth.
>
> (W. Shakespeare, *Henry VI*, Part I)

But not all disorders have been viewed with such dread. E. P. Thompson points out, in his seminal work *The Making of the English Working Class*, that many riots have popularly been regarded as just and their leaders viewed as heroes, while others have claimed that dissent and revolt should be welcomed as harbingers of change and reform.

> Disobedience in the eyes of anyone who has read history, is man's original virtue. It is through disobedience that progress has been made, through disobedience and through rebellion.
>
> (O. Wilde, *The Soul of Man under Socialism*)

The 1981 Brixton disorders were not a rebellion in the sense of an organised attempt to overthrow the lawful government, for they were an unpremeditated outburst of anger and resentment against the police in a context of social and economic deprivation (Scarman, 8.11–8.12). And although Lord Scarman stressed that nothing could justify or excuse 'the terrifying lawlessness of the crowds' (Scarman, 4.97), he found that reforms and improvements are necessary.

In April 1982, one year after the Brixton riots, a conference was held at the University of Leicester to consider Lord Scarman's diagnoses and prescriptions. It was organised by the Continuing Education Unit of the University's Department of Adult Education, and during three days twenty-three speakers addressed an audience drawn from the police service, community groups, central and local government, churches, education, pressure groups and the media. Over 260 participants explored the issues from a wide variety of viewpoints during nearly twenty hours of debate.

Many of the essays in this book are based on contributions made at the Leicester Conference, and my thanks are due to all who participated and helped to make the discussions so lively and stimulating. I am especially grateful to the authors of the chapters which follow who, despite the considerable demands on their time, willingly revised and updated their essays.

It is a pleasure to pay tribute to all the members of the Department of Adult Education who took part in the organisation of the conference. I would like to thank particularly my fellow Conference Director Colin Bourn, who is Head of the Continuing Education Unit, the Department's Secretary John Cunningham who unassumingly and dependably shouldered the administrative responsibilities, and the Conference Secretary Beryl Penny who smoothly and efficiently dealt with the avalanche of applications. Without them there would have been no conference and hence no book.

I would also like to express my appreciation for their help and encouragement to colleagues at the University of Leicester and in particular to William Forster, Director and Head of the Department of Adult Education, Professor J. E. Spence, Pro-Vice-Chancellor, and John Day, Head of Politics. The research of government publications was greatly assisted by Mr. A. R. Siddiqui, an Assistant Librarian at the University of Leicester. I would like to thank my friends in the Department of Politics at the University of Warwick for their help, Pauline Maniscalco, my secretary, for her assistance, and Mrs. K. E. Richardson of Pergamon Press. I am especially grateful to Mrs. Cindy George of Pergamon for her advice and helpful comments on the production of this book. I also gratefully acknowledge the financial support of the Commission for Racial Equality, an organisation which deserves more credit and appreciation than it often seems to receive. I would particularly like to thank Lionel Morrison for his help.

My biggest debt is to Jane Hodgkin who produced the transcript of the conference, which was over 430 pages in length, and typed the revised and edited chapters. She also played a large part in the preparation of the index. I am very grateful to her for doing this work so quickly and for managing accurately to interpret the weird hieroglyphics which were sometimes set before her. I benefited greatly from her perceptive comments about the book.

Finally I would like to thank Coleen, Joseph and Danielle for their good humour and forbearance during the last few months; without this I would have sunk without trace, and the book with me.

Leicester   JOHN BENYON

Acknowledgements

The editor and publisher wish to thank the following for permission to reproduce material:

The Times

Daily Mail

Daily Mirror

The Guardian

Daily Telegraph

Daily Express

The Sunday Times

The Observer

The Times Higher Education Supplement

Manchester Evening News

Independent Television News

The Political Quarterly

Lion Publishing PLC for permission to reproduce material from *Weep for the City* by Colin Bedford.

Cambridge University Press for permission to reproduce material from 'The Economic Contradictions of Democracy' by S. Brittan, published in the *British Journal of Political Science*.

The Controller of Her Majesty's Stationery Office for permission to use extracts from *The Brixton Disorders 10–12 April 1981* (Cmnd 8427), The House of Commons Official Report (Hansard) and other publications in Crown copyright.

The Sun was unable to grant permission for copyright material to be used in this book.

Contents

The Contributors

JOHN BENYON is Lecturer in Politics in the Department of Adult Education at the University of Leicester and was previously at the University of Warwick. He was an elected member of Warwick District Council, 1979–1983, and his publications include articles in *Public Administration*, *New Scientist* and *Local Government Studies*.

PAUL BOATENG has been Member for Walthamstow and Chairman of the Police Committee of the Greater London Council since 1981. He is a practising solicitor, a governor of the Police Staff College, Bramshill, and he was Labour Party Parliamentary Candidate for Hertfordshire West in the 1983 election.

JOHN CLARE was appointed the British Broadcasting Corporation's first Community Affairs Correspondent in 1977. Before moving to the BBC, he worked for Independent Television News (ITN), *The Times*, the *Daily Mirror* and *The Observer*.

ALAN GOODSON, OBE, QPM, has been Chief Constable of Leicestershire since 1972 and was President of the Association of Chief Police Officers 1979–1980. After graduating from Kings College, London in 1951 he served for fourteen years in the Metropolitan Police.

GEORGE GREAVES is Principal Community Relations Officer of the Council for Community Relations in Lambeth and is a member of the Community Police Consultative Group for Lambeth which was established in 1982. He gave oral evidence to phase two of Lord Scarman's Inquiry.

BASIL GRIFFITHS was Vice-Chairman of the Police Federation until his retirement in 1982. He was born in Cardiff and completed his thirty years' police service in the South Wales Constabulary; he has now taken up an appointment as full-time Conservative Agent in the Newport West constituency.

GRAHAM MURDOCK is Research Associate in the Centre for Mass Communication Research at the University of Leicester. He has published extensively on the news media and social violence and he co-authored *Demonstrations and Communication* and *Televising Terrorism*.

MICHAEL NALLY is Northern Correspondent of *The Observer*. He is based in his home city of Manchester and has spent most of his life in the North of England. He worked as a reporter and news editor for the BBC and has contributed to a number of publications such as *New Society*.

KENNETH OXFORD, CBE, QPM, is Chief Constable of Merseyside and was President of the Association of Chief Police Officers for England, Wales and Northern Ireland, 1982–1983. He was born in Lambeth and served in the Metropolitan Police for twenty-two years from 1947.

USHA PRASHAR has been Director of the Runnymede Trust since 1977. The Trust aims to contribute to the elimination of all aspects of racism and discrimination and to the promotion of racial justice. She previously worked at the Race Relations Board after graduating from the University of Leeds.

RUSSELL PROFITT is Race Relations Adviser for the London Borough of Brent and has been Labour councillor in Lewisham since 1975. He came to Britain from Guyana at the age of thirteen and was a deputy headmaster before taking up his present post.

THE RT. HON. TIMOTHY RAISON has been Conservative member of Parliament for Aylesbury since 1970. From 1962 to 1968 he was editor of *New Society*, having previously been on the editorial staff of *New Scientist*. He was Minister of State at the Home Office from 1979 to 1983 when he became Minister for Overseas Development. While at the Home Office his responsibilities included immigration and nationality, race relations, human rights and broadcasting.

JOHN REX is Director of the Social Science Research Council Research Unit on Ethnic Relations and visiting Professor at the University of Aston in Birmingham. He was Professor of Sociology at the University of Warwick 1970–1979. His books include (with R. Moore) *Race, Community and Conflict; Race Relations in Sociological Theory; Race, Colonialism and the City;* (with S. Tomlinson) *Colonial Immigrants in a British City; Social Conflict;* (ed.) *Apartheid and Social Research.*

KENNETH ROBERTS is Senior Lecturer in Sociology at the University of Liverpool. The most recent results of his research in the fields of work, leisure and unemployment were published as Research Papers by the Department of Employment: *Unregistered Youth Unemployment and Outreach Careers Work.* His books include *Leisure, From School to Work, The Working Class* and *Youth and Leisure.*

THE RT. HON. LORD SCARMAN, OBE, has been a Lord of Appeal in Ordinary since 1977. He was Chairman of the Law Commission, 1965–1973, and he chaired the Tribunal of Inquiry into the violence and civil disturbances in Northern Ireland in August 1969. He conducted the inquiry into the 1974 Red Lion Square disorders (Cmnd 5919) and three years later he chaired the Court of Inquiry into the Grunwick dispute (Cmnd 6922). His books include *Law Reform: the New Pattern* and *English Law—the New Dimension.*

MARGARET SIMEY is Chairman of the Merseyside Police Authority and serves on both Merseyside County Council and Liverpool City Council. She authored *Charitable Effort in Liverpool in the Nineteenth Century* and, jointly with her late husband Professor T. Simey, *Charles Booth.* A Scot by birth, she has lived for many years in the heart of Granby ward which includes Toxteth.

STAN TAYLOR is Lecturer in Politics at the University of Warwick and was elected to serve as a Conservative councillor in Coventry in 1983. His books include *The National Front in English Politics, Social Science and Revolutions* and *The Politics of Unemployment.*

DEVON THOMAS works in the South Bank Inner City Centre, London which he helped to establish to focus on the employment and economic needs of inner city communities. He has lived in Brixton since his family arrived from Jamaica in the 1950s and he was a prominent figure in the Brixton Defence Campaign which was set up to give support to those who were arrested, and their families, during the events of 1981.

KEN YOUNG is Senior Fellow at the Policy Studies Institute and has taught at the Universities of London, Kent, Bristol and Cambridge. He jointly edited *Policy and Politics* from 1972 to 1978 and his books include *Local Politics and the Rise of Party, Strategy and Conflict in Metropolitan Housing, Policy and Practice in the Multi-racial City* and (co-editor) *Ethnic Pluralism and Public Policy.*

PART 1

The Riots: Reactions and Explanations

CHAPTER 1

The riots, Lord Scarman and the political agenda

JOHN BENYON

Despite the royal wedding and its concomitant national euphoria, 1981 will surely long be remembered as the year of the riots. Civil commotions in Britain, as elsewhere, have of course occurred intermittently over the years, particularly amongst young people, but the 'ferocity' (Scarman, 3.109) of the 1981 disorders seemed to many people to be a new development.

The first riots of the year occurred in London. On 2 March a demonstration by the New Cross Massacre Action Committee was held to protest against the alleged failure of the police to investigate adequately a tragic fire in Deptford. This fire, in January, had caused the deaths of thirteen young black people, and many local residents regarded it as arson. The demonstration numbered some 10,000 and, as the march wound through Fleet Street, violence occurred: 23 arrests were made and 17 police officers were injured. The next day the national newspapers printed stories the like of which were to recur many times during the next five months.

Reactions to the riots

The violence which led to Lord Scarman's inquiry took place during the weekend of 10–12 April, and reactions were swift. The commonest view seems to have been one of shock and bewilderment. As a tense and shaken Home Secretary put it as he surveyed the scene in Brixton on Sunday 12 April: 'how completely and utterly senseless this is'.[1]* Lord Scarman described how 'the British people watched with horror and incredulity' (Scarman, 1.2) the pictures on their television sets, although the *Sunday Telegraph*'s columnist Peregrine Worsthorne claimed that the public's response was rather one of rage and frustration.[2]

---

* Superscript numbers refer to Notes at end of chapters.

Both these reactions were evident in the comments made in the House of Commons.[3] The Home Secretary used the words 'disappointment' and 'sadness', while John Fraser, MP for Norwood, told of his 'regret and shock'. However, the Member for Putney, David Mellor, stated, 'is it not grossly wrong and unfair to talk about social protest? What we should be talking about is sheer criminality.' Mr John Stokes (Halesowen and Stourbridge) concluded that 'riots on this scale have not happened for 200 years. Are not these riots something new and sinister in our long national history?'[4]

The response of a number of opposition MPs was to point to the poor state of police–community relations in Brixton. Roy Hattersley stated that 'the breakdown of the relationship between the police and the public is an undoubted fact' and he called for a fundamental review. One of the two MPs whose constituencies covered Brixton, John Fraser, spoke of 'a deep disaffection about relations with the police' and this factor was developed in media coverage during the following days.

Two other strands of opinion were also apparent. Many Labour MPs tended to see social deprivation as a prime cause of the disturbances, while some other Members considered that they must have been premeditated and organised by subversives. David Alton, MP for Liverpool Edge Hill, asked whether evidence of the involvement of extreme groups had come to light, and Eldon Griffiths suggested that the petrol bombs used by rioters 'must have been manufactured beforehand with malice aforethought'. The Member for Streatham, Mr William Shelton, was more forthright. He asked the Home Secretary whether he was aware

> that evidence is mounting that what sparked off the business on Saturday might have been a planned trap for the police?
>
> . . . Does he realise that the vast majority of the community in Lambeth is sick and fed up with Left-wing agitators taking advantage of the genuine grievances of many youngsters to further their subversive aims?[5]

The conspiracy theory was put forward outside Parliament as well. A number of newspapers proposed it and Sir David McNee, Commissioner of the Metropolitan Police, was quoted on Sunday 12 April as suggesting that outside troublemakers might be behind the events. However, Lord Scarman found that the riots 'originated spontaneously. There was no premeditation or plan' (Scarman, 3.108).

The second major outbreak of rioting began in early July. On 3 July in Southall a pitched battle occurred between hundreds of skinheads and local

Asian people. That same evening disorders began in Liverpool, but whereas the Southall disturbances lasted one night, those in Toxteth continued intermittently until the end of the month. During July violent confrontations also occurred again in Brixton, in Manchester and elsewhere.

The reactions were similar to those in April, with increased attention focused on the relations between the police and local communities. Conservative spokesmen tended to blame criminality, lack of parental control and subversion and sedition. In Parliament, Mr Ian Lloyd (Havant and Waterloo) asked:

> Since ... there is no necessary or convincing correlation between poverty and the rioting ... should we not seek an explanation for those deplorable events in some of the seditious, sociological claptrap that is passed on in our schools as education?[6]

The Prime Minister replied that she very much agreed with her Honourable Friend and she refused to accept that poverty was a cause of the disorders. Indeed Mrs Thatcher's repeated comments during this period seemed to imply that anyone who suggested a cause for the riots was in some way seeking to excuse them. Her view was that nothing 'would condone the violence that took place. One must totally condemn it.'[7] Furthermore, 'it is totally inexcusable and unjustifiable'.[8]

The Streatham MP, Mr William Shelton, again found evidence of subversion: 'the police are victims of a campaign of hatred organised by elements that wish to disrupt our society'.[9] The newspapers took up the conspiracy theory just as they did in April, but seemingly with greater zeal. Ronald Butt, in *The Times*, blamed 'mischief-makers and do-gooders'[10] while the *Daily Mail* went after 'the masked motorcyclists'.[11] Local figures and police chiefs spoke of 'political motivation' and 'agitators' while Mrs Shirley Williams revealed that the Militant Tendency was involved in riot areas.[12]

Labour spokesmen reacted to the July riots by again pointing to deprivation and to police–community relations. The Shadow Home Secretary, Roy Hattersley, 'utterly' condemned the arson, looting and 'mindless violence', but he drew attention to the deprivation which existed.[13] He listed unemployment and particularly escalating youth unemployment, abysmally inadequate housing, unacceptably low levels of social services and decaying central areas. The Government must act to ameliorate 'the despair and disillusion that were a major cause' of the chaos. The Home Secretary though considered that there could not 'be any reason or any excuse for mindless violence in a free society'.[14]

Trade union and church spokesmen tended to stress the importance of social and economic conditions and these views were articulated by some newspapers and on television. The majority of commentators though seemed agreed that Southall was a special case. Both inside and outside Parliament the predominant view was that Asian residents had been provoked by violent skinhead youths and they had responded to a racist threat. The attacks on the police were deplored, but it seemed generally agreed that the response of the Southall residents to the racial attack on their community was understandable.

Criticisms of the police

Only Enoch Powell[15] and certain newspaper journalists seemed prepared to argue that racial tension played a major part in the other disturbances. Most opinion leaders stressed that Brixton, Toxteth and Moss Side were not race riots but confrontations between young people—black *and* white—and the police.

While the Labour front bench tended to concentrate on the social and economic context of the riots, a number of Labour MPs and some Liberals and Social Democrats drew attention to the question of police relations with local people in the riots areas. Robert Kilroy-Silk (Ormskirk) told the House: 'there may be something seriously wrong'[16] with these relations in Toxteth, while the MP for that constituency, Dick Crawshaw, stated:

> I believe that these events came about because, rightly or wrongly, there is a genuine belief not only in the black community but in the white community that in that area the enforcement of law and order is not even-handed.[17]

Outside the House of Commons this appeared to be a widespread explanation of the riots. It was claimed that in Toxteth 'everyone on the streets had a personal grudge against the police',[18] and similar views were put forward about Moss Side.[19] As the Scarman Inquiry held its hearings between 15 June and 10 July 1981 more and more criticisms were made of the police. Indeed the volume of complaints about police behaviour had been growing since the riots in the St Paul's district of Bristol on 2 April 1980. During 1981 the media regularly reported accusations of 'heavy-handed' police activity which appeared to many as at best unpleasant bullying. Opinion polls showed that many people considered police behaviour to be a cause of the disturbances. In one poll, black and Asian people placed this factor second (33 per cent) after unemployment (49 per cent).[20] In another poll while only 13 per cent of white respondents chose police action as the main reason for the Brixton riots, 37 per cent of blacks pinpointed it.[21]

However, a study in the Handsworth–Soho area of Birmingham, where disturbances occurred on 10–12 July 1981, reported different findings.[22] The survey was locally based and included only males between 16 and 34.

Handsworth is noted for being an area which pioneered 'community policing' under Superintendent David Webb,[23] and it is also an area characterised by ethnic diversity and by many of the features of once-prosperous inner city areas.[24] The survey found that racial tension or police harassment were not cited as particular problems. The perceived causes of the local disturbances covered a variety of factors, but unemployment emerged as the most commonly chosen reason (43 per cent). 'Police harassment' was chosen by only 9 per cent: '3 per cent of Asians saw it as a cause, compared to 15 per cent of whites and 14 per cent of West Indians.'[25]

Whether or not these findings in Birmingham were a special case, during 1981 a frequent response to the riots was criticism of the police. Senior members or ex-members of the service tried to deflect the comments; for example, the Chief Constable of Lancashire, Mr Albert Laugharne, spoke against 'simple bashing of police'[26] while the former Metropolitan Commissioner, Sir Robert Mark, complained that the police were being blamed because

> by tradition, by judicial and administrative restriction, they were unlikely to defend themselves effectively or to be able to divert public displeasure to others with a less direct but infinitely greater responsibility.[27]

The Police Federation told Lord Scarman that activists were encouraging young black people 'to believe they are victims of police oppression'.[28]

However, these claims by members of the police service were not furthered when a sensational raid on houses in Railton Road, Brixton took place shortly after the end of the first phase of the Scarman Inquiry. On 15 July some 170 officers broke into eleven houses acting on information received. They were looking for petrol bombs and illegal drinking, but found neither. The next day pictures were seen, in the press and on television, showing wreckage and destruction in the houses. Lord Scarman was shown visiting the scene of the havoc, surrounded by visibly upset residents. Following the outcry which resulted, an inquiry was established under Deputy Assistant Commissioner Dear. In his report, some of which was made public three and a half months later, he exonerated those involved, although it was announced that some compensation would be paid.[29] Formal complaints against the police resulted in the Director of Public Prosecutions deciding to take no action.

Many police officers, politicians and commentators claimed that the police were becoming the scapegoats for the disorders. Other opinion leaders argued that police behaviour was a central factor. Some saw police harassment as a primary cause of the riots: confrontation and provocation had led to the propensity 'to hit back'. Others considered that while police actions triggered off the events in Brixton and Toxteth, the fundamental

causes were social and economic deprivation. These were some of the
arguments presented to Lord Scarman during the summer of 1981.

'The lord they love to laud'

The Scarman Report was published on 25 November 1981 and it
generated an avalanche of reactions. The reception was generally favourable, although to describe it as 'a wave of adulation'[30] seems something of an
exaggeration. The opinions expressed in the national newspapers were
mixed;[31] the *Daily Mirror* called it 'one of the great social documents of our
time', but *The Guardian* considered that Lord Scarman had failed to grasp
'various crucial nettles'. *The Daily Telegraph* typified a number of views; it
called his description of the riots 'brilliant' but was less generous about his
ideas on policing and critical of his opinions on the problems of the
multi-racial inner cities: 'vague liberal sentiments are all very well, but not
likely to be effective when things turn nasty'.

Like most papers, *The Times* devoted considerable space to the Report. In
its leader it called the Report 'commendably judicious' and 'a great help' but
'it could not, and it has not, come up with instructions either for politicians
or for the general public on how to prevent riots'. The *Daily Mail* concluded
that Lord Scarman's description of the events was 'masterly', with 'a
wonderful pace and clarity'. But it criticised his views on positive action and
on police discretion; 'as a text for our tense times, his report is required
reading. As a sermon, it raises as many questions as it answers.'

Also in the *Daily Mail* the paper's legal correspondent, Mr Fenton
Bresler, announced that 'this report is more what one might have expected
from a representative of the National Council for Civil Liberties' and it is
clear that this was not meant as a compliment. He could find just one aspect
for commendation and that was the recommendation for an independent
element in the police complaints system. Another view in the *Mail* was
expressed by Mr Paul Johnson. He considered that perhaps an inquiry
should not have been held at all, and certainly not one by a judge. But 'it was
to be expected that an indecisive Home Secretary like Mr Whitelaw, who
was taken aback by this year's riots—most events appear to come as a
surprise to him—should have turned to a judge, and Lord Scarman in
particular, for help'.

The mixture of reactions was seen again in the Sunday papers on 29
November, although on the whole the Report was applauded. According to
The Sunday Times it was 'masterly . . . lucid and compelling' and it
contained 'the most lethal critique of policing ever made by a judge', while
The Observer thought it was rational, optimistic and pragmatic.

Politicians generally welcomed the Report too.[32] William Whitelaw
spoke of the 'considerable debt' which the country owed Lord Scarman and

in an unusually quick reaction to such an inquiry he accepted many of the recommendations. Roy Hattersley offered Lord Scarman 'the Opposition's deep thanks for the historic work' and declared that the Labour Party willingly accepted all the recommendations. John Fraser (Norwood) commended the 'firm, forthright and specific' proposals and asked whether the Government would act with 'the same vigour and speed', while Edward Gardner, at that time holder of the largest Conservative majority in the country at South Fylde, spoke of the 'wise and useful report' but stressed the importance of the police being 'allowed to maintain law and order in all parts of the country fairly, impartially and, above all, effectively'.

Most politicians seemed to find at least one specific proposal to pick out while commending in general terms the Report. John Tilley (Lambeth, Central) drew attention to local people's 'great affection for and confidence in Lord Scarman' and stated that their expectations had been fully met by his 'radical and balanced report'. The Chichester MP, Anthony Nelson, supported this description and he drew attention to the comments on the role of the media, while David Steel, Liberal Leader, highlighted the proposals to tackle racial disadvantage in this 'outstandingly thorough and extremely important report'.

Outside Parliament the general view was favourable although plenty of criticism could be found. The Chairman of the Commission for Racial Equality, David Lane, called it 'a brilliant analysis',[33] whereas the leader of Lambeth Borough Council, Mr Ted Knight, dismissed it as 'a bitter disappointment' merely 'paying lip service' to racial problems and the police and offering nothing new.[34]

Sir David McNee, Commissioner for the Metropolitan Police, welcomed the Report as fair and thorough and conceded that 'some of the criticisms must be right'. He said:

> My message is that good will is required on both sides. The community have to come towards the police and the police towards the community.[35]

Other police reactions tended to be similarly conciliatory, although with a number of reservations. The President of the Association of Chief Police Officers, Barry Pain, accepted that there had been mistakes in policing, but local and central government needed 'to remove the breeding ground of discontent' in the cities.[36] James Jardine, the Chairman of the Police Federation, accepted the 'historic' report 'completely'[37]—but with many qualifications.[38] The weekly *Police Review* called it a book 'that will change your life',[39] while the December issue of *Police*, the journal of the Police Federation, said that the Report was fair and Lord Scarman's achievements were immense.

The views of members of the black community in Brixton were divided.

Darcus Howe, editor of *Race Today*, said that the report was 'way off beam', for Lord Scarman had failed to realise the need for radical action to correct the gross imbalance of powers between police and the black community. The recommendations were 'mere tinkering'.[40] Courtney Laws, director of the Brixton Neighbourhood Community Association, was more charitable—he called it 'honest, fair and constructive'[41] and he told the *Jamaican Weekly Gleaner* that his decision to co-operate with the Inquiry had been vindicated.[42]

Herman Ouseley, who was Lambeth's principal race relations adviser, said that Lord Scarman's denial of institutional racism meant that the Report was 'fundamentally flawed', but Rene Webb, director of the Melting Pot Foundation, welcomed the 'fair' Report and supported many of its recommendations. George Greaves, Lambeth's principal community relations officer, thought that the Report was a reasonable summary of the problems, but Devon Thomas, for the Brixton Defence Campaign, said the Report avoided the main issues and 'has legitimised the action that the police took'.[43]

For several days after its publication the Report was widely discussed in both local and national media. Despite this extensive coverage an Opinion Research Centre poll showed that among the respondents, 24 per cent of whites, 23 per cent of Afro-Caribbeans and fully 38 per cent of Asians were unaware of the Scarman Report. However, the poll showed 'massive support' among the rest for Scarman's proposals.[44]

Against this background the House of Commons debated the Report on Thursday 10 December.[45] Fulsome praise was heaped on its author, leading Michael White in *The Guardian* to dub him 'the lord they love to laud', although in fact a number of MPs were critical of Lord Scarman and his findings. Mr John Stokes declared that 'many of the conclusions are wrong and dangerous' and in 'a number of public houses' which he visited he had found:

> The report was regarded by people as a typically trendy and liberal viewpoint that took into account all opinions, except those of ordinary English people, who, despite massive brainwashing by some honourable Members and by the media, still cling stubbornly to their deep-felt views and beliefs.[46]

Mr Ivor Stanbrook found the Report 'flawed' on the question of law and order and Mrs Jill Knight had a number of reservations, particularly concerning positive action.

Despite these aberrations, the general consensus was one of approbation. There was much less agreement, though, on the policy implications of Lord Scarman's proposals and on the willingness of the Government to implement them. The Opposition doubted the Government's resolve to put the recommendations into effect, while Home Office Ministers declared their commitment to tackle the problems.

This concern over whether, and how, the Report's recommendations would be implemented has been a recurrent theme since its publication. Certainly some changes have been introduced, often with considerable publicity, but it has been claimed that much of this is 'mere window-dressing'. Indeed, some of the views expressed in this book suggest that while the Scarman Report placed a number of issues on the political agenda, it failed to ensure that action would be taken. The wheels of the government machine usually turn slowly and may grind to a halt altogether unless pressure continues to be applied. The riots and Lord Scarman may have set the machinery in motion, but whether the activity is sustained remains to be seen.

The political agenda

Many of the questions raised by the 1981 urban disorders have been problems for a long period. In our cities there has been a history of complaints about policing matters and deprivation, but scant attention appears to have been paid to them outside the areas affected. Racial disadvantage and racism have also failed to command 'the resolute approach'.[47]

The political agenda is made up of matters which are considered to be in need of attention and action by government.[48] It is clear that there is a limit to the number of issues with which any agenda can cope and although at the level of government a large number of concerns can be handled, factors such as finance, legislative time and politicians' predilections constrain the agenda. Resources are finite while the number of problems is almost unlimited, and proponents of particular problems must compete with others who are seeking to advance different demands.

Issues are problems which are generally recognised as unsatisfactory and in need of improvement. Clearly these may be matters of dispute: when is a problem unsatisfactory; can anything be done about it? How can these improvements be brought about; is the price too high? Is it a problem with which government should properly deal, or should it be left to individuals' actions and the free market? William Solesbury has suggested that there are three separate stages through which a problem must pass if it is to be successfully resolved. First it must command attention, second it must claim legitimacy, and finally it needs to invoke action.[49]

The riots were obviously events which commanded considerable attention. The survey of newspaper coverage shows the extent of this attention, which lasted intermittently from April until the end of the year with the publication of the Scarman Report, and beyond. Television coverage too was extensive and had a considerable impact. The riots were the topic of the year, entailing debates, ministerial statements and questions in Parliament.

However, it was a matter of opinion which issues were raised by the disorders. As the selection of reactions cited earlier shows, opinion leaders interpreted the events differently. For example, while many emphasised the problem of 'insensitive' policing, others stressed the lack of discipline and self-control of the young rioters. Others blamed the problem of unemployment, while many said it was 'sheer criminality'. So while the events themselves commanded attention, there were considerable differences of opinion on the problems which lay behind them. Lord Scarman's Inquiry helped to sort out the gallimaufry of explanations, itemising and clarifying a number of problems in the inner city areas.

There are many ways whereby problems can gain attention and be placed on the political agenda. They may be highlighted in campaigns by political parties, pressure groups, trade unions or employers. The growth of professions means that many areas of public policy have institutions willing to champion alleged wrongs. Other channels may be less visible but more effective, such as civil servants, ministers and other parts of the government machinery.

Access to the political agenda is not equally available to all who seek it. Some groups and individuals have far greater power to place issues on the agenda than others. Indeed it has been argued that certain types of problems and many people are systematically excluded from participation: there is a 'mobilisation of bias' whereby 'some issues are organised into politics while others are organised out'.[50] Many people living in Brixton and Toxteth seem to have been less effective in terms of furthering their interests than, for example, many of those living in Finchley or Penrith.[51] To those with little political power the opportunities to draw attention to wrongs and problems may be very limited. Indeed, Sir David McNee's remarks seem apposite. 'That is what it's all about. Power. Power to dictate. Power to shape lives.'[52]

Legitimising political action

Although political attention is a necessary requirement for problems to reach the political agenda, it is not on its own sufficient to ensure that an issue will be successfully pursued. Problems must be seen as ones with which government can, and should, concern itself and what is or is not a proper matter for public action is likely to be a subject for debate.

The aftermath of the riots included considerable argument over which issues were legitimate ones for government action. As discussed earlier, many of the political reactions were to condemn the disorders as 'sheer criminality'. Viewed in this way, the proper response of society was to deal firmly with those involved and not to capitulate to their demands. Some politicians seemed to believe that even holding the Scarman Inquiry was not a proper response; one view was: 'does not the inquiry itself appear to make the violence worthwhile?'[53]

A similar response was the frequent reference, by politicians, police officers and particularly the press, to 'conspirators' and 'agitators'. The implication appeared to be that problems raised by the rioting were smokescreens for subversion. The Prime Minister's repeated assertions that the disorders were 'inexcusable and unjustifiable' sometimes seemed to imply that since the riots were illegitimate, so too were suggested remedies.

One means whereby nascent issues can be legitimised is through an official inquiry.[54] Public inquiries can focus attention on particular problems and are able to make influential recommendations. Such pronouncements are likely to be seen as authoritative and 'objective' and issues so highlighted are thus successfully legitimised.

Lord Scarman's Inquiry can be seen in this way: his findings and recommendations, while not legally binding, have considerable political and moral force: they *ought* to be put into effect as they are sanctioned by an eminent authority after a lengthy investigation. This was the point of view put forward by the Labour Shadow Home Secretary when he urged the Government to implement the proposals in full. He said that Lord Scarman's repetition of the policy recommendations 'adds a dimension of authority and objectivity that elevates the whole question above the disputes of party politics'.[55]

The final stage through which issues must pass is that of action being taken. Arguably this is the most difficult stage for the proponents of an issue, for it is here that delay and partial responses may occur, resulting in loss of public and political interest. At the time of its establishment many sceptics viewed the Scarman Inquiry in this way, and for good reason.[56] A frequent response to political problems is to set up an inquiry—often a Royal Commission—thereby appearing to investigate the matter seriously, but in fact delaying action until the problem fades away. As Lawrence Marks wrote:

> The scenario was familiar. Both the law-and-order lobby and its liberal critics would be reassured that the outbreak was not being ignored, the politically weak black community would be divided, the media would soon lose interest—and in the autumn there would be a judicious report on race relations in the inner city to place along side all the other judicious reports on the same subject in the Home Office library.[57]

Some might argue that this is broadly what has happened, but it was certainly not possible in November 1981 for the Government to be seen quietly shelving the Report. Possibly this was because rioting recurred in July, keeping the problems in the public eye, or perhaps it was because Lord Scarman won the confidence of many Brixton people and ran his public inquiry in such a way as to encourage interesting and informed public debate. As the reactions to his report show, not everyone, by any means, was pleased with the final outcome, but a number of issues were clarified and identified as in need of political action. This did not though ensure that action would be taken.

Action to tackle political problems can take a number of forms.[58] First, there can be a serious attempt to implement policies to solve the problems. However, the success of such an attempt is likely to depend on accurate problem definition, reliable and comprehensive information and whole-hearted commitment. Many people sincerely believe Mr Whitelaw's commitment 'to see the evils of extremist racialist activity isolated and eliminated'—a pledge reiterated by the ex-Minister of State at the Home Office, Timothy Raison, in this book—but the past and present activities of the Home Office and some other government departments do not seem likely to achieve this, or indeed to realise 'a society in which people are treated according to their merit and as fellow citizens'.[59]

The problems of racial disadvantage and urban deprivation were highlighted by the riots and criticised by Lord Scarman. But over many years policies to improve the position have been characterised by half-heartedness and incrementalism. Political commitment and a full under-standing of the problems are needed if success is to be achieved. To take one example, information on the employment of members of the ethnic minorities is needed if an equal opportunities policy is to be implemented successfully. However, this kind of monitoring has not been practised by most public and private employers. Proper monitoring reveals the type of position found in Liverpool where, in 1981, only 169 local authority employees out of 26,000 were black.[60]

The more one examines policies in the areas of urban deprivation, racism and racial disadvantage, the more clear it becomes that many government policies have been ill-conceived, *ad hoc* and based on partial or inaccurate information, and these criticisms seem appropriate to some policing policies too.

Emasculation, delay and political inaction

A second basis for political action may be a search for agreement. Rather than a serious attempt to solve the perceived problems, this approach is one of consensus seeking, and as such it is likely to involve compromise and cosmetic changes. Policies based on this approach may well involve increased consultation so that at least some critics are satisfied. This kind of action will also usually involve a partial implementation of proposals, in an attempt to avoid more fundamental changes. Some of the ideas in the 1982 Police and Criminal Evidence Bill[61] seemed to be based on an attempt to mollify police interests while incorporating moves towards consultation of local people. Co-optation of 'moderate' critics into parts of the process, it is argued, may lessen the clamour for further, more radical, changes. Similarly, cosmetic changes in the police complaints procedure may diminish the campaign for a wholly independent investigative machinery, as suggested by Lord Scarman (Scarman, 7.18–7.29).

This second approach to action may be motivated by an attempt to reconcile different groups or by a desire to avoid committing additional resources. The responses of a number of governments to the problems of the cities seem to have been based on a strategy of appearing to act while in fact doing little. For example, frequent reference is made to section 11 aid under the Local Government Act, 1966, and to the Inner City Partnership schemes, thus giving the appearance of taking firm action upon which all can agree. But despite this apparent consensus, on examination it becomes clear that the resources involved, substantial in absolute terms, are really relatively small in comparison with the investment which is needed in jobs, housing and infrastructure.

A third approach involves management of the evidence which is used in support of an issue.[62] A redefinition of the basis of statistics may do much to remove a problem 'at a stroke'. Some have suggested that the new basis of collecting unemployment data, introduced by Mr Norman Tebbit in 1982, was an attempt to define away the problem. Others have viewed the Youth Training Scheme introduced in 1983 as a means of removing from political visibility a large number of young unemployed people.[63] Furthermore, it was estimated that measures introduced in the Budget on 16 March 1983 would mean some 100,000 less people registering as unemployed.

As most people are aware, 'there are lies, damned lies, and statistics', and this expression increasingly appears appropriate when applied to data used on the one hand by government spokesmen and, on the other, by advocates of particular causes. Crime statistics can be viewed in this way, for it appears that selective use of these highly dubious figures can justify almost any point of view on law and order policies.

Finally, political action on an issue may involve no action. Besides outright rejection, there are several ways of delaying implementation of recommendations, even if they have been legitimised by an inquiry such as Lord Scarman's. A common strategy is to carry out further investigations, and this has been a frequent ploy of the Home Office. One example is the series of working parties to consider police complaints. One was established in 1971, a review was held in 1974, the position was monitored after the establishment of the Police Complaints Board, a Home Office working party reported in March 1981, and following the riots yet another internal investigation was started.[64]

Another means of delay is for the Government to accept proposals 'in principle', but to plead lack of funds or the need for consultation. This postponement frequently means abandonment or emasculation of the recommendations. As time elapses, the urgency of action is likely to diminish as public interest switches to new concerns. David Owen, the Social Democratic MP, was concerned that the Scarman Report was likely to suffer this fate:

> This country has become more expert than almost any other in suffocating a report and in embracing a report with general praise and generalised endorsement of its philosophy but not following it through with the most detailed implementation.[65]

The riots, Lord Scarman and the political agenda

A study of issues and the political agenda tends to suggest that quite frequently problems invoke only partial responses or delay and procrastination. Pious statements by government ministers, however powerful, do not in themselves result in decisive action. Some issues are resolved, but many appear merely to fade away, perhaps to recur in the future. As Solesbury points out:

> It can be true of government, as of philosophy, that old questions are not answered—they only go out of fashion.[66]

Interest in problems needs to be sustained if they are to pass successfully through the tortuous decision-making processes of government. Even powerful sponsorship, by such as ministers, political parties or peak pressure groups, cannot ensure that committed action will be taken, but this kind of support clearly increases the chance of problem resolution. And if the costs of inaction appear too great and public interest is sustained, through continued debate or a recurrence of dramatic events, the likelihood of serious attempts to cure the problems will be enhanced.

This book is concerned with problems placed on the political agenda by the riots and by Lord Scarman in his report. It seeks to consider the main issues from a variety of viewpoints, and some of the contributors seem to share the fears of Dr Owen quoted above, for they consider that a number of Lord Scarman's prescriptions have been emasculated or abandoned. Others consider that Lord Scarman did not go far enough with his recommendations, while yet others feel that his criticisms were unjustifiably radical.

The book aims to assess lessons which can be learned from the disturbances and what should be done about the problems which were highlighted by the riots and subsequent discussions. It is a contribution to what should be a continuing debate about how urban violence and injustice can be eradicated. The book also tries to evaluate some of the action—or inaction—which has been apparent since Lord Scarman's proposals were published in November 1981.

In the next chapter Stan Taylor considers some explanations which have been offered for collective violence. He distinguishes a number of theories and he relates these to three political approaches. This analysis provides a particularly useful means of evaluating the political perspectives which can be discerned underlying reactions and responses to the riots and other contributions to this book.

The book falls into five parts. Part 1 is intended to set a context for the chapters which follow, and the five contributions in Part 2 consider what happened in the disorders and how they were reported. Part 3 concentrates on the policing issues raised during the riots and highlighted by Lord Scarman. The fourth section is concerned with questions of racial disadvantage, unemployment and deprivation in English cities and the concluding chapters in Part 5 consider some of the responses to Lord Scarman's proposals and recommendations.

In short, these essays reflect on the riots and their aftermath and they seek to assess Lord Scarman's diagnoses and remedies. This is a book about what needs to be done to eradicate the injustices and unequal treatment and the policing problems—the 'basic flaws' (Scarman, 9.4)—in our society.

Notes

1. Quoted by Sir David McNee in the *Sunday Mirror*, 31 October 1982, p. 10.
2. *Sunday Telegraph*, 29 November 1981.
3. William Whitelaw, the Secretary of State for the Home Department, made a statement to the House of Commons on Monday 13 April 1981. The quotations given here are taken from the discussion on this statement. See House of Commons Official Report, Parliamentary Debates (*Hansard*), Vol. 3, No. 87, 13 April 1981, cols. 21–31.
4. It is difficult to agree with Mr Stokes' assessment if one considers British history. Since the infamous Gordon riots of 1780 there have been many serious disorders such as those at Spa Fields and Ely (1816), Bristol (1831) and the Birmingham Bull Ring (1839). The Captain Swing riots of 1830–1 resulted in 505 people being transported and 19 being put to death.
5. *Hansard*, 13 April, col. 24. Mr Shelton later became Under-Secretary of State at the Department of Education and Science.
6. House of Commons Official Report, Parliamentary Debates (*Hansard*), Vol. 8, No. 138, 9 July 1981, col. 575.
7. *Hansard*, Vol. 8, No. 136, 7 July 1981, col. 258.
8. *Hansard*, Vol. 8, No. 138, 9 July 1981, col. 576.
9. *Hansard*, Vol. 8, No. 135, 6 July 1981, col. 27.
10. *The Times*, 9 July 1981.
11. The account of masked motorcyclists being seen in several places where rioting occurred became well known and John Fraser MP (Norwood) referred to them in a speech in the House of Commons:

I have heard stories about the four motorcyclists of the Apocalypse going from place to place throughout the United Kingdom stirring up the riots. Anyone who knows, knows that that is a ludicrous explanation (*Hansard*, 16 July 1981, col. 1245).

But the *Daily Mail* was not to be deflected; in November it was still suggesting that conspirators were behind the riots—white faces 'in the shadows among the rampaging blacks' (*Daily Mail*, 26 November 1981, p. 6).

12. M. Kettle and L. Hodges, *Uprising!*, Pan, 1982, p. 188. See also *The Times*, 11 July 1981.
13. *Hansard*, Vol. 8, No. 135, 6 July 1981, col. 22.
14. *Ibid.*, col. 23.
15. On 13 April the Official Unionist member for Down, South asked the Home Secretary and the Government whether they would bear in mind 'that they have seen nothing yet' (*Hansard*, 13 April 1981, col. 25). After the July riots he appeared on radio and television to draw attention to the racial factor as he saw it. In the House of Commons he intervened during Prime Minister's questions to speak of 'hysterical men, terrified of what is happening' (*Hansard*, 9 July 1981, col. 577). In a speech on 16 July, which was frequently interrupted, Enoch Powell claimed that the causes of the riots were racial tensions, and these would continue to grow unless the size of the black population in British cities stopped increasing (*Hansard*, 16 July 1981, cols. 1413–1419). His views received almost unanimous disapproval.
16. *Hansard*, Vol. 8, No. 135, 6 July 1981, col. 30.
17. *Ibid.*, col. 24.
18. Quotation attributed to the Liverpool 8 Defence Committee in *The Times*, 13 November 1981.
19. See the Hytner Report: *Report of the Moss Side Enquiry to the Leader of the Greater Manchester Council*, 1981.
20. *The Standard*, 11 May 1981. While white respondents also placed unemployment first, they placed blacks' behaviour as the second cause.
21. Reported in *The Times*, 14 May 1981.
22. P. Southgate, 'The disturbances of July 1981 in Handsworth, Birmingham: a survey of the views and experiences of male residents', in *Public Disorder*, Home Office Research Study, No. 72, HMSO, 1982, pp. 41–72.
23. Superintendent David Webb left the police service at the end of 1981 citing disillusionment with colleagues' support for 'community policing'.
24. For a detailed study of Handsworth see J. Rex and S. Tomlinson, *Colonial Immigrants in a British City*, Routledge & Kegan Paul, 1971.
25. P. Southgate, *op. cit.*, p. 50.
26. *Police Review*, 6 November 1981.
27. Sir Robert Mark, 'Police are easy scapegoats', *The Observer*, 12 July 1981, p. 14.
28. *The Times*, 9 July 1981.
29. See *Hansard*, 28 October 1981, cols. 993–1000.
30. M. Kettle and L. Hodges, *op. cit.*, p. 208.
31. For a selection of comments on the Report see the account compiled by Mary Venner: 'What the papers said about Scarman', *New Community*, Vol. ix, No. 3, Winter 1981/Spring 1982, pp. 354–363. Some of the following comments are drawn from this account. The newspaper quotations are from the editions on Thursday 26 November 1981 or Sunday 29 November, unless otherwise indicated.
32. These quotations are from *Hansard*, Vol. 13, No. 16, 25 November 1981, cols. 891–900 unless otherwise stated.
33. Commission for Racial Equality press release, 25 November 1981.
34. Quoted in a number of newspapers on 26 November 1981, e.g. *The Times*, pp. 1 and 5; *Daily Mail*, p. 2.
35. Interview on Thames Television, 25 November 1981.
36. Quoted in *The Times*, 26 November 1981, p. 5.
37. Article in *Police*, December 1981.
38. *Ibid.*, and also see *The Times*, 26 November 1981.
39. *Police Review*, 4 December 1981, editorial.

40. Darcus Howe, 'My fears after this failure', *The Times*, 26 November 1981, p. 14.
41. *Daily Mail*, 26 November 1981, p. 2.
42. *Jamaican Weekly Gleaner*, 2 December 1981.
43. These quotations are from *The Times*, 26 November 1981, p. 5.
44. These interviews were carried out on 27 and 28 November in Brixton and ten other areas using non-probability (quota) sampling; 320 whites and 301 non-whites were interviewed. See Muhammad Anwar, 'Public reaction to the Scarman report', *New Community*, Vol. ix, No. 3, Winter 1981/Spring 1982, pp. 371–373.
45. House of Commons Official Report, Parliamentary Debates (*Hansard*), Vol. 14, No. 27, 10 December 1981, cols. 1001–1080.
46. *Ibid.*, col. 1056.
47. This slogan has been displayed at Conservative Party Conference and is sometimes used by, and to describe, Mrs Thatcher.
48. For discussions of the political agenda see: R. W. Cobb and C. D. Elder, *Participation in American Politics: The Dynamics of Agenda-building*, Allyn & Bacon, 1972; D. A. Schon, *Beyond the Stable State*, Temple Smith, 1971; D. Braybrooke, *Traffic Congestion goes through the Issue Machine*, Routledge & Kegan Paul, 1974; J. J. Richardson and A. G. Jordan, *Governing Under Pressure*, Martin Robertson, 1979.
49. W. Solesbury, 'The environmental agenda', *Public Administration*, Winter 1976, pp. 379–397.
50. E. E. Schattschneider, *The Semi-Sovereign People*, Holt Rinehart & Winston, 1960, p. 71. See also P. Bachrach and M. S. Baratz, *Power and Poverty: Theory and Practice*, Oxford University Press, 1970.
51. Finchley is the Prime Minister's constituency and Penrith and the Border was that of Mr William Whitelaw who was Home Secretary, 1979–1983.
52. 'Sir David McNee's own story', *Sunday Mirror*, 31 October 1982, p. 10.
53. William Benyon MP (Buckingham) speaking in the House of Commons. *Hansard*, 13 April 1981, col. 23.
54. This point is developed further by Solesbury, *op. cit.* See also K. W. Wheare, *Government by Committee*, Oxford University Press, 1955; G. Rhodes, *Committees of Inquiry*, Allen & Unwin, 1975.
55. Roy Hattersley MP in *Hansard*, 25 November 1981, col. 893.
56. 'Many a dusty committee report must be lying on the shelves of Whitehall departments labelled "problem gone away" (or at least "no one of political importance interested in problem")': J. J. Richardson and A. G. Jordan, *Governing Under Pressure*, p. 87.
57. Lawrence Marks, 'Brixton's sideshow became star event', *The Observer*, 13 September 1981.
58. For further discussion of some of these factors see Solesbury, *op. cit.*, and Joan K. Stringer and J. J Richardson, 'Managing the political agenda: problem definition and policy making in Britain', *Parliamentary Affairs*, Vol. xxxiii, No. 1, 1980, pp. 23–39.
59. *Hansard*, 16 July 1981, col. 1407.
60. Mr Roy Hattersley, quoting Mr Anthony Rampton writing in the *Secondary Education Journal*, 1981; *Hansard*, 10 December 1981, col. 1012.
61. The Bill received its second reading in November 1982 and entered Standing Committee where, during the first four months of 1983, many of its provisions were vigorously opposed. Although the Government accepted some amendments the Bill was still viewed as unsatisfactory by a variety of interests and it failed when the general election was called for June 1983. A new bill is expected to be published late in 1983 and the indications are that it too will fail to satisfy many interested parties. Attempts at consensus-seeking often seem to satisfy very few groups indeed.
62. See Stringer and Richardson, *op. cit.*
63. The four-year corporate plan, presented to ministers in March 1983, showed that spending by the Manpower Services Commission would be some £2000 million by 1984–5. £1000 million will be spent on the Youth Training Scheme to provide 460,000 year-long courses for school-leavers; see *The Guardian*, 10 March 1983.
64. Kettle and Hodges, *op. cit.*, pp. 224–226.
65. David Owen MP (Plymouth, Devonport); *Hansard*, 26 November 1981, col. 1021.
66. Solesbury, *op. cit.*, p. 396.

CHAPTER 2

The Scarman Report and explanations of riots

STAN TAYLOR

The explanation of collective violence may be approached from a variety of theoretical and political perspectives involving different appreciations of the causes and nature of such violence and thence of the means of preventing its occurrence in future. The purposes of this chapter are to elicit the explanation of violence contained in the Scarman Report on the disorders in Brixton on 10–12 April 1981, to locate this and the recommendations stemming from it within the general corpus of perspectives on collective violence, and to suggest some of the grounds upon which the Report might be criticised on the basis of the exclusion of alternative explanations of disorders. The chapter is divided into five parts. In the first, the major theoretical approaches to the study of violence utilised by social scientists are summarised briefly. Secondly, these are related to what are described as conservative, liberal and radical perspectives on collective violence. The third part is devoted to an exposition of Lord Scarman's explanation, and in the fourth section this is typologised in terms of the preceding discussion of theories and perspectives on violence. In the final section various criticisms which can be made from theoretical and political standpoints other than that adopted by Scarman are set out.

Some theoretical approaches to the explanation of riots

The most useful way of ordering the numerous theories of rioting is to consider them as far as possible within the framework of the particular social science from which they are derived, and, in some cases, the sub-disciplinary approaches deployed.[1]* On this basis it is possible to outline two types of sociological approaches, two sociopsychological kinds of

---

* Superscript numbers refer to Notes at end of chapter.

theories, an economic or rational choice approach, several variants of political theories, and another category of explanations relating to the temporal and spatial effects of initial riots upon the chances of later riots.

The first group of theories comprise those which are *sociological* in character, i.e. stress the importance of the dynamics of social relations, social institutions and social systems as causes of riots. Such theories diverge according to whether they are predicated upon a functionalist or a conflictual conceptual framework.[2] The former perspective embodies a notion of society as a set of individuals and groups held together by a moral consensus as to the appropriate social, economic and political values governing the social order. In order for society to survive, this consensus has to be maintained by a social system which will adapt to new demands, achieve goals, socialise new members of society into prevailing values and norms and exercise social control.

On occasion, social systems fail to fulfill these functions adequately, and existing modes of social interaction are perceived by individuals and groups within society as inappropriate given their particular situation. Smelser[3] has used this framework to analyse the causes of riots (which came under his category of 'hostile outbursts'). Riots were a consequence of the malfunctioning of the social system, of its inability to adapt to new demands, coupled with the growth of generalised beliefs which provided an account of why the system had failed and offered a new basis for reconstituted social action. These factors yielded a *potential* for collective violence: this became *actual* violence following the occurrence of a *precipitator*, some development which put discontent into a specific, and reinforcing, context, leading to a build-up of fear and antagonism which was eventually expressed in rioting.

A similar account has been produced by Johnson,[4] although he stressed the role of coercion in inducing dissensus. The failure of a social system was, he suggested, initially followed by the sustaining of authority by coercion. If this continued over a long period, the regime became delegitimised as it was seen to depend upon organised violence as distinct from consent. A 'power deflation' of this kind created a potential for violence; this was, however, only realised following the occurrence of an 'accelerator event', an event which provided an immediate and proximate focus for discontent, and sparked off violence.

Both of these theorists regarded the malfunctioning of the social system as a temporary phenomenon: riots and the like were mere hiccups which took place when social systems were unable to adjust immediately to new demands, and collective violence invariably diminished as social systems were stimulated by that violence to change the institutional structures of society. This approach to violence was used by a number of American social scientists who attempted to account for the Black Riots of the 1960s, most notably Lieberson and Silverman,[5] White[6] and Downes,[7] all of whom suggested that variations in the responsiveness of local social systems to demands from blacks account for differential patterns of rioting between cities. They found that differences in the openness of municipal political structures to black demands were positively correlated with rioting, although it should be noted that this interpretation has been strongly contested, notably by Spilerman.[8]

The other sociological approach is through the medium of a conflictual model of society. In this, society is seen not as an entity cemented by moral agreement and a stability-functioning social system, but as an arena within which dominant and subordinate groups compete for wealth, status and power. One variant of this is of course associated with Marxism, with society conceived in terms of struggles betweeen classes defined by their relationship to the means of production which ultimately lead to successful revolution by the proletariat. This perspective, which Tilly[9] at least occasionally seems to espouse, suggests that riots must be seen as the early conflicts by which a nascent proletariat begins to lash out against capitalist exploitation. It is, of course, problematical to apply these theories straightforwardly to cases involving race riots (in that these exhibit racial rather than class characteristics), but this can be variously overcome by redefining rioters as a 'class fraction',[10] as a class exploited by 'internal colonialism',[11] or, more dubiously in Marxist terms, as an 'underclass'.[12]

Another approach within the conflictual mould is to retain an emphasis upon groups as structurally-defined entities, but to regard the range of such entities as extending beyond classes defined in conventional Marxist terms to include other types of groups such as race groups. In this context, races take the place of classes, and phenomena such as riots are held to instances of protest by exploited races which herald racial revolution. Such a model was, of course, apparent in at least the rhetoric of Black Power[13] in the United States. The third variant within this framework abandoned the notion that groups were structurally determined, but retained the idea that society can be seen in terms of groups with competing interests. Thus classes (defined in terms of life-chances rather than by relation to the means of production), religious or ethnic groups compete within the political system for available resources, and some groups win while others lose. In this case, riots and like phenomena can be described as the protests of consistent losers anxious to obtain some redistribution of resources in their favour. This latter perspective was apparent in a number of studies of the race riots in the United States, including some of those which found their way into the *Report of the National Advisory Commission on Civil Disorders*.[14]

The second cluster of theories are those which are sociopsychological, which seek to explain riots as individual behaviours determined by particular psychological processes. Some theorists base their accounts in cognitive psychology, in particular Festinger's[15] theory of cognitive dissonance. This started from the assertion that all individuals have cognitive systems which comprise their knowledge, opinions and beliefs about themselves, the environment and behaviour. Where the various components of cognitive systems are consistent with each other, individuals are in a state of cognitive consonance, which is one of relative psychological harmony: where inconsistencies arise, individuals move to a state of cognitive dissonance, which is psychologically disturbing, and which motivates behaviour designed to reduce dissonance and alleviate psychic tension.

Theorists such as Eckstein,[16] Geschwender[17] and Schwartz[18] have used this theory to explain collective violence. They argue variously that, if the performance of economic, political or social systems falls short of expectations, this stimulates dissonance between normative and reality-based cognitions: individuals thus experience tension, and are motivated to alleviate this by adopting behaviours designed to realign appropriate cognitions, behaviours which could include rioting.

The second strand of sociopsychological theorising over riots stems from a different tradition within psychology, that associated with the frustration-aggression model of behaviour pioneered by Dollard *et al.*[19] The contention here is that individuals who are prevented from achieving their goals become frustrated, and sustained frustration leads to psychological tension which is automatically transmuted into aggression and thence violence. Davies,[20] Gurr[21] and Bwy[22] have all advanced models of riots in which individuals are held to be frustrated because of past, present, or expected relative deprivation; such frustration is changed into aggression, and individual catharsis is achieved through participation in riotous violence. It may be noted that both of these sociopsychological explanations of rioting involve a notion of individuals acting non-rationally, as being spurred towards violence by unconscious, and uncontrollable, mental processes.

The 'economic' models of rioting suggest the precise opposite—that riot behaviour can be analysed in terms of individuals making rational choices between courses of action upon the basis of maximising the net differential between gains and costs. Ireland,[23] Tullock[24] and Silver[25] have approached collective violence by making the usual assumptions necessary to apply rational choice theories (that individuals can always make decisions between alternatives, have known and transitive preferences, always act so as to maximise the achievement of the most preferred outcome, and faced with the same alternatives will always make the same choice) and then constructing equations specifying the costs and benefits of particular courses of action (rioting, not doing anything, helping the police). The components of equations include the private benefits flowing from alternatives (for example from looting), the entertainment value of courses of action, the chances of incurring costs (being caught) and the costs which could be imposed (fines, suspended sentences, jail sentences of varying lengths). On these models, rioters are individuals who have decided rationally that the profits of looting and the 'fun value' of rioting are worthwhile given the balance of risks and penalties. While very little research has been undertaken on this interpretation of rioting, it is perhaps worth noting that Aldrich,[26] who examined patterns of riot damage to shops in American cities, found that such damage was not randomly distributed (as might be expected from angry men lashing out) but that targets had been carefully selected with a view, among other things, towards stealing the most expensive portable goods available.

A fourth set of theories stress a variety of political variables which can explain rioting. The first and most simple of these is that riots and like phenomena are engineered by extremist political groups who wish to encourage violent confrontations for nefarious purposes varying from mobilising support to promoting repression in the hope of destabilising the political system. A second political variant relates to the adequacy of the institutions of the political system in dealing with the issues presented to it. The economic or social environment may change rapidly: but, as Huntington[27] has noted, political institutions take time to adapt and incorporate new groups or channel resources towards them. Riots in this sense may be seen as a response to the failure of institutions to manage new conflicts, as a reflection of bureaucratic inertia in the face of external changes.

The third political theory has some similarities to this, although the non-incorporation of new demands in the political system is seen as a matter of choice rather than the inherent difficulties of inducing institutional change. Bachrach and Baratz[28] have argued that there are 'two faces' of power, one relating to the ability to determine the outcome of conflict on issues accepted as legitimate within the political system, the other the ability to keep particular demands outside the system, i.e. refuse to allow them on to the political agenda. They suggest that political élites may mobilise bias to make non-decisions, decisions not to let particular demands become an accepted part of the policy process. For any group thus excluded, riots offer a way of forcing demands into the political system, of accomplishing by violence what they see themselves as unable to achieve by more conventional means. In this sense, Bachrach and Baratz suggest that riots are the ballot box of the poor, and they present a case study to show how their analysis could explain riots in the United States, in particular those in Baltimore.

The final political model is concerned with political repression as a cause of riots. Gurr,[29] Bwy[30] and Russell[31] have all argued that, over the shorter term, there is a positive relationship between the level of repression or coercion used by regimes and counterviolence by mass populations, the latter increasing with the former. In the longer term, coercion builds up to a level at which continued collective violence becomes so costly that it begins to diminish, and, in a totally repressive society, may almost disappear. With respect to riots, Gurr's detailed empirical study suggested that there was a strong relationship between the occurrence of riots and the adoption by regimes of increased coercion.

Finally, there is a group of theories which cannot be classified under the previous headings which suggest that riots may be caused by other riots in three ways. Firstly, there may be a *geographical* contagion in so far as a riot in one city, or one part of a city, may become known locally, and stimulate riots in neighbouring areas. This was one of the central effects identified by the American National Advisory Commission on Civil Disorders.[32] Secondly, there may be *media* contagion whereby the publicity given nationally to a riot provides a cue for 'copycat' riots in other, geographically remote, cities. Thirdly, it has been suggested that riots will be more likely where there is a *tradition* of rioting which either sanctifies such behaviour as normal or minimally provides some positive reinforcement for riot behaviour. It may be noted that these possibilities were exhaustively investigated for the Black riots in the United States by Spilerman,[33] but he found that the temporal and spatial patterns of those riots were inconsistent with the patterns projected on the basis of the contagion/riot tradition hypothesis.

This completes the brief survey of social scientific theories of rioting. It should be stated that this is not intended to be comprehensive, and, for example, neither normative political theories of rioting[34] nor anthropological[35] or ecological[36] accounts have been considered. These omissions are not, in the author's opinion, critical, as these theories are generally considered to be peripheral to the main social scientific models outlined.

Political perspectives on the explanation of riots

These theories stand as genuine attempts to explain riots; but, as Button[37] has argued, they may also be regarded as supportive of, or associated with, various political perspectives on riots, with conservative, liberal or radical interpretations of this phenomenon. The conservative view starts from the presumption that, in modern democracies, existing institutions are adequate to advance the interests of deprived groups within society. Electoral systems provide opportunities for the expression of discontent through the ballot box, and policy-making is regarded as pluralist in character, i.e. the decision-making process is accessible to groups within society who can always mobilise political resources to further their interests and block policies counter to those interests. Given this, collective violence is unnecessary to achieve group goals, and must reflect other factors. Individuals who indulge in violence are the unwitting dupes of power-hungry extremists (as implied by the political conspiracy theory of rioting), or motivated by personal gain (as in the economic theories) or find rioting entertaining (again as specified in the economic theories), or are acting on uncontrollable and irrational psychological impulses (as suggested by the sociopsychological explanations of collective violence) or are merely imitating the behaviour of others (as noted in the media contagion, geographical contagion, and traditions of rioting theories). The prescription for violence viewed in these terms is a combination of (1) better intelligence to combat extremist groups, (2) improved policing and more severe sentencing to penalise looting to the extent that it becomes unprofitable, (3) the inculcation of moral values embodying a respect for property, the law and the police: values which will counteract any tendency towards irrationality, (4) the adoption of police tactics to ensure that individuals at some psychological snapping point do not have the opportunity to coalesce as a maddened mob, and (5) self-restraint by the media to minimise the exposure given to riots and thence the chances of inducing imitative behaviour. To the conservative, riots are instances of manipulated, morally degenerate and irrational mass behaviour: they are to be avoided by effective policing, moral regeneration, and the exercise of responsibility by the media.

The liberal view of collective violence is predicated upon the assumption that, while the social and political arrangements of societies usually provide for the incorporation of deprived groups and their interests, this is not axiomatic and there are certain circumstances in which some groups remain unrepresented in the power hierarchies of a particular country. This may be because social and political institutions have failed to adapt homeostatically to the demands of new groups (as in the functionalist or 'institutional lag' theories) or because dominant groups have proved unwilling to allow subordinate ones a fair share of resources (as implied in the non-structural variant of the conflictual theories) or because political élites have refused to consider groups' interests (as in the 'non-decision' model of the exclusion of particular interests from the pluralist bargaining process). Given this, the answer to collective violence lies, on the one hand, in reforming social and political institutions so as to enable group interests to be adequately represented, and on the other, in securing some shift of resources towards deprived groups. To the liberal, the sources of riots lie in societal institutions or social injustice and the solution to them is reform and redistribution.

The third perspective on collective violence is the radical view. This presumes that societies are organised and structured so as to sustain a dominant class (as in Marxist theories) or other groups (as in the second conflictual model) and to enable it to effectively exploit other groups and secure its control over them. Riots, on this view, are a form of collective action by the exploited in pursuit of their group interests. While they may be defused initially by increased coercion, reforms or concessions, these are ultimately meaningless in so far as they fail to relate to the causes of violence which are embodied in the basic economic, social and political structures of society itself. The only solution to riots and like phenomena is the fundamental transformation of society to create a new society in which exploitation and inequalities are abolished. Thus the radical sees the causes of collective violence in terms of macrostructures of power, wealth and status, and believes that only successful revolution can create a society from which violence will vanish.

The Scarman Report

In order to locate the Scarman Report within the matrix of theories of and political perspectives on collective violence identified in the previous sections, it is necessary to consider Scarman's causal analysis. Scarman made a distinction between those factors which had, over the longer term, contributed to a high *potential* for collective violence in Brixton, and a shorter-term precipitant which translated potential into actuality. Four major factors and one minor one were held to be responsible for creating a general potential for violence. Firstly, the population of Brixton was disproportionately composed of deprived and vulnerable sections of the population as a whole—the very young, the very old, clerical, semi-skilled and unskilled manual workers, one-parent families, low-income households, the mentally ill and the handicapped (Scarman, 2.13). This was, in large measure, a reflection of the second factor, that Brixton was an inner city area at an advanced stage of economic and social decay, with consequent high unemployment, an impoverished and depressing environment, major housing stress, and an absence of facilities for leisure and recreation (Scarman, 2.1–2.11). These sources of deprivation were compounded among the large ethnic minority—mainly West Indian—communities of Brixton by the third factor of racial problems, in particular the difficulties of adjusting to the British way of life, the impact of British social conditions upon traditional structures of community life, educational under-achievement by minorities, very high rates of unemployment among them, especially the young, and the alleged root cause of these and many other difficulties, racial discrimination. Scarman summarised the position of the ethnic minorities in that:

> ... overall they suffer from the same deprivation as the 'host community' (i.e. the white population), but much more acutely. Their lives are led largely in the poorer and more deprived areas of our great cities. Unemployment and poor housing bear upon them very heavily: and the educational system has not adjusted itself satisfactorily to their needs. Their difficulties have been intensified by the sense they have of

a concealed discrimination against them, particularly in relation to job opportunities and housing. Some young blacks are driven by their despair into feeling that they are rejected by the society of which they rightly believe they are members and in which they would wish to enjoy the same opportunities and to accept the same risks as everyone else. But their experience leads them to believe that their opportunities are less and their risks are greater. Young black people feel neither socially nor economically secure (Scarman, 2.35).

Scarman described how young blacks, without close parental support, unemployed and with few recreational facilities, made their lives on the streets and in the seedy clubs of Brixton, and in some cases drifted into a life of crime. This brings in the fourth major factor identified by Scarman, crime and community–police relations. He outlined a policing dilemma in Lambeth stemming from, on the one hand, the duty of the police to prevent and detect crime, and on the other, the need to create and sustain good relations with the ethnic minorities. There was nothing inherently contradictory in these objectives. However, the police, in their efforts to maintain law and order, in an area with a high incidence of crime, had created the suspicion among the ethnic minority communities that their actions were dictated less by the impartial enforcement of law than by racial prejudice. Scarman traced the process by which, over a period of years, successive police attempts to combat crime had undermined their standing among the ethnic minorities and eventually resulted in a lack of confidence in the police force in Brixton (Scarman, 4.1–4.46). In addition to these major causes of a potential for violence, Scarman also briefly mentioned a fifth factor, that of feelings of political insecurity and rejection among the ethnic minorities, this being caused variously by the absence of black representation in elective political institutions and the fact that the law allowed extremist right-wing groups to march and demonstrate in favour of tougher immigration controls and the repatriation of blacks (Scarman, 2.36).

Thus a combination of a high incidence of deprived groups in the population, the difficulties of living in the inner cities, the economic, social and political disadvantages of the ethnic minorities, and the latter's complete loss of confidence in the police, were held to have created a sense of grievance among the inhabitants of Brixton which constituted a *potential* for collective violence. Scarman regarded 'Operation Swamp'—the operation which began on 6 April 1981, to enforce law and order by a massive and visible police presence—as the accelerator event which triggered *actual* political violence. Following this, any relatively trivial incident could have occasioned a riot. In fact, that incident happened on Friday 10 April, when police attempts to help an injured black youth were misinterpreted, conflict developed, police reinforcements were called in, and blacks began to defend themselves. Scarman described this as 'a spontaneous act of defiant aggression by young men who felt themselves hunted by a hostile police force' (Scarman, 3.25), and this initial confrontation quickly escalated into a riot. On the following day, a similar incident involving the police, trivial in itself, sparked off a second wave of rioting, the basic raw material of which, Scarman claimed, was 'the spirit of angry young men' (Scarman, 3.78). However, this source of riot behaviour was complemented by three others. The rioting on Friday had apparently indicated that there was some 'fun value' in rioting, and young blacks 'found a ferocious delight in arson, criminal damage to property, and in violent attacks upon the police, the fire brigade and the ambulance service' (Scarman, 3.109). Additionally, looting started, and there were a number of attacks upon retail and commercial premises and public houses from which goods were stolen. Scarman noted that some of the witnesses had charged that the looters were from outside Brixton and 'were simply taking advantage of the disorders for their own criminal purposes' (Scarman, 3.61). Presumably it could have been criminals who provided the measure of organisation identified in the Saturday riot, including the setting up of a 'factory' for petrol bombs: alternatively, extremist groups might have been using the riots to further their own ends. The third day of rioting was the Sunday. The riot was, as on the previous days, started by a minor incident in which the police were involved: this riot, however, was held to lack the intensity of social and political protest manifest earlier, and 'outsiders, some no doubt attracted by media coverage of Saturday's events, were more in evidence: there was more systematic and opportunistic looting' (Scarman, 3.92). The Sunday riot was the last of this wave of riots in Brixton, although there were further minor disturbances on Monday 13 April.

This, then, was Scarman's causal analysis of the riots, and this explanation was accompanied in his Report by various recommendations. These were, briefly (1) the adoption of a more effective coordinated approach to tackling the problems of the inner cities, (2) the adoption of a policy of positive discrimination, particularly in education and employment, to combat racial discrimination among ethnic minorities and lessen racial disadvantage, (3) reform of the police force and the introduction of new methods of policing, including better tactics and equipment for handling riots, and (4) various changes in the laws relating to powers of arrest, police complaint procedures and political demonstrations.

Discussion

It is clear that the Scarman Report embodied several of the approaches to the explanation of collective violence set out in the first part of this paper. He specified the longer-term causes of the Brixton riots variously in terms of a functionalist-type model (systems, particularly the educational system, failing to adapt to new demands), a non-structuralist conflictual approach (loser groups including the deprived, the deprived in the inner city, and the ethnic minority-deprived in the inner cities attempting to gain resources), a coercion approach (ethnic minorities threatened by allegedly racist policing), and a political exclusion model (blacks felt that they had been systematically ignored by a political system within which they were not represented).

The precipitant of violence was identified as a dramatic increase in police visibility, the actual trigger incidents involving the police. The Friday riots were held to be a spontaneous expression of group grievances, but Scarman identified economic components in the Saturday and more particularly the Sunday riots (people motivated by the desire to have fun/reap profits) as well as political conspiracy; additionally, he suggested a media contagion effect. It is evident from the discussion in the second part of this paper that this analysis involved components of both the liberal perspective on collective violence (an attempt to achieve social justice by a deprived group) and the conservative one (people rioted at the behest of extremists or criminals, or to imitate others, or for fun or personal gain). This same duality of approaches was apparent in Scarman's recommendations. On the one hand, he enjoined media caution in publicising riots and advocated new tactics and equipment for the police in order that they could control riots more quickly and effectively, two recommendations which would seem to reflect a conservative perspective on violence; on the other, he suggested reforming institutions (the police, the political institutions involved in the making and implementation of inner city policy) and tilting the balance of resources towards deprived groups (positive discrimination), solutions to riots normally associated with the liberal perspective on collective violence.

This would seem to imply that, if Scarman is to be criticised, criticisms could come from three directions—the 'pure' liberal perspective, the 'pure' conservative perspective, and the radical approach to collective violence. The liberal would attack Scarman in so far as his Report deviated from a stress upon riots as the product of economic, social and political deprivation. He would argue that the conspiracy allegations made were ill-founded, and provided too convenient an explanation for those who did not wish to tackle the basic social and economic problems which had given rise to the riots in the first place. The liberal would suggest that the 'fun' and 'profit' motives for rioting could not be considered independently of the social setting in which the riots took place: if people had to find their enjoyment by this means, it was an indictment of a system which did not provide adequate alternatives, and looting had to be seen against the background of an intensely deprived group living in a highly materialistic society (which, in fairness, Scarman did mention in paragraph 2.23 of his report). Given this, the liberal would suggest that Scarman's recommendations should have related more strongly to causes of riots lying within society, and should perhaps have gone rather further in calling upon policy-makers to make an immediate, and substantial, contribution to the alleviation of the problems of the inner cities and of racial disadvantage. The liberal would regard the recommendations concerning the strengthening of the police capacity to handle riots as at worst irrelevant—they in no way related to the causes of the collective violence—and at best provocative in so far as increased potential coercion was likely to further increase the insecurities of the ethnic minorities and, if anything, stimulate violence. The liberal would limit the reforming of the police to proposals designed to change police practices in order that they might relate more fully to the needs of a multi-racial society, and would, for example, stress the recruitment of black officers or the screening of recruits to weed out those with racist dispositions.

The conservative would start from the perspective that, no matter how deprived people felt, there were institutions—the electoral system, parties, pressure groups, bodies such as the Commission for Racial Equality—through which demands could be expressed non-violently. Given the availability of these channels, the conservative would argue that, if the rioters' behaviour were in some sense related to deprivation, they represented the outcome of irrational psychological forces, or, alternatively, that they were not related to deprivation at least as strongly as Scarman seems to suggest, but were determined by other motivations. This latter point might be held to be supported by the contention that Scarman's analysis of the longer-term causes of riots was inconsistent with the overall pattern of riots in England in 1981. Scarman himself had noted that 'some of the disorders occurred in areas which could not be described as seriously deprived' (Scarman, 2.24), which does not suggest that deprivation was a necessary condition for riots to take place. Further, with respect to the element of racial disadvantage, the conservative would note that it was not the case that rioting was always undertaken by the ethnic minorities: in particular, the large-scale riots in Liverpool seemed to involve young whites to a considerably greater extent than young blacks.

The conservative would be unwilling to accept that repressive policing was a factor motivating the riots. After all, these had occurred in the West Midlands, where Scarman had found that 'the relationship between the police and the local community seems generally, although not universally, to be more favourable (than elsewhere)' (Scarman, 2.30). Thus the conservative would suggest that the evidence for the social conditions/police repression long-term causes was open to question. He would stress, alternatively, that the most salient general characteristics of the riots were that they involved the young (black or white) in Brixton or in other cities, and that sections of this generation were morally degenerate compared to previous ones, reflecting variously the decline of religion, the break-up of the traditional family, the encouragement provided by the welfare state to look for rewards without work. In this sense, the riots were merely an outburst of immoral behaviour, the manifestation of a warped sense of 'fun' and of greed for consumer goods. In addition to irrationality and immorality, the conservative might argue that Scarman did not give enough weight to the role of criminal or political conspiracies in starting or sustaining the riots. With regard to political conspiracy, the conservative could point to the evidence of a build-up of left-wing activities in Brixton prior to the riots,[38] or, for example, the unusually high numerical strength of the extreme left in Liverpool.

On the basis of this overall analysis, the conservative might reject Scarman's social and economic recommendations: these did not get to the roots of irrational or immoral behaviour, in fact they could encourage rioting by providing rewards for it. The conservative would also dispute the recommendations for changing police practice towards a multi-racial society on the same grounds: these would not only reinforce perceptions that the police were 'soft', but, by restricting their ability to enforce law and order, give a further licence to crime in areas where the streets were already unsafe to walk by day or night. The conservative solution would be moral regeneration—in particular action by parents to inculcate respect for property, law, order and the police—coupled with improving the ability of the police to detect crime and to prevent the coalescing of irrational mobs in riots as well as the imposition of stiffer penalties to deter rioting for fun or for profit.

The final critic would be the radical, whose perspective was not embodied in the Report. He, if he were of the Marxist variety, would argue that Scarman completely failed to take account of the macrostructural framework of the riots, that of the role of blacks in British capitalism at a particular stage of its decline. Blacks had, in the 1950s, been brought to Britain as cheap labour to fill jobs which the indigenous working class were not prepared to take. When, in the 1960s, British capitalism began to be subject to economic decline, the monopoly capitalist class had accorded the blacks two other roles, one as the scapegoat for decline (attributed to too many immigrants rather than capitalist overexploitation), the other as an instrument to divide the working class (providing a focus for them to identify as white and British rather than simply proletarians). Thus blacks were exploited and deliberately subjected to racial discrimination and racial disadvantage in order to sustain British capitalism. Given this, it is not surprising that they protested by rioting. The radical would see no possible solution to this within the capitalist system: it will only be when black and white workers realise their common interests in overthrowing capitalism and fundamentally transforming British society that the root cause of rioting—exploitation—will be abolished.

The non-Marxist radical would make a similar argument, except that he would suggest that the structures of society are organised to maintain whites as the dominant group exploiting blacks, but he too would see revolution as the only basis of achieving equality and thence avoiding riots and like instances of collective violence. Given this, the non-Marxist radical would view the Scarman Report as irrelevant, and suggest that if anything, it ought to be considered as a trick by which the dominant class/whites seek to suggest that solutions are possible within the existing framework of society and thence deflect the further mobilisation of proletarian or black revolutionary consciousness.

Conclusion

This chapter has attempted to set the Scarman Report in the context of both general theories of collective violence and political perspectives upon such violence and how it may be avoided in future. It was argued that the Scarman Report embodied a variety of theories, and, in political terms, combined both the liberal and the conservative perspectives on violence. Some indications of possible lines of criticisms were discussed, these stemming from the 'pure' liberal and conservative views of violence, as well as the radical approach. It may be noted that, while the final set of radical criticisms seems unlikely to be amenable to empirical analysis, both the liberal and conservative critiques are predicated upon interpretations which are open to dispute on factual grounds, and it is hoped that the reader will find some basis for choosing between them in the material presented in the remainder of this book.

Notes

1. See S. Taylor, *Social Science and Revolutions*, Macmillan, 1983.
2. This distinction is perhaps most clearly explained in S. M. Lipset, *Revolution and Counter-Revolution*, Heinemann, 1971, pp. 121–158.
3. N. Smelser, *Theory of Collective Behaviour*, Routledge, 1962.
4. C. Johnson, *Revolutionary Change*, University of London Press, 1968.
5. S. Lieberson and A. Silverman, 'The precipitants and underlying conditions of race riots', *American Sociological Review*, **80**, 1965.
6. J. White, 'Riots and theory-building', in L. Masotti and D. Bowen (Eds.), *Riots and Rebellion*, Sage, 1968, pp 157–168.
7. B. Downes, 'Social and political characteristics of riot cities: a comparative study', *Social Science Quarterly*, **49**, 1968, pp. 504–520.
8. S. Spilerman, 'The causes of racial disturbances: a comparison of alternative explanations', *American Sociological Review*, **35**, 1970, pp. 627–649.

9. C. Tilly and L. Tilly (Eds.), *Class and Collective Violence*, Sage, 1981, but see C. Tilly, *From Mobilization to Revolution*, Addison-Wesley, 1978, where this is combined with a political perspective.
10. See A. Phizacklea and R. Miles, *Labour and Racism*, Routledge, 1980.
11. The classic statement of this position is R. Blauner, 'Internal colonialism and ghetto revolt', *Social Problems*, **16**, 1969, pp. 393–408.
12. See J. Rex, 'Black militancy and class conflict', in R. Miles and A. Phizacklea (Eds.), *Racism and Political Action*, Routledge, 1979, pp. 73–92, and J. Rex and S. Tomlinson, *Colonial Immigrants in a British City*, Routledge, 1979, pp. 275–295.
13. Although there is a debate as to how far the Black Power analysis was based in a structuralist or a pluralist appreciation of the problems of blacks in America.
14. *Report of the National Advisory Commission on Civil Disorders*, Bantam Books, 1968, particularly pp. 136–137.
15. L. Festinger, *The Theory of Cognitive Dissonance*, Stanford University Press, 1978.
16. H. Eckstein, 'On the etiology of internal wars', *History and Theory*, **4**, 1965, pp. 133–163.
17. J. Geschwender, 'Explorations in the theory of revolutions and social movements', *Social Forces*, **42**, 1968, pp. 127–135.
18. D. Schwartz, 'A theory of revolutionary behaviour', in J. Davies (ed.), *When Men Revolt and Why*, Free Press, 1971, pp. 109–132.
19. J. Dollard, L. Doob, N. Miller, O. Mowrer and D. Sears, *Frustration and Aggression*, Yale University Press, 1974.
20. J. Davies, 'Towards a theory of rebellion', *American Sociological Review*, **6**, 1962, pp. 5–19.
21. T. Gurr, *Why Men Rebel*, Princeton University Press, 1970, and 'Psychological factors in civil violence', *World Politics*, 1968, pp. 245–278, and 'A causal model of civil strife', *American Political Science Review*, **62**, 1968, pp. 1104–1124.
22. D. Bwy, 'Dimensions of social conflict in Latin America', in Masotti and Bowen (Eds.), *op. cit.*, pp. 201–236.
23. T. Ireland, 'The rationale of revolt', *Papers in Non-Market Decision Making*, **1**, 1967, pp. 49–66.
24. G. Tullock, 'The paradox of revolution', *Public Choice*, **xi**, 1971, pp. 89–100.
25. M. Silver, 'Political revolutions and repression', *Public Choice*, **xvii**, 1974, pp. 63–71.
26. R. Berk and H. Aldrich, 'Patterns of vandalism during civil disorders as an indicator of selection of targets', *American Sociological Review*, **17**, 1972, pp. 533–547.
27. S. Huntington, *Political Order in Changing Societies*, Yale University Press, 1971.
28. P. Bachrach and M. Baratz, *Power and Poverty*, Oxford University Press, 1973.
29. T. Gurr, 'A causal model of civil strife', *op. cit.*
30. D. Bwy, *op. cit.*
31. D. Russell, *Rebellion, Revolution and Armed Force*, Academic Press, 1974.
32. *Report of the National Advisory Commission on Civil Disorders*, *op. cit.*, especially pp. 38 and 66.
33. S. Spilerman, *op. cit.*
34. As, for example, in Barrington Moore Jnr., *Injustice: The Social Bases of Obedience and Revolt*, Macmillan, 1979.
35. B. Siegel, 'Defensive cultural adaptation', in H. Graham and T. Gurr (Eds.), *Violence in America*, Vol. II, US Government Printing Office for the National Commission on the Causes and Prevention of Violence, 1969, pp. 593–603.
36. G. Carstairs, 'Overcrowding and human aggression', in H. Graham and T. Gurr (Eds.), *op. cit.*, pp. 603–620.
37. H. Button, *Black Violence*, Princeton University Press, 1978, pp. 4–9.
38. See P. Shipley, 'The riots and the far left', *New Community*, **9**, 1981, pp. 194–198.

PART 2

The Riots: Perceptions and Distortions

CHAPTER 3

The riots: perceptions and distortions

JOHN BENYON

As any police officer knows, witnesses often differ in their descriptions of even reasonably straightforward events. Riots, of course, are anything but simple, and reports of such complex occurrences must necessarily be highly selective. An observer of a tumult can only see some of what occurs, and much of what he or she does view takes place amidst confusion, possibly in darkness or partially obscured by smoke. The observer is only able to record or remember a small part, and this selection is greatly determined by predispositions and prejudice. George Orwell pointed out that even the best-intentioned reporter must cope with 'the ignorance, bias and self-deception from which every observer necessarily suffers'.[1]*

The survey in Chapter 1 makes clear that the accounts and interpretations of the urban disorders varied greatly. A number of perceptions seem to have been particularly partial, but this should come as no surprise for it has been pointed out that 'we only believe what we see; unfortunately we only see what we want to believe'.[2] Perhaps this helps to explain why some, such as the *Daily Mail*, repeatedly saw conspiracy and subversion while others saw unemployment, urban deprivation or police harassment.

Lord Scarman's perceptions

Lord Scarman's Report overcame some of the problems of perception and distortion which were evident in much of the media coverage. The substantial volume of evidence presented to the inquiry enabled him to piece together partial accounts to construct a more comprehensive view. Even so, his inquiry suffered from not hearing the views of rioters themselves, and attention has been drawn to the Kerner Commission's different methods of investigation.[3] This inquiry used teams of researchers who went into the riot areas in the American cities to interview many of those who had been involved in the July 1967 urban violence. The

---

* Superscript numbers refer to Notes at end of chapter.

Commission's Report thus included information derived from the participants themselves, adding an important dimension to the analysis.

Despite these omissions, the Scarman Report describes the riots, and the
build-up to them, in vivid detail, and very few serious criticisms have been
made of this section. Lord Scarman describes how the first disorder began
on Friday 10 April 1981 after a police constable had tried to stop and then
help a black youth (Scarman, 3.4–3.12). This seemingly minor incident
sparked off an hour-long riot, which led to a hastily-convened meeting
between the police and local community leaders (Scarman, 3.13–3.22),
including George Greaves, author of Chapter 6.

Lord Scarman's comments on this first flare-up are particularly telling:

> Nothing that happened on Friday could have taken the police by
> surprise—until they were stoned. Tension between the police and
> black youths was, and remains, a fact of life in Brixton. Young black
> people, as well as many local people of all ages and colours, lacked
> confidence in the police. The worst construction was frequently put
> upon police action, even when it was lawful, appropriate, and
> sensible. . . .
>
> . . . the crowd of black youths felt, with some reason, that they were
> being pursued. They turned and fought. Their action was criminal, and
> is not to be condoned. It was not, however, planned. It was a
> spontaneous act of defiant aggression by young men who felt
> themselves hunted by a hostile police force (Scarman, 3.23–3.25).

Although a serious disturbance in itself, the Friday riot was merely the
prelude to the disorders on Saturday 11 April. During nearly six hours of
violence, arson and looting, 82 people were arrested, 279 police officers and
at least 45 members of the public were injured, 61 private vehicles and 56
police vehicles were damaged or destroyed and 145 premises were damaged,
28 of them by fire (Scarman, 3.74). The majority of the rioters were young
black men, although a significant number were white. The looting in the
centre of Brixton, several hundred yards from the main disorders, was
generally carried out by people who were not involved in the riots
themselves. Many of the looters were older whites, some of them seen
arriving in cars, particularly after the Saturday evening television news.[4]

The trigger which set off the Saturday disorders was the incident outside
the S & M Car Hire office (Scarman, 3.28–3.38). Two officers in plain
clothes, working in the infamous Swamp 81 operation, searched a minicab
driver and his car. The officers were white and young—24 and 20 years
old—and the driver was black. It is difficult to read Lord Scarman's
account, or the descriptions of others, without concluding that the police
constables' behaviour during this incident was at best foolish and inept.
Lord Scarman decided that whilst not unlawful, their actions lacked 'the

discretion and judgement which maturer years might have brought', for they failed 'to strike the correct balance between enforcing the law and keeping the peace' (Scarman, 3.79).

Sunday brought further disturbances although the attacks on the police were generally less intense. 165 people were arrested, 122 police officers and 3 members of the public were reported injured, and 61 police vehicles and 26 other vehicles were damaged or destroyed. Monday 13 April was the last day of these disturbances, with a further 29 arrests (Scarman, 3.81–3.94). Over 7000 police officers had been involved in quelling the disorders.

The riots in Liverpool 8 and elsewhere

Lord Scarman was able to piece together a detailed and graphic account of the April riots only after hearing the statements of many different observers. No such authoritative descriptions of what happened during the July disturbances are available. The Hytner Report[5] details the Moss Side riots, but this investigation was hampered by the refusal to participate by Mr Anderton, Chief Constable of Greater Manchester.

The first disorders in July occurred in Southall. As described in Chapter 1, this confrontation on Friday 3 July 1981 was initially between white skinheads and young Asians, although the police quickly became embroiled. Petrol bombs were used, some 20 arrests were made, and about 130 police and members of the public were injured.

That same night, in the Liverpool 8 area of Merseyside,[6] an apparently minor incident occurred when police chased a young black man on a motorcycle. This was the spark that set off rioting in Toxteth from 3 to 6 July. The worst violence took place on the Saturday night when the police officers suffered a concerted attack of terrible ferocity. The Rector of the Toxteth Team Ministry in Liverpool, Colin Bedford, described his experience of the events in his book *Weep for the City*.

> It was 2 am on Monday 6 July 1981. . . . We were horrified at the sight before us. About forty separate fires were burning on the skyline. . . .

> We stood and watched the roof of the Rialto store collapse. We heard shots in the distance. . . . CS gas was being used by the police, because of the brutality and ferocity of the attacks. . . .

> I had been out on the streets earlier in the evening and seen lines of police being battered by rioters. . . .

> In the light of the morning, I travelled round the area and surveyed the immensity of the destruction. I heard how patients in the Princes Park hospital had been evacuated by taxi drivers, how rioters had got in and looted many of the geriatric patients' personal possessions. I saw the

burnt-down shops, garages and small businesses in the area, and learned that damage totalling over £10 million had been done, jobs had been lost and a community terribly scarred and hurt.[7]

This was the perception of one local witness who knew the area well. Others, such as Alex Bennett, a black community worker, claimed it was a newspaper lie that anyone touched the hospital.[8] As in Brixton, it was argued, the arson targets in Liverpool 8 were chosen selectively—such as the Racquets Club and Swainbank's furniture store. These perceptions, though, could be interpreted as attempts to justify what happened and, besides the problem of appearing to condone arson, some of these accounts seem to suffer from selective omissions.

On the Sunday night alone, 282 police officers were injured and 46 needed to remain in hospital. Looting was extensive and, according to witnesses, involved a large number of young and old whites. There are many stories of farcical episodes during the riots, such as the lady holding up a piece of stolen carpet and asking all those around whether it was 6 feet by 4 feet, or the case of the man with a looted washing machine staggering up the stairs of a Mill Street high-rise, with the police in pursuit, because as usual the lift wasn't working.[9]

The police suffered particularly vicious attacks in Liverpool 8—as the extent of officers' injuries made clear. They were bombarded with bricks and other missiles, and attacked by youths wielding a variety of weapons including 10-feet-long scaffolding poles. Beer barrels, oil drums and gas cylinders—with the valves open—were rolled at them, and fusillades of petrol bombs assailed them. A vivid account of the perceptions of the police was given by James McClure in *The Observer*. It consists almost entirely of personal reflections by police officers, telling stories of fear, bravery and kindness. And even in the depths of chaos and violence there was humour:

> There was this young bobby in the line, y'know, and he's takin' a batterin' for five hours and his bottle goes—he's away, shield, the lot, down a side street, cryin'—gets into this doorway with his shield over him. He's sobbin' away, y'know, and there's this voice behind him, 'Come on lad. On yer feet. Let's see yer back up there!' 'I can't sarge,' he says. 'I'm not your sergeant,' the voice says, 'I'm a superintendent.' The bobby jumps up: 'Bloody hell,' he says, 'I didn't realise I'd run that far!'[10]

The violence in Liverpool 8 had subsided temporarily by Tuesday 7 July, the day it broke out in Manchester. Disorders also occurred in north London and by the end of the week in Handsworth, Birmingham and other towns such as Sheffield, Nottingham, Hull and Slough. Disturbances continued to spread during the weekend with reports of trouble from areas such as Leeds and Bradford, Blackburn, Leicester, Derby, Aldershot, High Wycome and Cirencester.

Then, following the questionably provocative police raid on houses in Railton Road, rioting again occurred in Brixton. Eleven days later further violence took place in Liverpool, from 26 to 28 July, and it was during this rioting that the only death occurred. A disabled man aged 23, David Moore, was hit and killed by a police vehicle. The policemen involved were charged with manslaughter and were found not guilty in April 1982; on the piece of waste ground in Upper Parliament Street where this happened a group of saplings has been planted. Two other men nearly lost their lives. Albert Fitzpatrick was set upon in his taxi and as he drove away he crashed into a tree, sustaining very serious injuries, and 18-year-old Paul Conroy was hit by a police Land Rover, causing his back to be broken, and was then allegedly thrown into a police van.[11] More police officers also suffered injuries which required hospital treatment.

The media under scrutiny

The July riots in Toxteth were the last to receive widespread media coverage, although further trouble was reported in August 1981. The images and impressions which they left behind in people's minds no doubt varied, but two seem to have been particularly prevalent: the violence of the disorders and the numbers of black youths involved. But, despite the tragic death and injuries, in comparative terms the English riots were not very violent. British history provides many more bloody confrontations such as those at Tonypandy, the Rhondda (1910), Liverpool (1911), Cardiff and many other towns (1919), and London and Birkenhead (1932)—to select just a few instances from this century. Riots in other countries tend to result in far more injuries and deaths than occurred during the 1981 disorders in England. For example, in the Detroit riot of 1967 over thirty people were killed in just one night. In February 1983 over three hundred deaths were reported in less than 2 weeks' rioting in Assam state in north-eastern India; in these riots at least three policemen were shot dead by other police marksmen. The violence of the English riots was terrible enough, but could have been far worse.

The press, in particular, rarely stressed this comparative dimension. They did, though, tend to emphasise the number of black people involved. However, the little hard evidence which is available on this point, notably Home Office statistics, suggests that a large majority of rioters were white. Figures for the July riots showed that of over 4000 arrested, 766 were described as West Indian/African, 180 as Asian and 292 as other non-white; at least 2762, or 70 per cent, were white. Some 66 per cent of those arrested were under 21 (20 per cent were under 17) and about half the total were unemployed.[12] The figures showed considerable variation between different areas, but this was the national picture: perhaps a rather different picture from that presented by the nation's media.

The role of the media during the riots, in particular those during July, came under considerable scrutiny. It was argued that a prime responsibility for the rash of rioting in English towns and cities lay with the press and television. Others felt that the coverage by particular newspapers and television programmes was partial and irresponsible. Many of the arguments about the role of the media were put at the August 1981 meeting of the Edinburgh International Television Festival. Some, such as Julian Critchley MP, stressed the 'copycat' effect—the media contagion mentioned by Stan Taylor in Chapter 2—while others such as David Nicholas, Independent Television News editor, pointed out the media's duty to report factual news, however disquieting. The effect of such news, he claimed, was to dispel rumours.

A number of MPs continued to express their concern at the effects of the media. Anthony Nelson (Chichester) pointed out 'the awesome power' which the media have; there is often only 'a fine dividing line between reporting the facts and influencing and inciting disorders'.[13]

A similar reaction occurred in the United States in 1967 and 1968 after the extensive urban rioting there. The Kerner Commission was particularly asked to look at this question, and it concluded that 'it would be imprudent and even dangerous to downplay coverage in the hope that censored reporting of inflammatory incidents somehow will diminish violence'. Kerner's views were similar to those of the ITN editor: the credibility of the media would be jeopardised by such self-censorship, enabling rumour mongers to exploit the information vacuum.

Other studies, too, have argued that the spread of civil disorder is not dependent on the media. Rudé, for example, points out how rioting spread in past centuries, despite the lack of mass media in modern terms.[14] However, it is difficult to believe that television, radio and newspapers did not have considerable impact in 1981. As Lord Scarman points out, these riots were graphically displayed before anyone who cared to switch on their television sets. He concluded that the media did bear a responsibility for the escalation of the disorders and for the imitative element. He urged the media:

> . . . to assess the likely impact on events of their own reporting of them, to ensure balance in the coverage of disorder and at all times to bear in mind that rioters, and others, in their exhibition of violence respond alarmingly to what they see (wrongly, but understandably) as the encouraging presence of the TV camera and the reporter (Scarman, 6.39).

The views of Lord Scarman, and others such as Mary Whitehouse and MPs who had drawn attention to the imitative effects of the media, were not received without question. The BBC and the IBA commissioned a report from Howard Tumber of the Broadcasting Research Unit at the British Film Institute. He conducted interviews with young people, police and broadcasters and he found that television had played a very minor role in the disturbances. Less than 10 per cent of the 12 to 19 age group watch television news, and information tended to be 'gathered in the classrooms, the streets and the pubs'. Indeed, said Tumber, during many of the riots, far from encouraging the disturbances, camera crews were attacked and their equipment smashed.[15]

Despite evidence such as that used by Tumber, criticisms of the media, in general, persisted. During the riots in July a number of allegations were made of foreign television crews in Toxteth and elsewhere actually paying youths to throw stones at the police in order to film 'the disturbances'. Another factor pointed out to Lord Scarman was the unfair reporting of areas such as Brixton. Both police officers and members of the black community agreed that the media focused on problems and difficulties, creating a bad image, rather than reporting positive things (Scarman, 6.40).[16]

Perceptions and distortions

Newspapers often seen to deal more with images than with reality. Selective reporting, it has been argued, is inevitable, but some of that which occurs amounts to dangerous distortion. The quality press tend to give more balanced coverage of events—although bias and partiality is still a feature—but grave distortion occurs frequently (some would say daily) in many of the popular newspapers. The sort of distorted image peddled by the unscrupulous press was seen in March 1982 and March 1983 following the release of racially-based crime statistics. One commentator in March 1982 observed:

> Londoners riding home on the proverbial Clapham omnibus— especially the Clapham omnibus—last week could have been forgiven for believing that they resided in a city racked by racial hatred, where black muggers loitered threateningly at every street-corner waiting to accost them.[17]

For this was the image portrayed by television and many newspapers, exemplified by stories such as those in the *Daily Mail* ('Prisoners behind net curtains'; 'Black crime: the alarming figures'), and the *Daily Express* ('On Britain's most brutal streets').

In 1983 similar figures were released 'through the malevolent offices of

Mr Harvey Proctor, the ultra-right-wing Conservative MP'. Once again, continued *The Guardian* leader, we have been treated to 'selective manipulation' and 'orchestrated distortion'.[18] But despite criticisms from such quarters, false and grotesque images are dealt out to millions. The daily circulation of *The Sun* alone, at 4.2 million, is some thirteen times greater than that of *The Times*.

Two respected and experienced journalists give their eyewitness accounts in the next two chapters. John Clare and Michael Nally report their perceptions of disorders in Brixton and Moss Side respectively. In the following essay George Greaves highlights some of the central features in the Brixton disorders and the build-up to them, and he comments on some of Lord Scarman's findings and proposals. The final chapter in this part of the book is concerned with the ways in which the media reported the riots and the impact which this had, and Graham Murdock provides a detailed analysis of the perceptions and distortions which were evident in the news media's coverage.

Notes

1. G. Orwell, 'The prevention of literature', in *Inside the Whale*, Penguin, 1971, p. 161.
2. P. Atteslander quoted in J. Friedrichs and H. Ludtke, *Participant Observation*, Saxon House, 1975, p. 26.
3. O. Kerner *et al.*, *The Report of the National Advisory Commission on Civil Disorders*, US Government Printing Office, 1968; see also R. M. Fogelson and R. B. Hill, *Who Riots? A Study of Participation in the 1967 Riots* (Supplementary Studies for the Kerner Commission), US Government Printing Office, 1968. A more recent evaluation of riots in the United States is provided by: United States Department of Justice, *Prevention and Control of Urban Disorders: Issues for the 1980s*, US Government Printing Office, 1980.
4. M. Kettle and L. Hodges, *Uprising!*, Pan, 1982, p. 112. This point was made by a number of people interviewed by the media after the April disorders, and is taken up by Lord Scarman (Scarman, 3.61).
5. *Report of the Moss Side Enquiry Panel to the Leader of the Greater Manchester Council* (Chairman, Mr Benet Hytner, QC), 1981.
6. Known as Toxteth, nationally and internationally, local people refer to the area as Liverpool 8, Princes Park, the South End, or Granby.
7. C. Bedford, *Weep for the City*, Lion, 1982, pp. 7–8.
8. Quoted in M. Williams, 'The tents at the gate of the city', *New Society*, Vol. 57, No. 974, 16 July 1981, pp. 98–100.
9. See Kettle and Hodges, *op. cit.*, pp. 159–161 and M. Williams, *op. cit.*, p. 99.
10. J. McClure, 'After the battle of Liverpool 8', *The Observer*, 12 July 1981, p. 15. See also J. McClure, *Spike Island: Portrait of a British Police Division*, Macmillan and Pan, 1980.
11. Kettle and Hodges, *op. cit.*, pp. 172–173.
12. Home Office Statistical Department, *Bulletin*, Autumn 1982.
13. House of Commons Official Report (*Hansard*), 25 November 1981, col. 898.
14. See G. Rudé, *The Crowd in History*, Wiley, 1967; D. O. Sears and J. B. McConahay, *The Politics of Violence: the New Urban Blacks and the Watts Riot*, Houghton Miflin, 1973; S. Field, 'Urban disorders in Britain and America', in S. Field and P. Southgate, *Public Disorders*, Home Office Research Study No. 72, HMSO, 1982.
15. Howard Tumber, *Television and the Riots*, British Film Institute, April 1982. See also Tumber's letter in *The Guardian*, 21 April 1982.

16. The same criticism is made of the media's attitude towards Liverpool 8. See, for example, C. Bedford, *Weep for the City*, Lion, 1982, chapter 6.
17. J. Shirley, 'Mugging: statistics of an "unacceptable crime"', *The Guardian*, 14 March 1982.
18. 'Black, white and full statistics', *The Guardian*, 24 March 1983.

CHAPTER 4

Eyewitness in Brixton

JOHN CLARE

A few weeks after the riots in Brixton, my teenage daughter presented me with a cartoon which she had cut out of one of the pop music papers which she reads. It shows a riot in full swing—crowds, bricks, bottles, smoke—and there, standing amid the smouldering ruins, are a reporter and a television crew. The caption reads: 'Now over to our community relations correspondent, for a gullible, white, middle-class, university educated, nonentity's view of today's events.' It is in that spirit that I would like you to consider what follows. . . .

Measured words or purple prose?

The reason for Lord Scarman's Report was that in Brixton one Saturday evening in April 1981 three or four hundred young people, most of them black, attacked the police. They did so after what they saw as considerable provocation. The trouble was mostly confined to a number of back streets. It lasted for four and a half hours. Intermittently during that period the crowd attacked the police with stones, bricks, bottles, and, in particular, petrol bombs. They set fire to buildings, destroyed vehicles, particularly those belonging to the police, and many shops in the centre of Brixton were looted. For much of the time the police stood in defensive cordons behind their riot shields. Subsequently the statistics showed that 279 policemen had been hurt, as well as 45 members of the public, and 28 buildings were damaged or destroyed by fire (see Scarman, 3.74). The following day there was more trouble, but nowhere near as serious.

Now that is one entirely factual and accurate way of describing the rioting in Brixton last April. One might add that no-one was killed or maimed. No bullets were fired, rubber or otherwise, and CS gas was not used either. Here is another way of describing those events:

> During the weekend of the 10th to the 12th of April . . . the British people watched with horror and incredulity an instant audio-visual presentation on their television sets of scenes of violence and disorder

in their capital city, the like of which had not previously been seen in this century in Britain. In the centre of Brixton, a few hundred young people—most, but not all of them, black—attacked the police on the streets with stones, bricks, iron bars and petrol bombs, demonstrating to millions of their fellow citizens the fragile basis of the Queen's peace. The petrol bomb was now used for the first time on the streets of Britain (the idea, no doubt, copied from the disturbances in Northern Ireland). These young people, by their criminal behaviour—for such, whatever their grievances or frustrations, it was—brought about a temporary collapse of law and order in the centre of an inner suburb of London. . . . For some hours the police could do no more than contain them. When the police, heavily reinforced, eventually restored order in the afflicted area, the toll of human injury and property damage was such that one observer described the scene as comparable with the aftermath of an air raid (Scarman, 1.2–1.3).

That, in case you are confused, is no media hype. That is not the portentous purple prose of the popular press—'Cor guv, it was like a battlefield'. Those are the measured words of a High Court judge. And yet I wonder if they trouble you as they trouble me. I wonder if the British people did watch 'with horror and incredulity', particularly as these were the sort of scenes of violence and disorder that British television scarcely bothers to show any more when they come from Northern Ireland. I wonder if we did learn anything from Brixton that we did not know before about the 'fragile basis of the Queen's peace'. I wonder even what that strange phrase is meant to mean. I wonder whether Lord Scarman really does believe that the scene was comparable to the aftermath of an air raid. An air raid surely conjures up scenes of widespread devastation, of high explosives, and charred bodies being carried out of ruins. I wonder, because I saw nothing like that in Brixton. And I wonder, too, what is actually in Lord Scarman's mind when he talks about a 'temporary collapse of law and order in the centre of an inner suburb of London', for it is a concept to which he keeps returning. Later in the Report, for example, he says of the police:

In Brixton over that terrible weekend they stood between our society and a total collapse of law and order in the streets of an important part of the capital (Scarman, 4.98).

Does he mean that but for the police in Brixton that evening, Buckingham Palace would have been put to the torch, the Houses of Parliament taken by storm, the gates of Brixton prison thrown open, and that the tumbrils would have rolled down Fleet Street? Well, maybe he does, because in a debate on law and order in the House of Lords in March 1982, Lord Scarman said this:

There was an occasion in Brixton on the Saturday, when a few unreinforced police stood between the Inner City of London and the total collapse of law and order. If that thin blue line had been overwhelmed, and it nearly was on that Saturday night, there is no other way of dealing with it but the awful ultimate requirement of calling in the Army.[1]*

A real battle?

In common with most experienced reporters, I would be the last to claim infallibility for eyewitnesses of even the most mundane scenes. Observers see only part of the whole and they do not even see that very clearly. Furthermore, they tend to distort the significance of what they have seen. But even allowing for all this, when reading and rereading the Scarman Report, I still find myself identifying with a young man called Fabrizio who is the hero of Stendhal's novel *The Charterhouse of Parma*. Fabrizio, you may remember, having been nurtured on romantic tales of grand battles, finds himself conscripted into a French regiment at the battle of Waterloo. But there, amidst all the mud and the noise, instead of the disciplined, ordered majesty of the charge and countercharge that he had been led to expect, of plans being executed, and heroic deeds being done, he finds only sporadic activity and overwhelming disjointed confusion. So much so that at one point he turns to a sergeant and says, 'Sir, this is the first time I have ever been in a battle. . . . But is this a real battle?' And that is precisely the question I sometimes find myself silently asking Lord Scarman. The sergeant replied, incidentally, 'It'll do till a real battle comes along'. (Perhaps I should add in parenthesis that Brixton was not the first riot I had reported on: I have covered a dozen far worse in Northern Ireland.) What I am stressing, in all humility, is that what I saw in Brixton over five hours that Saturday night in April 1981 was not, in some crucial respects, what Lord Scarman sat down to describe at the end of his marathon inquiry. In particular, I did not then, and I do not now, see any evidence for his repeated assertion that only a thin blue line prevented a total collapse of law and order in our society. Let me emphasise, however, that I do not now, and I did not then, minimise either the violence of the rioting or its significance.

This now is how—and let me emphasise this—*still very close to the heat of the moment*, I reported that riot (with actuality inserts) on the morning after:

> Crouched behind their riot shields, the police withstood many such
> barrages of bottles, bricks and petrol bombs during the five hours the
> rioting lasted. When there was a lull they advanced, first giving
> ominous warning of their intentions by drumming on their riot shields

* Superscript numbers refer to Notes at end of chapter.

with their truncheons. The last big push came in Railton Road, just before 9.00 p.m. In tortoise formation, shoulder to shoulder, their shields over their heads, three lines of police moved cautiously up the road, past a barricade of overturned and smouldering cars, and on towards the flames and clouds of black smoke. As I followed, the road was littered with shattered glass and broken bricks. . . . *They are advancing up two streets now at the same time. On my right there are forty or fifty police crouched behind their riot shields. There is a burning tyre in the middle of the road, and down in front of me there are 150 or 200 police, their riot shields over their heads. Buildings are burning on both sides of the road, one on the right hand side quite gutted.* . . . Earlier, across fifty yards of no man's land, councillors and community leaders had attempted to mediate between the rioters and the police. One of them, Mr Tony Morgan, returned to give the local police commander an urgent account of the mood behind the barricades. . . . *There's overturned cars in the street, there's Molotov cocktails and if something is not done at the present time there is going to be a highly explosive situation, and the only way to defuse the situation is by decreasing the presence of the police within the area at the present time, because they see the police as their target, as the target that they want to attack.* Police commander: *I understand exactly what you're saying, and I appreciate what you have already done, but there is no question, and it is my decision at the moment, there is no question of withdrawing the police from here.*

A few minutes later, a Lambeth councillor, Mr John Boyle, told me that the rioters had another demand: *They want an interview with the TV and radio. They want to put their grudges to you personally. Would you be prepared to let them have access to you?* . . . So I went back with Mr Boyle across no man's land. He was carrying a loud hailer and was careful to announce us. . . . On the other side a black man in his mid twenties was waiting, a half brick in either hand, a white scarf tied across his face muffling his voice: *We want all the prisoners that have been nicked down here, we want them released, and we want them down here, right? Number two, we want all those policemen to move off, go somewhere else, go about their business, you understand?* But the police would have none of it, though their casualties were mounting by the minute. Petrol bombs still curled viciously out of the darkness. I must have seen twenty policemen dragged back out of the smoke, their legs trailing along the road, blood pouring down their faces.

It ended as suddenly as it had begun. The firemen moved in to damp down the smoking remains of gutted pubs and shops, and the police were able to give some attention to the scores of shops that were being freely looted by passers by. Most of the 500 or so who took part in the rioting were black, aged between 15 and 25, but among them I saw a substantial number of young whites, their faces carefully masked. So, what had started with a simple arrest in the early afternoon turned into a prolonged and vicious riot, quite unlike anything London has seen. Blacks I talked to were in no doubt about what had caused it. Like this shopkeeper in Railton Road, they put it down to constant harassment by the police: *We don't really want to have a row with the police, but if they are antagonising us like that—if I left my shop now and walked down the street, there is a ten to one chance that five or six policemen will stop me, for nothing.* However, the Commissioner of the Metropolitan Police, Sir David McNee, had another explanation: *We have unconfirmed reports that what you have seen tonight was not spontaneous, but has been orchestrated and very well planned. You don't find petrol bombs and the kind of missiles that have been thrown at my officers just by chance.*

Of course that last statement by Sir David McNee has since been shown to be without foundation, as they say. The Report finds that the rioting was spontaneous and not premeditated (Scarman 3.108–3.110). And as for the alleged involvement of outsiders, the evidence for that (if evidence is not too strong a word) is confined to one woman with an American accent, and a couple of sightings of people described as 'strangers' (Scarman, 3.101–3.103).

An exaggeration of the seriousness of the violence

Now you may conclude from my heat-of-the-moment account that it was indeed a real battle and that Lord Scarman was right to portray it as such. Let me try to disabuse you—on two counts in particular, First, as I have already hinted, I believe that Lord Scarman's estimate of the relative seriousness of the violence is heavily exaggerated. Horror and incredulity might well have been the feelings of a policeman cowering behind his riot shield as he watched the bricks and petrol bombs rain down upon him, and the police, many of whom gave evidence to the inquiry, were right to emphasise it. However, that is not the vantage point from which the Report is supposedly written. Also, the sudden raw reality of urban violence might well have come as a shock to an upper class judge who commutes between the hushed tones of the High Court and the quieter reaches of Chelsea, but those are not the reference points of most of the rest of us. Furthermore, working class people, especially if they are elderly or black, are forced to live with the daily threat of random violence, of mob hooliganism, racial harassment and urban crime. The shock, therefore, of a street riot is somewhat dulled. Similarly, I believe they, like the rest of us, have learned to make allowances for what they see on their television screens, especially for that distorted melodrama which sometimes passes for news. It is not, I think, an allowance Lord Scarman has made. In fact, far from stepping back from what happened and judging it coolly, he has propelled himself into the very thick of it and been overcome by the smoke.

Secondly, I believe Lord Scarman has misunderstood the nature of the rioting in Brixton. It was highly localised. In other words, there was no evidence at the time, nor has any been produced since, that the rioters intended to storm the West End. The rioting arose immediately out of specific grievances of police harassment. In the short term, there were those 943 stop and searches in Brixton on the preceding five days—'Swamp 81'— and the fact that on the Saturday afternoon, hours before any violence was threatened, there were no less than 84 police officers, most of them in plain clothes, patrolling the streets of Brixton, as well as three police vans driving round and round in what was seen as a menacing manner. And finally, the rioting had a specific target—the police—and a stated objective (by the rioters) to drive them out of the back streets of Brixton.

It is true that the rioters did take the opportunity to pay off some old scores. Some of the arson targets for example were quite deliberately selected, and there was a good deal of entirely opportunistic looting (little of it by the rioters themselves), but that is all. It was not (contrary to the fevered claims of a small band of romantic Marxists in Brixton) an insurrection, a revolt, a rebellion, an uprising, or even as Lord Scarman colourfully suggests, an incipient revolution mercifully strangled at birth by a thin blue line. It is only fair to add though that both the romantic Marxists and Lord Scarman are in very good company. In June 1855 Karl Marx watched an angry London crowd staging a noisy occupation of Hyde Park. They were protesting against two Parliamentary Bills that proposed closing all places of public amusement on Sundays, including the pubs, which were only to open on Sunday evenings. The next day, Marx wrote:

> We witnessed the event from beginning to end, and believe we can state without exaggeration that yesterday in Hyde Park the English revolution began.[2]

The real lesson of the disorders

To argue, as I am doing, that the seriousness of the rioting in Brixton has been exaggerated, and its intention distorted, is not however to play down its significance; quite the opposite. My concern is that the significance of what happened has been so roundly misrepresented that we are in danger of being blinded to the real lesson. And nor is that the only danger. For what, I ask you, are the lessons that have most notably been drawn from the Scarman view of Brixton? They are, first, that the police urgently need to be equipped with stocks of CS gas and rubber bullets (which they now have been) and second, that the blacks, as Mr Powell has been proclaiming for the past 15 years, are an alien, potentially revolutionary wedge in our inner cities. You may incidentally be interested to learn that Sir Kenneth Newman, the Commissioner of the Metropolitan Police, and one of the founders of Scotland Yard's Community Relations Branch, apparently adheres to the *genetic* theory. In a recent interview with the American *Police Magazine*, he is quoted as saying this:

> In the Jamaicans, you have a people who are constitutionally disorderly. It's simply in their make-up. They are constitutionally disposed to be anti-authority.*

That would explain everything.

In truth though, these are not the lessons of Brixton at all. But, they are the lessons that are very likely to be drawn from a report that pretends that the intention and scale of the violence that weekend was such that our society for a time teetered on the brink of total collapse. The real lesson of course, of Brixton as of Bristol and Toxteth, is much simpler: if you lean too heavily on a socially and economically hard pressed community, it does not take much to make it snap, whether it is the foolish harassment of a minicab driver on the Front Line, a heavy handed raid on a black café in St Paul's, or the chase and arrest of an innocent motorcyclist in Upper Parliament Street.

Whether Lord Scarman has actually added much to our already considerable knowledge of why such relatively trivial incidents turn into riots is something I must leave others to judge. But a final point which intrigues me is why Brixton but not Bristol was accorded the full rigours of an establishment analysis. After all, in Bristol in April 1980 you will remember, the violence lasted 6 hours, 50 policemen were injured, and a total of 21 buildings were damaged or destroyed by fire. And yet afterwards very little was said and virtually nothing done. Indeed, I remember Mr Timothy Raison, Minister of State at the Home Office, remarking that it was not the sort of problem you could throw money at. Toxteth, on the other hand, where of course the rioting was most severe and prolonged, received little analysis, but it did get the Secretary of State for the Environment for one day a week, and many promises of much money. Brixton, I suppose, got Lord Scarman because it has served for so long as Britain's prime symbol of black settlement and therefore racial tension. And, as I have tried to suggest,

---

* *Police Magazine*, Criminal Justice Publications, January 1982, p. 18. Sir Kenneth subsequently denied the remarks attributed to him, claiming that the journalist concerned, Bruce Porter, 'totally distorted the whole point of what I was saying'. Mr Porter denied it. He told the *Daily Mirror* that he was 'quite certain that (Sir Kenneth) said the words quoted'. *Daily Mirror*, 30 June 1982.

Lord Scarman rose to the occasion with an appropriately cataclysmic analysis.

Postscript: changes in Brixton

On 1 November 1982 I again found myself in Brixton watching buildings burn and people throwing stones at police in full riot gear. But it was a small-scale affair, provoked by the demolition of some derelict houses in the Front Line, and quickly suppressed by an efficient police operation. Other things have changed too. Much of the area around where the 1981 riots occurred has been demolished to make way for new housing and there are elaborate plans for better amenities, including a black social centre. Policing of the area, despite a high crime rate, has been much more sensitive and careful— thanks in part, no doubt, to the vigorous, twice-monthly meetings of the new Community/Police Consultative Committee. In the local government elections of May 1982, four black people were elected to Lambeth Borough Council where previously there had been none. And the unemployment situation has changed too. According to the annual report of Lambeth's Community Relations Council, published in August 1982, three black youngsters out of four in Brixton are now without a job. The report found that in the 12 months after the riots, unemployment among black youths in the area rose by 79 per cent. *Plus ça change* . . .

Notes

1. Parliamentary Report, *The Times*, 25 March 1982.
2. 'Riot acts', *The Times Educational Supplement*, 5 March 1982.

CHAPTER 5

Eyewitness in Moss Side

MICHAEL NALLY

The riots were 'mainly carnivals of the young', according to a polytechnic lecturer, writing in *Socialist Worker* a few months after the debris had been cleared away.[1]* I thought that was nonsense when I first read it, the author confirming a right-wing caricature of his profession as clown. On reflection, however, I am not so sure.

The reflection was prompted partly by some lines which appeared about the same time in *Big Flame*, a rival left-wing publication. They are from a poem by 'an unemployed mother of two' from Toxteth. It begins:

> On the morning after the riots
>   my washing had been out all night and smelled of bonfires.

And it includes this verse:

> You can see through the riot-shields made of polythene
> the police are angry and vicious
> the people are angry and happy
>   swinging their power like a lantern in the night[2]

She writes with more conviction than a knee-jerk poetaster, and Larkin might like the line about the washing. She made me think again: perhaps you can have a desperate carnival, just as you can have a lively wake.

Certainly, some of the rioters in Toxteth and Moss Side choose to remember the events of July 1981 as celebrations of sorts. That was made plain to me often in later months, when I spent time in both districts, reviewing in relative peace impressions recorded during the riots.

Youths I talked to—some I recognised from the days and nights of the riots, others were convincing in their recollections of incidents in which they claimed to have taken part—relished the memories, like too many older men relish memories of war. The statements of the most jubilant of them can be summarised thus: they knew their interests and those of the police were incompatible because they wanted the freedom of the streets, day and

---

* Superscript numbers refer to Notes at end of chapter.

54

night, and the police wanted them indoors at night; they were elated when it seemed to them that they had the run of the streets, if only for a few hours.

The villainy of those hours was discounted—there was unprovoked and mindless violence, and it was not always directed against the police and those who declared for them, and there was looting motivated only by greed. What mattered was that they had challenged the police, against whom they believed they had legitimate and provable grievances, and for a time they bettered them. They were as jubilant as the Provos in Amsterdam in the 1960s, again if only for a short time.

Many of their views were simplistic of course. They ignored other factors and motives which had to be taken into account when reporting what could be seen and heard and what might be the meaning of it. (I take that to be the reporter's basic task on any story.) Nonetheless, it would be unwise not to try to see the riots from the narrow angle favoured by the youths.

'Tooling up'

Moss Side is a sprawl of a place. The parliamentary constituency so named at the time stretched from a deprived ward in the north-east, on the edge of the centre of Manchester, to relative affluence in the south-west. The deprived ward had a population of about 11,800, and more than one in five of them were on the dole at the time of the riots. Of the 2179 members of ethnic minorities registered as unemployed in February 1981, 1120 were of West Indian origin, 800 of Asian.

The riots began in the deprived ward in the early hours of Wednesday 8 July 1981. Groups emerged from pubs, clubs and shebeens to gang up with youths already on the streets. Windows were smashed, fires broke out and there was looting.

During the day, given what had happened in Toxteth during the previous three days and nights and reactions to it in Moss Side, it became obvious that there was a risk of more serious trouble. I went round the district for a lunchtime drink to learn from a number of sources that both potential rioters and the police were 'tooling up'. The phrase was used by a plainclothes detective, who added that he did not think the vice squad would be over-busy that night.

A woman who worked in further education with some of the youths preparing for confrontation feared the worst. Toxteth was on many people's minds, she confirmed, and the police were throwing their weight about. Everyone was anticipating trouble; community leaders and workers were meeting, then meeting the police, and senior police officers were meeting among themselves.

Police plans were amended as a result of one meeting, which was attended by James Anderton, Chief Constable of Greater Manchester. He agreed with the community leaders that there would be no 'excessive' policing so long as 'hotheads' were restrained. There was later controversy about the meeting, and Anderton was accused of 'politicking'. In turn, he talked of 'some terribly ulterior purpose'.

He and some local officers were already established in the demonology of the streets. His authoritarianism and narrow-mindedness and the arrogance and prejudice of certain officers were cited as the main reasons for the recent and rapid deterioration in relations between sections of the community and the police.

I now live in a 'softer' suburb, about three miles from Moss Side, and it did not seem a good idea to drive back there that night and park, certainly not remembering what had happened to some vehicles in Toxteth. Apart from that, taxis have other advantages: their drivers are advised by colleagues over their radios about the movement of other traffic and obstructions. The driver I hailed ruled against the normal route before we had gone a mile. The word was that marked police vehicles and unmarked vehicles driven by 'God-knows-who' were 'tearing around', and at least two roads were sealed off.

'Under attack—send assistance'

We reached Whitworth Park, near the Manchester University campus, whose expansion has coincided with change in Moss Side, and agreed left at Denmark Road was the safest bet. The road leads into Greenheys Lane, and as we reached the junction, we realised that we had lost the bet. The district police station across the lane was under attack.

It was the end of the ride. I paid the fare, and the taxi did a rapid U-turn as I approached a group of people watching the mayhem, about fifty yards from the front of the station. It was about half past ten, and the rioters had first hit the station minutes before. Hurling abuse and bricks, they were now advancing again, as the officers inside, eleven men and three women under the command of a male superintendent, locked doors and prepared for a siege.

They called for help by telephone and radio, as bricks shattered windows in the station's reception area. The note of one call read: 'We are under attack. Send assistance.' No-one could recall a similar message being sent before. My impression was that someone would be killed if the attack was sustained.

But it was not. It ended after about another ten minutes, with one group peeling away, to be followed by others, as the assistance—a marked van from a nearby station—swerved through to block the entrance. More missiles were thrown during the retreat. One group tried to dislodge a grid cover for a final throw. It held though, and they ran. The police flailed at laggards, but they seemed more intent on clearing the station area than on taking prisoners.

The rioters moved quickly towards the junction of Princess Road, Moss Lane West and Moss Lane East, about a quarter of a mile away, to regroup with others on grass opposite a pub known throughout Manchester and beyond as the Big Alex. I reckoned there were three to four hundred from the attack or picked up on the move, and about four times as many already on the grass and around it.

The grass, sometimes referred to as the Mound or the Meadow, might have been sited and landscaped for the stand-off and chases that followed. There is room on it for a shrewd command to deploy forces in file and phalanx, with support from snatch squads from the sides and the rear. Police deployment and demeanour were hesitant at first, but they became more confident. The rioters were disorganised and restless. Some of them were disconcerted by looting, which had begun again along the road. A few shouted against it, arguing that it was weakening the anti-police effort and bringing the rioters into disrepute with non-combatant locals and the media.

The stand-off was prolonged. It was broken by skirmishes and noisy chases. Officers in police vans threw open their doors, shouting and banging; previously uninvolved locals screamed in fear and anger. A line of police wearing black crash helmets, first issued for support-duty in Toxteth, stood shoulder to shoulder. Two groups wearing conventional helmets with plastic visors moved in front of them.

Why is it happening?

There was time to ask why, and for a while no shortage of youths willing to answer. A black youth, who was high on the excitement of the attack and eager to join in any future fray, spoke passionately and, I believe, for many other attackers. It is worthwhile reporting his words directly. He said: 'I'm here to see the pigs get theirs. They've done this for years. Now they know what it's like to be hit back. We had the bastards in there shitting themselves. We nearly got hold of a couple of them before they shut up the shop and screamed for help.'

Like others who spoke later, he refused to give even his Christian name; he swore, invoking the 'Holy Lord', that the police would not hesitate to take reprisals against anyone they suspected of taking part in the attack. All he would volunteer was his age—he was seventeen. Pressed, he added that he lived nearby, worked occasionally in a record shop and liked to mind his own business.

We were joined by friends of his, a mixed group, who were blunter. One white youth threatened to use a short wooden shaft tucked into his belt under his bomber jacket. He said: 'You piss off and write what the hell you like. Say it's political or something. What the fuck would you do if you lived here?'

That conversation finished abruptly, and the youths jogged on to the grass in search of action. But there were umpteen other conversations, enough to indicate the origins, characters and motives of most of the most militant rioters. They were local or from other southern suburbs, and they were on the streets to protest against alleged harassment and ill-treatment by the police, over months and years some claimed.

Others were using the heat they were generating to draw attention to the deprivation around them. They described Moss Side as looking 'a damned sight better than it is'. And many were there for kicks and/or profit, some emboldened by drink and drugs. Those looting for profit were able to take advantage of apparent police lack of interest in all but the action on and around the grass for much of the night.

Three youths squatted in the window of a shop, pocketing goods picked up from among the splintered boards and shards. Two were black, one white. They seemed to be having a ball. One of the blacks jumped out of the window to walk down the road, where another window had been shattered. I had taken out my pocket tape recorder to try to capture the sounds of the night—the like of which I had only heard before in Northern Ireland—and he spotted it. He asked which shop I got it from. Unabashed to be told I was a reporter, not another looter—there were one or two who looked nearly as old as me—he said: 'If they just want to fight the police, that's up to them. I can't see the point, unless they're already after you.' He was 15, bright, but obviously ready for bed. He had not slept since he joined in the earlier looting, and I do not suppose he slept the following night either.

'Hellholes'

The white youth with the 15-year-old whistled to a white girl, promising her a present if she was nice to him. The girl was the only one to respond directly to a question about the political motives of some of the rioters. She said: 'They've been here all day, selling their stupid newspapers. They're all Commies, we think. No-one's taking much notice of them. We know how bad it is here. Half of us don't work, and some of us live in hellholes. We don't need to be told that, do we?'

Two white youths wearing anti-Thatcher badges were watching the grass from the shelter of a car park by the district community and shopping centre, which has been the scene of much vandalism and theft. They were not locals and refused to say where they were from. One said: 'You can see for yourself what this is all about. Half of this lot haven't got jobs, and they're getting it from the police. There'll be plenty more of it unless there's a big change.'

That warning was repeated by a middle-aged black woman, who was wandering around the centre. She was looking for her son and daughter. She feared they had been involved in some trouble during the night and might be looking for more. She said: 'They're too young. He's only 13, and she's 16. I don't mind so much if he's with her, but she's got these mates. They're trouble, they've been praying for this.'

An officer moved her on, saying it was for her own good. Then, he stood and watched his colleagues come under fire again from a group hurling bricks and other missiles. Two vans hurtled down Quinney Crescent, which runs along the back of the grass, towards a group standing on the pavement, or so it appeared from where we were standing. The group split and panicked, and one of the two vans brushed two people aside. A third person—it may have been a man or a boy—was hauled somehow into the van as it turned the corner. The officer said: 'God knows we've had bloody aggro here for ages. But this is something else. It's as if they want to burn everything to the ground.'

It was about five hours after the station attack before Moss Side cooled down. And even then, we heard of running skirmishes down side streets, and there was still a cacophony of shouting, tinkling glass, horns and hammering and a confusion of smells.

I separated from some locals with whom I had been discussing the night, and decided to wander towards the city centre. I made good time over the first few hundred yards, being chased by about half-a-dozen black youths when I was daft enough to turn down a side street. They did not catch me, but they could have done if they had wanted to. Perhaps I was not worth catching, or maybe it was something to do with carnival spirit.

Police attitudes and activities

The next night, Anderton swamped the district. About thirty vans and numerous other vehicles circled the grass and cut down streets and across crofts to try to stop movement and drive as many people as possible indoors. Their main targets were youths, but older people complained of harassment and manhandling. I was warned more than once to get out or else.

There was no more rioting, and the Chief Constable attributed that to 'good' policing. Community leaders alleged that the police were trying to frighten anyone who wanted the right to the streets. Some youths were shaken by what they had taken part in earlier; others were 'out of steam', but they boasted that they would soon be ready for more.

The attitudes and activities of the police were crucial to analysis of the rioting. That was acknowledged in the report of a panel under Mr Benet Hytner QC, which was appointed by Greater Manchester County Council to 'do a Scarman' on Moss Side, and boycotted by Anderton. The Report paid tribute to the police but pointed out that the panel's opinion would be 'supremely irrelevant' to a black youth of good character who was racially abused and manhandled.[3]

In a supplementary paper, Hytner wrote: 'We were satisfied that for some time prior to the summer of 1981 a number of officers misused their powers to stop and search subjects. . . . We were satisfied that on many occasions, particularly but not only in Moss Side, black youngsters have been racially abused. . . . Officers offering it (racial abuse) may not appreciate how deeply wounding it is to the recipient, and in consequence the lasting damage it does to relations between the police and the public.'[4]

But harassment and abuse continued. Senior officers condemned 'excess'; but some foot and mobile patrols ignored guidance and orders. 'Sus' was abolished, but there were other weapons. A group of community workers wrote to *The Guardian* complaining of 'the almost unbelievable behaviour' of some officers, who careered through the streets in vans, beating their truncheons against the sides of the vans and chanting slogans, such as 'Nigger, nigger, nigger, oi, oi, oi!'[5] One worker, who won an appeal against a conviction for a breach of the peace during the rioting after evidence that he had acted as peacemaker, complained of personal harassment and brutality.

Cynicism and uneasiness

Attempts by central and local government to reduce the deprivation in Moss Side and Toxteth were woefully inadequate. In Westminster, Whitehall and the town halls of Manchester and Liverpool, they were still quoting the 'Principle of Unripe Time' to excuse lack of imagination and generosity.

I reported cynicism about the appointment and work of Michael Heseltine, the Minister responsible for inner city areas after the riots.[6] He denied that it was widespread. That was nonsense, even on reflection.

By the time he was moved to Defence in January 1983, more than a year after the first of his series of carefully publicised 'initiatives' on Merseyside, he had made no impact where it mattered most, on the streets. There were more trees in Toxteth, ready for the fire next time; public corporations were 'interested' in 'considering' some projects; and businessmen were trying to raise the wind of profit from redevelopment of Liverpool's old docks. But unemployment in the riot areas was higher; statutory, municipal and voluntary services were tightening their belts or starving; and the youths still loathed the police.

Shortages of time and money were certainly factors, but lack of will was important too. We knew about that as long ago as December 1981, when *The Economist*, a magazine with excellent contacts with both factions of the Government, quoted a 'dry' minister noting 'the heat is off on this one'.[7]

But for how long? There was uneasiness in Moss Side and Toxteth throughout 1982. Few people forecast further trouble on the same scale in the near future, if only because the police were more alert and better deployed, and trained and equipped to face another challenge—but no-one ruled out minor clashes or incidents.

Kenneth Oxford, Chief Constable of Merseyside, established a special 'Toxteth Section', ostensibly to meet demands for community policing. Older locals praised the work of officers involved; young adults and teenagers were suspicious of their presence, in uniform on foot patrol, and their backup mobile squads, in a variety of guises and vehicles. Oxford referred in a report on the section's operations to 'the vicissitudes of policing a partly hostile community'.[8]

He remained unapologetic about his force's undisciplined response with CS gas during the riots, the first time that the weapon had been used on the British mainland, and the Merseyside Police's stock of plastic bullets. (Despite the outcry against the use of the bullets by the security forces in Northern Ireland, where they were blamed for at least eleven deaths, mainland police forces had built up their stocks to a total of about 10,000 bullets by the beginning of 1983. Only 10 of the 43 police authorities had rejected their use in riots.)[9]

Police readiness and weaponry were not the only factors contributing to the uneasy peace. The mood on the streets had changed, too. The experience of 1981 had clearly been cathartic for some rioters, traumatic for others. Many were under pressure from relatives and acquaintances not to risk themselves again. There was agreement that there would have to be exceptional provocation locally or disturbances elsewhere before there was major conflict.

There was fire again in Toxteth within three weeks of the first anniversary of the riots in the summer of 1982. I could see flames as I drove into Liverpool from the east at the end of a week of sporadic disturbances. From one angle it looked as though the city's Roman Catholic cathedral was on fire. But the arsonist's target turned out to be Myrtle Gardens, a tenement block which was to be refurbished to provide flats for sale. The prices would have been modest only for the middle-class, and there are not many of them on those streets in Toxteth.

A black youth watching experts examining the block next morning said: 'Who's losing, man? They were no good for us any more, were they?'

And there were other questions, most of them rhetorical, some echoing the last verse of the poem I quoted earlier:

Why did it only happen once?
We can take our power back—
why are we afraid to go on?

Notes

1. *Socialist Worker*, 13 March 1982.
2. *Big Flame*, February 1982.
3. *Report of the Moss Side Enquiry Panel to the Leader of the Greater Manchester Council*, 30 September 1981.
4. *Manchester Evening News*, 8 January 1982.
5. *The Guardian*, 9 December 1981.
6. *The Observer*, 9 August 1981 and 11 July 1982.
7. *The Economist*, 26 December 1981.
8. 'The Toxteth Section', *Report of the Chief Constable to the Police Committee*, 25 January 1983.
9. *Daily Express*, 1 February 1983.

CHAPTER 6

The Brixton disorders

GEORGE GREAVES

The myth still persists that the bad police–community relations in Brixton are the result of the interaction between alienated *young* black people and young, inexperienced and frightened policemen. Lord Scarman seemed to support that contention when he stated that

> it would be surprising if they (young black people) did not feel a sense of frustration and deprivation. And living much of their lives on the streets, they are brought into contact with the police who appear to them as the visible symbols of the authority of a society which has failed to bring them its benefits or do them justice (Scarman, 2.23).

But Lord Scarman went further when he wrote that

> a significant cause of the hostility of young blacks towards the police was loss of confidence by significant sections, though it should not be assumed by all, of the Lambeth public in the police (Scarman, 4.1).

'Bad behaviour' by the police

There is no doubt in my mind that large sections, particularly of the black community, regarded the police as an oppressive force which disregarded their civil rights and dignity as human beings. That view was shared by the Counsel for the Tribunal, Mr R. Auld QC, an independent participant, in the sense that he did not represent any of the parties. His role was to assist the Tribunal in the preparation of its report and in the making of its findings and recommendations. Mr Auld in his closing address said that there were two main reasons why relations between the community of Brixton and the police had gone so badly wrong. He saw as the first reason the style of policing: they had failed 'to achieve the difficult but necessary balance between the effective prevention of crime and the keeping of the goodwill and support of the community'.

He went on to say that

> the second main reason for things having gone so badly wrong which I invite your Lordship to consider is bad behaviour by police constables. That there has been a widespread failure, I think, is putting it too high, and I should say that there has been a failure—at police constable level to behave to the community, particularly the young blacks, in the way that they should and in which their senior officers have trained and instructed them. I put that in basic, neutral terms—'bad behaviour'. It has had its expression in the evidence given to your Lordship most frequently in the word 'racism' or 'racialism'; and it is taken up largely by that aspect of the problem. But whether it is racialism or some other behaviour, it is bad behaviour—a way in which no person should behave to another, whether a police officer or otherwise.

Approaching a point of confrontation

It was in 1976 that I had the first real premonition that relations between the police and the black community of Brixton were approaching a point of violent confrontation. The incident which caused me to come to that conclusion involved the police and a black man in his late fifties. The man was on his way home along Railton Road, which forms part of 'the front line' when he was stopped by police and questioned about a parcel of groceries which he was carrying. He was man-handled, and his groceries scattered in the roadway. A pregnant young woman intervened but she was rebuffed with such force that she fell to the ground. The incident was witnessed by the young people who frequent the 'front line'. So intense was the anger generated in those who witnessed the incident that they marched as a body to Brixton Police Station to complain, and it was a spontaneous demonstration without any prompting from community leaders or community activists. The significance of that demonstration was not lost on those of us who were familiar with the area. The black youths were giving notice that they were no longer prepared to rely on intermediaries to win for them the justice which they felt was being denied them. They were prepared to act on their own behalf and in their own way.

On Monday 12 February 1979 three members of staff of the Council for Community Relations in Lambeth (CCRL) were arrested at the office and taken to Brixton police station in connection with a fracas in a local pub the previous Friday evening, when two plain clothes officers and a black barman were stabbed. The only link between the CCRL staff who were arrested, and the suspect, was that they wore sheepskin coats. That incident played a large part in the decision of the Executive Committee of CCRL to withdraw from the CCRL/Police Liaison Committee which had been formed in the previous October (see Scarman, 4.26).

The arrest of CCRL staff was only one of several questionable police actions taken over the weekend of that stabbing. For example, a young black woman returned to her flat on the Sunday evening from Luton where she had spent the weekend, to discover that her flat had been forceably entered. She called the police who, when they arrived, asked her questions relating to her boyfriend. They were looking for him as they felt that he might have information about the stabbing incident. She was invited to accompany them to the police station to make a statement. That she readily agreed to do. When they got there it was discovered that the officer who wanted to question her had gone off duty. She was then locked in the cells overnight. It was a callous and illegal act against someone who was not even a suspect. There was also the case of the woman who was kept in the police cells from the Saturday to the Monday with her 7-year-old child.

With one exception none of the informants who related the treatment received at the hand of the police that weekend wanted to use the police complaints procedure. Some were afraid of reprisals by the police, others had no confidence in the procedure. The CCRL workers started civil actions against the police which were still, in April 1983, waiting to be resolved.

The arrest of the CCRL staff received wide coverage in the press and elsewhere, but significantly in none of the reports was the question of its effect on the black community of Lambeth raised. It was mostly the older members of that community who contacted CCRL members and staff with words of sympathy. It was evident that the incident had increased further their sense of insecurity. They had felt that as a quasi-government body the CCRL would be immune from such off-hand police conduct. As one man said, 'If they can do that to you, now you can see what we have to put up with.'

For over a decade the police in Lambeth, of which Brixton is a part, have persisted in resorting to saturation policing in an attempt to combat street crime. During these operations substantial increases occur in the number of officers policing a specific area, and these are either local constables deployed from other areas within the District, or supplements (including the Special Patrol Group) brought in from elsewhere. Operation Swamp '81 which took place the week preceding the riots in April 1981, was one such operation, and it depended upon an extensive use of the 'stop and search' powers of the Metropolitan Police.

The police persisted in this method of policing even though the evidence showed that the level of success in combating street crime was minimal. The police usually went to great lengths to keep secret the knowledge of any imminent saturation exercise, but of course the element of surprise, which justified the secrecy, was short-lived. It did not take the criminal element long to realise what was happened, with the consequence that they moved to other parts of the borough, or to the neighbouring boroughs. The lack of success of the operation in dealing with street crime was matched by the tension it created in the saturated area, and the anger it generated in the minds of law-abiding citizens who resented the manner in which they were dealt with by the police when stopped. In some instances it may be argued that one result of saturation policing is to create crime, in the sense that the outcome of a 'stop' is a charge of 'obstructing a police officer in the execution of his duty' or 'assault on police'.

The 'Sus' law: unjust and inflammatory

Even more damaging to relations between the police and the black community was 'Sus'. 'Sus' was the shorthand for the charge of being a suspected person under section 4 of the Vagrancy Act 1824, and it was used more extensively in Lambeth than most other London boroughs. It was used particularly to prosecute young males of West Indian origin. For the three years 1977, 1978 and 1979 about three-quarters of those arrested for 'Sus' were black. In the second quarter of 1978 Lambeth topped the league in the use of the 'Sus' law when compared with other London boroughs with a similar sized West Indian population. The figures were:

Lambeth—65

Brent—14

Haringey— 2

The most significant feature of section 4 of the Act was the fact that the burden of proof on the prosecutor was very low: all that was required was for two officers to give corroborative evidence of what they had witnessed to gain a conviction. They did not need to present a potential victim or an independent witness, and they rarely did so. The police would tell the court for example that they saw the young man put out his hand to a woman's handbag as she stood in the bus queue. They might describe the handbag and what the woman was wearing at the time, but there was no necessity for them to produce the woman in court, and this produced major difficulties for the defence, and the bench.

In the cases where the defendant had the good sense, and the means, to be legally represented, his lawyer was faced with an uphill task. In the absence of other evidence he had to prove beyond all reasonable doubt that of the two conflicting stories—the one told by the police and his client—the latter was the truthful one. He might, for example, try to bring out inconsistencies in the police statements by skillful cross-examination. Other devices would be to try to throw doubt on the accuracy of police observations, or on the conclusions they had drawn, perhaps by arguing that the defendant was not the sort of person likely to be attempting to steal from handbags at a bus stop. In many ways the verdict reached by the magistrates related more to the court hearing than to the facts of the alleged offence, and the success of the devices used by the defence depended on the attitude of the bench towards police evidence, the character of the defendant and the proficiency of the defence counsel.

So apprehensive had some parents become that their children might be charged as suspected persons that they either kept them indoors, particularly after dark, or arranged for them to be escorted by an adult if they had to be out. For example, parents would take turns to meet a group of children and escort them to their houses from the youth club.

The relevant parts of section 4 of the Vagrancy Act 1824 were repealed by section 8 of the Criminal Attempts Act 1981. It is interesting to note that while the Metropolitan Police were contending that they needed 'Sus' if they were going to deal effectively with street crime, the Chief Constable of Manchester in a letter to *The Guardian* of 6 January 1979, described section 4 of the Vagrancy Act 1824 as an 'unnecessary controversial piece of legislation' rarely used by his force.

In his closing address to the Inquiry, Mr Michael Beloff QC, Counsel for the Council for Community Relations in Lambeth, said:

> It is respectfully noted that the Council came before the Inquiry wearing, unhappily, the mantle of a prophet. In a letter dated 7 February 1980, written more than a year before the disturbances, Mr Greaves warned Commander Adams, 'The long term consequences of your policy are that you will increasingly have to rely upon coercion rather than consent. This could ultimately degenerate into open and physical conflict between police and some members of the community in which people, both from the community and the police, will be injured.'

The Brixton eruption

With regard to the rioting itself, I write as someone who knows the area, and who, over the years, has observed the dynamics of the community. Yet, in honesty, I must confess that I was surprised by the scale and ferocity of the disorders. Stones, iron bars, bricks and petrol bombs were used to attack the police, and although the hostility of the crowd was directed mainly at the police, the rescue services also came under attack. It was believed that ambulances were ferrying in police reinforcements, and the belief that the fire brigade might be actively assisting the police was reinforced when Chief Superintendent Robinson and some of his men commandeered fire hoses from the firemen and turned them on the crowd in a desperate attempt to prevent themselves from being over-run (see Scarman, 3.70).

In the early stages of the disturbances damage to business premises conformed to a pattern which anyone familiar with the area would have anticipated. It was those businesses with a known reputation for exploiting their black customers and for subjecting them to a variety of indignities, which were first singled out for attack. These business enterprises must not be confused with those more distant from the area of the disturbances which were looted by opportunists who took advantage of the fact that the police had more urgent things to attend to (Scarman, 3.61 and 4.95–4.96). The fact is that in the main the people who were fighting the police were a different set of people from those who were looting on the main road of Brixton. There has been some attempt to see the causes of the disorders as the poverty and lack of employment opportunities existing in Brixton, and some of those who subscribe to this belief point to the widespread looting as evidence which supports their contention. My recollection is that many of the looters were decently clad, and certainly did not seem to represent the poorest sections of the society. I still retain the memory of seeing the spoils from a looting expedition being hurredly loaded into the boot of a white Rover car which was then driven off at high speed.

An early statement by the Commissioner of Police for the Metropolis, Sir David McNee, stated with certainty that the disorders were instigated by extreme left-wing political agitators from outside the Brixton area. If that statement were true it would follow that the riots were premeditated, but Lord Scarman said that the evidence he had heard indicated that the disorders originated from spontaneous crowd reaction to police action, which the crowd believed to be harassment of black people (Scarman, 3.109). To the young people present, the actions of the two police officers outside the S & M Car Hire firm on the Saturday afternoon was the 'straw that broke the camel's back', and they reacted immediately in the only way which they felt was open to them. Their complaints in the past, formal and informal, about police misconduct had gone unheeded, and as no one was helping them solve the problem of continued police harassment they therefore felt that they had to seek their own solution.

Once the conflict had started, leadership and organisation quickly developed. Some white people became involved, some as part of the crowd confronting the police, some seemed to be acting as scouts, while others were egging the crowd on. Evidence was given at the Inquiry that white people were seen assisting the black youths in the manufacture of petrol bombs (Scarman, 3.104).

Commissioner McNee in his statement credited the political agitators with much greater influence over the black youths than they have in reality. Radical political activists are attracted to Brixton, but their influence, so far, has been minimal. Much of their activities are concentrated around Brixton tube station where they sell their newspapers. They are very much on the fringe of the local and community politics.

More than one person when giving evidence before Lord Scarman referred to the carnival-like atmosphere which marked the earlier stages of the disturbances. There was much laughter and ribaldry coming from the young people who were actively engaging the police. Such behaviour—bizarre in the circumstances—seems difficult to explain, but I would venture to suggest that going through the minds of those young people were divers emotions. A situation which they may have contemplated in the past and partially discarded had now become a reality. There must have been a feeling of *release*, as they could now given vent to the anger which they had suppressed for so long. Mingled in with the other emotions must have been the feeling of *power*: did they not put the police, who until then were inviolable, on the defensive? There was also *fear*, as they had entered into a pursuit fraught with many dangers in its execution: they were entering uncharted waters not knowing at the time where it was leading.

Institutional racism: Lord Scarman's blinkered view

In his report Lord Scarman wrote:

> It was alleged by some of those who made representations to me that Britain is an institutionally racist society. If by that is meant that it is a society which knowingly, as a matter of policy, discriminates against black people, I reject the allegation. If, however, the suggestion being made is that practices may be adopted by public bodies as well as private individuals which are unwittingly discriminatory against black people then this is an allegation which deserves serious consideration, and where proved, swift remedy (Scarman, 2.22).

Later in the report he stated that ' "institutional racism" does not exist in Britain; but racial disadvantage and its nasty associate racial discrimination have not yet been eliminated' (Scarman, 9.1). In June 1982, at a meeting of the Black Rights Movement (United Kingdom and the USA) which was organised by the *Caribbean Times*, Lord Scarman seemed to have modified his position slightly when he said that the debate was 'a matter of semantics'.

However, British society can be shown to be institutionally racist even on the narrow definition of 'institutional racism' used in the Scarman Report. The concept of patriality introduced in the Commonwealth Immigrants Act 1968 was a device used specifically to prevent Asian East African United Kingdom passport holders from entering Britain. The patrial clause gives free entry to intending immigrants if they can prove that their parents or grandparents were born in Britain. In passing this Act, Parliament knew full well that the chance of an East African Asian being able to satisfy that criterion was small.

I do not accept Lord Scarman's narrow definition, for to do so would mean ignoring the customs, administrative practices and attitudes which have governed the workings of the institutions and which often discriminate against black people and work to their disadvantage. 'Institutional racism' may be intentional or unintentional, direct or indirect. Lord Scarman only needed to look at his own profession to see institutional racism at work. Black barristers find it inordinately difficult to be taken into Chambers. The existing system gives the Clerk of Chambers enormous powers to influence who is accommodated in the Chambers, and under the British system solicitors are not permitted to negotiate directly with barristers. Initial negotiations and the distribution of the work to members of the Chambers are undertaken by the Clerk. The fact that he is not salaried but on commission must incline him towards conservatism and rationalisation of any negative attitude he may have about black people. The consequences of that system are that black barristers do not find it easy to join established Chambers, and as a result they do not have access to libraries and other resources.

Lord Scarman summed up black inequality and alienation thus:

> Some young blacks are driven by their despair into feeling that they are rejected by the society of which they rightly believe they are members and in which they would wish to enjoy the same opportunities and to accept the same risks as everyone else. But their experience leads them to believe that their opportunities are less and their risks are greater. Young black people feel neither socially nor economically secure. In addition they do not feel politically secure. Their sense of rejection is not eased by the low level of black representation in our elective political institutions. Their sense of insecurity is not relieved by the liberty our law provides to those who march and demonstrate in favour of tougher immigration controls and 'repatriation' of the blacks (Scarman, 2.35–2.36).

The feelings of frustration and insecurity are not just limited to young black people, for they are experienced by the vast majority of black people living in Britain, regardless of age. It is important to ensure that the scale of the problem is not forgotten, although, in the context of the Inquiry, it was natural for Lord Scarman to concentrate on the plight of the young, for it is they who are most likely to be in the vanguard of any open confrontation with the authorities.

In order to appreciate fully the complex nature of the causation of the disorders it is necessary to look beyond Brixton to the national scene. We must examine the way black people in Britain are regarded by British society, and equally important are the perceptions of black people of the status accorded them by that society.

It is my opinion that racism and the power of white institutions arbitrarily to shape the destiny of black people constitute the main ingredients in the explosive mixture which erupted in Brixton and elsewhere in 1981. Police policies and practices which sparked off the Brixton disorders were easily identified, but they are only part of the problem. Would the service provided to black people by the social service agencies stand up to critical examination? Are black mothers being malicious when they lament that the advice which their children are receiving from social workers creates unnecessary discord in the household? Black people are hardly ever in a position to influence decisions made about them—decisions which sometimes alter the course of their lives in fundamental ways. They are hardly ever consulted about matters which affect them, and on the rare occasions when they are consulted they feel their advice goes unheeded. If they protest they are then accused of 'having chips on their shoulders'.

Lord Scarman's denial of the existence of institutional racism was a good example of the blinkered approach to matters about race which can affect even well-meaning white people.

Brixton in 1983: few serious changes

Lord Scarman pointed out that although a 'section 32 inquiry' is essentially concerned with policing matters, it must also take account of the social context. He thus tried 'to identify not only the policing problem specific to the disorders but the social problem of which it is necessarily part' (Scarman, 1.5).

It is now over two years since the Brixton disorders occurred and eighteen months since the publication of Lord Scarman's report. But what steps have been taken to deal with the social and policing problems which he identified?

Unfortunately it seems that very little has been attempted or achieved, and some problems such as unemployment have deteriorated further. The local newspaper, the *South London Press*, reported on 4 March 1983 that

> More than forty people are chasing every job vacancy in Lambeth. Latest figures show that there are 23,645 unemployed in the borough—up 4 per cent on the previous month. And of all youngsters out of work, 52 per cent have been on the dole for more than six months.
>
> Lambeth has 18 per cent unemployment—highest in London, and nearly 5 per cent above the national average.
>
> Unemployment in the borough has risen by 18 per cent in a year.

Lambeth Borough Council has made attempts to improve the environment and amenities in the vicinity of Railton Road—'the front line'. The adventure playground is being extended, and some additional open spaces and traffic-free streets are proposed. Some of the houses which were damaged during the disturbances are being rebuilt, and other properties are to be renovated. New locations have been found for some of the small shopkeepers. The number of crimes committed remains high, with burglaries and auto-crime heading the list. The clear-up rate is low—only about 8 out of 100 burglaries are solved. There are some encouraging signs that street crime may be starting to diminish.

The Community-Police Liaison Group for Lambeth has been in existence for over a year. It has broad community representation, but there are one or two important local organisations which have not sought membership. The Group is slowly trying to come to grips with the mammoth task of helping to improve police–community relations. Its efforts have not been assisted however by the Government's Police and Criminal Evidence Bill, which was before the House of Commons from November 1982 and until May 1983 when it failed on the dissolution of Parliament. In the Bill police powers were being extended in those very areas, for example stop-and-search, which bring the police and members of the community into conflict. It is to be hoped that any legislation brought forward by the new Government is more conducive to good police–community relations.

The attempts so far to tackle the problems of Lambeth identified by Lord Scarman are slight relative to their scale and complexity. The community nevertheless seems to be returning to normality, and is waiting to see how the authorities intend to deal with those matters which affect the quality of life in the area. The people of Brixton interpret their situation as one of neglect over the years. It is to be hoped that the authorities will use the breathing space now being afforded them to demonstrate that the expressed and observed needs of the community will be catered for. Time is not on the side of the authorities, because the community is not likely to slip back into the state of apathy which existed before the momentous events of April 1981.

CHAPTER 7

Reporting the riots: images and impact

GRAHAM MURDOCK

This chapter sets out to answer two basic questions. Firstly, how did the national press and television news report the urban riots of July 1981—what images and explanations were given the greatest prominence and what factors shaped the coverage? And secondly, what impact did the reporting have—did it influence the course of the riots themselves, and if so how, and how far did it set the agenda for the debate on policing and public order that followed?

A great deal more was said about the riots and their causes than appeared in the major news media of course. They were extensively discussed in current affairs programmes and documentaries and in the weekly and monthly magazines. Nevertheless, most people gained a great deal of their information and impressions about the events from the national press and television news, and as we shall see, the images they offered shaped both the political debate and public opinion. Recent American research suggests that the news coverage of spectacular challenges to order, such as large scale rioting or political assassinations, can play a key role in fuelling fears about the breakdown of society and in mobilising popular support for tough counter measures.[1] * The summer riots were just such a formative moment.

Depicting disorder—images of Toxteth

The news coverage of the 1981 riots crystallised on Monday 6 July when all the national dailies carried front page stories of the weekend's disturbances in Toxteth. This drew on a range of images and welded them into a powerful perspective which provided the framework for much of the coverage and debate that followed. This perspective cut across the normal divisions of stance and style and converged around a single dramatic image of an under-equipped police force struggling to protect property and the

---

* Superscript numbers refer to Notes at end of chapter.

Queen's Peace in the face of a rioting crowd, most of them young and a lot of them black, using barricades, bricks and petrol bombs to drive them off the streets, and taking the chance to loot shops and burn buildings.

This image appeared in its starkest form in the *Daily Mail*, whose front page headline 'BLACK WAR ON POLICE' appeared directly above a large photograph of the police lines (shot from behind) confronting stone throwing youths and captioned: 'Facing the fury of the mob: Row upon row of police behind their riot shields at Toxteth'. Immediately above the headline was a quotation from the Chief Constable of Merseyside, Kenneth Oxford, claiming that: 'For 100 years we haven't had a problem—now they're hell-bent on confrontation.' The question of who exactly 'they' were was promptly answered in the main story which began with another quote from Oxford, blaming the violence on gangs of 'young black hooligans' whom he later described more fully as 'a small hooligan criminal element hell-bent on confrontation', adding that 'their fight was with us, the police, a symbol of authority and discipline which is anathema to these people'.

The *Daily Mail* image was reinforced and extended by the double page spread on pages 2 and 3 headed: 'Weapons of hate in the city of fear'. One page carried a large photograph of the police lines preparing to 'advance towards a trouble spot', and a smaller picture of a policeman's head, bandaged and bloodied under the visor of his protective helmet, entitled 'riot victim'. Opposite Kenneth Oxford was shown sitting behind a table littered with pick-axe handles and other items captioned: 'the armoury of destruction'. By invoking the imagery of warfare, this description suggested that the police were fighting an external non-British enemy. This impression was strongly reinforced by the emphasis on how 'the people of Upper Parliament Street, Liverpool 8, counted the cost of the riot', based on a young woman's eyewitness account of the looting of her family's grocery store. Although she pointed out that 'more whites were looting our store than blacks', this qualification was offset by an adjacent article headed 'Violent Streets' which listed 'the recent record of race riots in Britain', placing Toxteth within this context.

Through these various devices—headlines, photographs, the descriptive language, the juxtaposition of items—the *Mail*'s coverage directed its readers towards three important conclusions. Firstly, it separated the rioters from 'the people of Upper Parliament Street', portraying them as an alien black presence threatening the property and safety of established residents. Secondly, it identified the action of the police with the interests of the community and depicted officers and locals as the common victims of mob violence. And thirdly, having established an image of exceptional threat, it called for exceptional control measures to deal with it. This 'solution' was outlined in a page 3 story entitled: 'Police: Give us riot gear' and backed by an editorial calling for the police to be provided with suitable vehicles, equipment and weapons, including water cannon, to enable them to vanquish future riots.

The basic pattern of the *Mail*'s coverage was repeated in three other major dailies, the *Daily Express*, *The Daily Telegraph*, and *The Sun*, though all three played down the 'race riot' angle in favour of other emphases. Like the *Mail*, the *Express*'s front page story, 'HELLBENT ON HAVOC', was built around Kenneth Oxford's description of the rioters as 'a band of hooligans who do not want to live in a civilised society' and his assertion that 'they will not win. We will uphold the law'. And like the *Mail*, the rest of the coverage elaborated these themes with three pictures of police facing rioters and a smaller photograph of an injured policeman captioned 'victim'. But unlike the *Mail*, the central comparison is with Northern Ireland rather than previous British 'race riots'. Hence the main story begins:

A policeman is near to being enveloped with flames as his shield is hit by a petrol bomb.

The bottle was thrown by the youth in the mask. The other, hooded rioter takes aim with a boulder.

He is filled with hate and he looks every bit as sinister as the gangs of Northern Ireland.

This Irish 'angle' was further underlined by references to 'terror' and 'masked mobs', in the caption to one of the main photographs—'the police retreat against a barrage of terror from the masked and hooded mob'—and in Eldon Griffith's feature article headed, 'Can we really afford NOT to arm our police?' which called for the British police to make use of the vast experience of the Royal Ulster Constabulary.

The Daily Telegraph's coverage also followed the same basic pattern as the *Mail*'s. The front page was based around Kenneth Oxford's view of events with two out of the four main headlines quoting him directly:

No no-go areas . . . black, yellow or white, they won't beat my men.
STREET RIOTS ERUPT AGAIN
Violence to 'thin blue line' worries Thatcher
Police Chief pledges to maintain order

Similarly, the inside coverage took up the core themes with a large photograph of the police holding the line against rioters, two portrait photographs of injured policemen, a picture of Oxford behind the desk of riot weapons, and a report of 'Jardine's pleas for riot gear', supported by an editorial call for better police equipment and tougher legislation. However, though the front page story quoted Oxford as saying that the trouble began with a 'crowd of black hooligans', it immediately added that white youths soon joined in, and the event was placed in the context of general images of teenage violence established by the coverage of 'football hooliganism'. Thus the rioters facing the police lines in the page one photograph were identified as 'an advancing mob of missile throwing youths' while the caption to a similar picture on page 2 described them as 'rampaging youths' renewing 'their orgy of violence against the police'.

The Sun's coverage on the other hand deftly combined references to Northern Ireland with generalised images of crowd disorder. The front page photograph mobilised the familiar Irish images of masked petrol bombers, while the lead story headed 'THE BLOOD FLOWS AGAIN' evoked fears of 'King Mob'.

The media's consistent interpretation

Nor was this perspective of the events confined to papers which support the present government. It was shared by the *Daily Mirror*, which has a long record of backing Labour. Above their main headline 'HAMMERED', the *Mirror* carried a small picture of a policeman's bandaged and bloodied face. Underneath was a much larger photograph of police with riot shields (one apparently on fire) with masked rioters in the background, captioned: 'Targets: Police under fire at Toxteth', and this was followed by the main story which opened by reporting the police call 'for Continental style riot gear after two nights of violence that left dozens of officers injured'.

Despite these differences of emphasis and elaboration, all the papers discussed so far shared the same underlying definition of events as an eruption of youthful violence and criminality, which the police just managed to contain and which could only be successfully combated by giving them better control equipment and greater powers. This perspective comprehensively wrong-foots the counter arguments that tough policing may be a cause of rioting rather than a cure for it. This view did appear in the press reporting of Toxteth but it was effectively contained by the general thrust of the coverage. The *Daily Star*, for example, featured a statement from the Merseyside Community Relations Council claiming that a heavy-handed police response to the original incident had served to escalate matters:

> There was an over-reaction by police. An excessive number of police vehicles converged on what initially was a minor matter. Deeply-felt anger and resentment was aroused and there followed a series of incidents of police cars being stoned.

This was immediately followed by Kenneth Oxford's denial that the area had been 'over-policed'. Similarly, on page 11 the *Star* printed a feature based on a black councillor's statement that 'the stop-and-search exercise before the Brixton troubles and the coroner's disastrous handling of the Deptford fire enquiry' had simply added to the feelings of alienation amongst black youth, and strengthened their hostility to the police. But before reaching this piece, readers had already been offered a quite different view of events, such as the front page photograph of police being attacked by petrol bombs, and the inside feature headed 'BLOODY FACE OF BRITAIN '81'. This included a picture of 'hard pressed police' scrambling 'desperately for shelter from the mob in Liverpool as petrol bombs explode against their riot shields', together with a portrait of an injured policeman and the picture of Kenneth Oxford displaying the 'hate weapons seized in Liverpool'.

The Guardian's major story also carried the Merseyside Community Relations Council's statement that the police had 'over-reacted', and (on page 22) a Jamaican community leader's claim that 'the real cause of the trouble is policing of the area and the lack of respect police have for people'. But here again these alternative views were offset by the main presentation which featured a large photograph of policemen retreating 'under a hail of missiles', together with a portrait of Kenneth Oxford and a main headline repeating the assertion that ' "Hooligans caused riots" ' (though the use of quotation marks does distance the paper somewhat from his views).

A similar displacement of critical perspectives on police behaviour was also evident in the television news coverage. The key police decision to deploy CS gas, for example, was presented as an entirely necessary and justified step, given the violence of the rioters and the inadequacy of standard police equipment. Here is how Independent Television News (ITN) described the situation on its *News at One* bulletin on Monday (6 July 1981) lunchtime.

> As police moved in to clear a barricade of milk floats strung across Upper Parliament Street, they were set upon by a mob of youths. With only riot shields and truncheons, they faced a barrage of petrol bombs, bricks and iron bars. As the intensity of attacks increased, the toll of police casualties climbed. A policeman who had this iron railing thrown at his head is lucky to be still alive, but faced with that sort of savagery, the police were forced to use CS gas for the first time on the British mainland.

This view was later underscored by the BBC in its major evening bulletin at 9 pm.[3] Subsequent investigations revealed that on at least one occasion when CS gas was used in Toxteth, police ignored the manufacturer's instructions, and aimed directly towards the crowd causing substantial

injuries to several people.[4] Although the evidence on this only came to light
some time afterwards, the television news men could have taken a more
critical stance towards the police handling of the situation and given more
space to alternative views, as they had in their reporting of the Brixton riots
in April.[5] In July, however, the coverage was constructed much more
centrally around the views of senior police officers, and the statements of
Conservative politicians who favoured a tough response. In his study of the
major evening bulletins on the two main channels, from 14 to 16 July,
Howard Tumber found that while government ministers received 373
seconds of air time and senior police officers 367, community leaders
received only 147 and the rioters themselves just 52 seconds.[6] They were
universally spoken about but rarely spoken to. The same pattern emerged
from Anders Hansen's analysis of reports in the *Mail*, *Mirror* and *Guardian*
from 6 to 12 July. In all three papers the statements of senior policemen
received more space than the views of any other group (more than twice as
much in the case of the two 'populars'), while the views of participants were
afforded very little space.[7]

The major news media then presented a highly consistent account of the
Toxteth disturbances centred around the image of a 'thin blue line' of police
defending the community against an unprecedented wave of violence and
lawlessness, and within this view the riots were defined as a criminal rather
than a political phenomenon, as street crime on a mass scale, to be dealt with
as such, through more effective policing and extended police powers. As we
shall see, this basic image was elaborated on in a variety of ways, as
commentators searched for explanations and explored solutions, and it
becomes clear that questions about the political roots of rioting and the
advisability of greater police powers have been edged out from the centre of
debate, with the focus instead on the argument that new and exceptional
threats to law and order require new and exceptional measures to deal with
them. But why did the initial coverage take the form that it did? Contrary to
the 'high' and 'low' conspiracy theories favoured by some critics of the news
media,[8] the answer does not lie in interventions from on high or in the
personal prejudices of journalists and editors, but in the routine business of
news production and the practical and commercial pressures which shape it.

Getting the story: news gathering

As Michael Nally points out in his contribution, the journalist's job is to
report what can be seen and heard and what might be the meaning of it. But
this is not always as simple as it first appears. What you see depends on
where you stand and what you hear depends on who you talk to, or who is
prepared to talk to you. The reason why police and government
spokespeople were prominently quoted while community leaders and

rioters got comparatively little space, has more to do with practicalities than with ideology. As news sources, senior policemen and politicians have certain distinct advantages. They are relatively easy to contact and skilled at providing material that can be turned into quotable tags: important factors in view of the tight production deadlines. Reporting their statements also confirms the newsmen's cherished image of themselves as the key channel of communication between the 'authorities' and the people, and being public servants they appear to speak for the community as a whole, rather than simply for themselves. Grass roots leaders and 'rioters', on the other hand, have none of these advantages. They are often difficult to contact and many are unwilling to talk to journalists or give their names (and an unnamed source always presents a problem for reporters). Some suspect that their views will be distorted by selective quotation and unsympathetic presentation,[9] while 'rioters' may fear that their statements will find their way to the police and be used against them later. A similar difference in ready access to sources also underlies the reporting of injuries. Any police officer receiving an injury (of whatever nature) must report the fact and the total figures are readily and rapidly available. In contrast, many participants with injuries never go to a doctor or a hospital, and so there is no reliable injury list. As a result, the injuries to police almost always appear greater than the injuries to the public and the participants.

Another aspect is the key role of photographs in the press reporting of the riots. All the 'populars' carried dramatic front page pictures of the police lines (shot from behind or from the side) facing a crowd throwing stones and petrol bombs, which both illustrated and confirmed the image created by the headlines and the text. But here again, the explanation has more to do with practicalities than with ideology. Press photographers tend to shoot from behind the police lines because this is usually the least unsafe place to be in a riot, and because the police actively offer them the protection of the cordon as a matter of policy. Photographs taken from this vantage point encourage the audience to see the event through police eyes by showing a thin blue line of officers protected only by helmets and riot shields facing a dense and threatening-looking mob.[10] Shot from behind the rioters, however, the same scene looks completely different. We see what appears to be a solid para-military phalanx bearing down on a crowd of ordinary-looking young people, and these contrasting images generate rather different lines of thought. The first image reinforces demands for more and better riot equipment to enable the police to cope more effectively with the threat to public order, while the second prompts us to ask why it is that the situation in our inner cities has deteriorated to such an extent that it take police in riot gear to control the local youth population.[11] Photographs of the second type were difficult to take during the riots, however.[12] Most participants did not want to be photographed and there were a number of cases of photographers and film cameramen being threatened, or having their equipment smashed. Consequently, most of the photographs available to editors showed the police lines facing the crowd, injured policemen, or (as with the picture of Kenneth Oxford behind the desk piled with weapons) scenes arranged by the police. Occasionally though, the closeness of press cameras to police operations can produce images which suggest a less favourable view of police performance. The most notable example from Toxteth was a picture of an officer, looking much more like a soldier in combat than a policeman, holding a shotgun used to fire ferret type CS gas cartridges, taken by John Sturrock of the Network Agency on the night of 8 July. This appeared too late to make the Monday editions and was never taken up in the mainstream coverage, though it did feature widely in the alternative press, where it was used to anchor arguments against the further extension of police powers.[13]

Making sense of it: news presentation

Having gathered the raw material, news organisations are faced with the problem of turning it into a story which will make sense to the audience and hold their attention. The problem of creating interest was easily solved by focusing on the clashes between police and rioters at the height of the disturbances, since these scenes had all the classic ingredients that are judged to make a 'good story': dramatic and violent action, a large number of participants and important political implications. Conversely, they paid comparatively little attention to the original incident that triggered the disturbances,[14] or to the allegations of a build-up of resentment at the way the area had been policed which, it was claimed, lay behind the disorders. Consequently, as a senior BBC newsman pointed out later, neither they 'nor anybody else were able adequately to explain why the riots were happening'.[15] But the news organisations had to provide their audiences with some sort of explanation and in the search for feasible frameworks they turned to images which were already firmly embedded in popular culture and consciousness. As a result the Toxteth disturbances were removed from their specific historical context and relocated within a network of imagery and explanation which touched on longstanding fears about the nature and sources of public disorder.

Rampaging crowds and sober citizens

From the beginning of the modern political system our view of popular participation has been dominated by two opposed images: the public and the crowd. The public is composed of individuals, each one making rational political choices and expressing their preferences through an electoral system based on universal franchise. By contrast the crowd appears as a degenerate form of political expression based on direct rather than electoral action and characterised by irrationality and extremism, rather than moderation and good sense. Moreover, so the argument goes, in a modern mass democracy with fully formed representative institutions, there can be little political rationale for the resort to direct action, and no rationale at all for the resort to crowd behaviour.

Against this, some commentators have argued that the British political system is currently undergoing a crisis of representation in which increasing numbers of people, particularly young people, no longer feel that the traditional parties and political organisations adequately articulate their interests and aspirations, and that consequently the riots must be seen, in part, as an alternative means of drawing attention to grievances and securing a political hearing. The dominant perspective, however, excludes this possibility and focuses attention firmly on the irrationality of crowd behaviour.

Within this framework 'mob' violence appears as an eruption of irrationality and animality brought on by the excitement of being in a crowd. As Charles McKay of *The Times* put it in 1852, 'men go mad in herds, while they only recover their sense slowly, and one by one',[16] a point which Gustav Le Bon later promoted in his best-seller *The Crowd*, first published in 1895 and still in print. According to Le Bon:

> . . . by the mere fact that he forms part of a crowd, a man descends several rungs in the ladder of civilisation. Isolated, he may be a cultivated individual; in a crowd, he is a barbarian—that is, a creature acting by instinct.[17]

This argument found many echoes in the coverage of Toxteth, most notably in the *Daily Mail*'s centre page spread on 6 July, headed 'Saturday night madness', a play on the title of the hit film *Saturday Night Fever*, also suggesting another way of looking at the riots—as a disorderly form of teenage leisure.

Dangerous streets and hooligan youth

Adolescence has long been seen as a particularly unstable and volatile period when young people are most likely to challenge established authority and early on these fears crystallised around the delinquent behaviour of juvenile street 'gangs'. This image of peer groups as predatory hordes was crystallised in the coverage given to the London Hooligans at the turn of the century. The original group was reputedly formed by Patrick O'Hooligan, a notorious Lambeth street fighter, but the term was soon applied to almost any 'gang' behaviour, as in this story from the *News of the World* of 1900, headed 'Hooligan Terror':

> For years past gangs of Hooligans have waged war in the streets of London either with rival gangs or with the police and peaceable citizens . . . and the authorities appear to be quite unable to deal with the ruffians who make the streets of the metropolis more dangerous to law-abiding folk than the streets of the most lawless mining camp.[18]

Soon afterwards, the term 'hooligan' became generalised still further to apply to almost any outbreak of public disorder in which young people played a prominent part, or in which adults failed to 'act their age' and behaved like adolescents. Hence when riots and looting occurred in Liverpool in the summer of 1919, following a strike by police, *The Times* headed their account 'HOOLIGANS IN LIVERPOOL', and went on to report that:

> The trouble began late on Friday night when several shops were wrecked. The hooligans of the Scotland Road and dock areas took advantage of the depletion of the police force and let themselves go. . . . Anarchy broke out. . . . Gangs of youths and young men proceeded along the thoroughfare stopping first at one shop and then another. The air resounded with the crash of huge plate-glass windows.[19]

In this perspective, rioting appears simply as an outbreak of adolescent 'hooliganism', as ordinary gang behaviour on a mass scale, to be dealt with like any other wave of street crime by tougher policing and stiffer penalties. This framework has proved remarkably resilient. The rhetoric of 'hooligan' is still widely applied to youthful deviance and especially to incidents of collective violence, as in the extensive coverage given to 'football hooliganism' in recent years. As we have seen, this rhetoric featured prominently in Kenneth Oxford's statements on Toxteth, and provided one of the major frames through which the news media reported the events. Despite the continuities in the language used, however, there was one very significant difference between perceptions of Liverpool in 1919 and 1981: the centrality of images of black youth.

The black tide and the blue line

The image of the black population as permanently alien and threatening to 'our' way of life is deeply ingrained in British popular culture and the presence of black youth adds a significant extra dimension to the established imagery of street crime and crowd disorders: 'Hooligans' become 'black hooligans' and 'mobs' become 'race mobs'. This rhetoric had been firmly established by the reporting of the disturbances at the Notting Hill carnival in 1976, and the riot in the St Paul's area of Bristol in April 1980, but it was given a fresh salience by the coverage of the clashes in central London in March 1981 between police and marchers protesting about the police and press handling of the fire at a teenage party in New Cross in January, which had killed thirteen young blacks. These clashes attracted headlines such as 'Police injured in clash with demo blacks', 'RAMPAGE OF A MOB', 'Riots and looting as marchers run wild', 'BLACK DAY AT BLACK-FRIARS', and 'WHEN THE BLACK TIDE MET THE THIN BLUE LINE'.[20] This last headline, from the *Daily Mail*, catches the echoes of empire which underpin this representation of events. It evokes visions of the thin red line of British 'tommys', familiar from countless adventure stories from G. A. Henty to *Zulu*, valiantly holding out and defending the British way of life against the encroaching 'black tide'.

There is, of course, a powerful counter-perspective to this, centred on the image of black youth as victims rather than victimisers, bearing the brunt of the current recession and forced to forego the chance of a decent job and reasonable prospects through no fault of their own. This view did appear in the follow-up coverage to Toxteth, most notably in the *Daily Mirror* and in the *Daily Star*, which carried a front page editorial on 7 July arguing that the main causes of the riots

> are unemployment, poor housing, inadequate education, the collapse of inner city areas and the feeling of utter despair that so many young people, black and white, feel in these times of crippling recession.

But here, as elsewhere in the popular press, the force of this argument was blunted by the strength of the 'law and order' framework already established and constantly returned to. Page 3 of that same issue of the *Star*, for example, also carried three photographs of injured policemen under the headline 'BLOODY BATTLE: nightmare on the streets of hatred' and a dramatic eye-witness account of the riots which described the rioters as 'howling as they drove the police down Upper Parliament Street' and 'jeering at ambulance-men evacuating the old folks' hospital' and presented CS gas as 'the only weapon in the meagre (police) armoury capable of halting the mayhem'. The same story also introduced another key theme with references to sinister 'masked men' handing out 'petrol bombs to their frenzied army of teenagers' and to the 'masked ringleaders behind the riots'. This idea that the youthful participants were encouraged by outside agitators played a prominent part in organising the news media's explanations of the riots.

Aliens and agitators

The notion that riots are fomented by foreign agitators or people possessed of 'alien' views and bent on undermining the 'British way of life' has been used to explain almost every incident of public disorder since the Gordon Riots of 1780.[21] It is dominated by the image of socialist subversives working away to weaken the British state. When unemployed labourers rioted in the West End of London in February 1886, *Punch*, for example, was quick to blame the trouble on left-wing agitators with a satirical ditty entitled 'Song of the Socialist Spouter'.

> Violence, sweet Violence!
> Beautiful brute Violence!
> Nice to see the dupes we've maddened to their practice led,
> Nice to see them stealing, smashing,
> Shop-fronts wrecking, faces bashing,
> While we hug our theories, and hurry home to bed![22]

In the same vein, two days after its dramatic report of the Liverpool riots of 1919, *The Times* printed a story headed 'PLOT FINANCED FROM ABROAD', claiming that 'the authorities' were convinced that the disorders were 'part of a definite conspiracy, which had its roots abroad, to subvert the present system of government in this country'.[23]

Riots, like accidents, clearly do attract outsiders to the scene and some of them belong to political groups, but firm evidence of an organised conspiracy or even of left-wing activists playing a significant role in directing the July 1981 riots was hard to come by. However, this did not stop the *Daily Mail* from making this the main theme of their follow-up coverage. The front page for Tuesday 7 July was dominated by the headline: 'The riots and political militants—Special Branch is called in. SEARCH FOR THE MASKED MEN.' The story featured eye-witness accounts of 'masked figures on motor cycles issuing instructions to groups of rioters' and 'Cockney and Scottish voices shouting from in the middle of the mob', backed by a statement from Merseyside's deputy chief constable saying that 'detectives were investigating this aspect of the rioting'. The theme was picked up by ITN the same day, with the flash headline 'Was someone directing the Liverpool riots?' between the chimes of Big Ben at the beginning of *News at Ten*. But their evidence was even thinner than the *Mail*'s. They claimed to 'have a picture of someone who *may have been trying to* direct the last riot' (my italics), but the film turned out to be of two youngsters on a motor bike who, it was claimed, were 'moving ahead of police charges, warning rioters of their positions'. Two days later, however, ITN returned to the theme with an opening headline 'Trouble in Woolwich—is it organised?' and the next day on *News at One* they established it even more firmly by asking the Home Secretary whether he thought 'that agitators have been causing some of the riots?' He answered with a provisional 'yes', and cited the opinion of Manchester's Chief

Constable, James Anderton, who had claimed in an ITN interview the previous day that he could not 'believe that it is within the intelligence and capacity of even many of the older groups of the young people involved to plan and organise an operation of this scale', and he thought 'there must be other people involved'.

This argument mistakes youthful alienation from official organisations such as clubs, churches and the mainstream political parties, for lack of organisation. Youth in the inner city are not disorganised, they are simply organised in a different way, built around informal networks and unofficial leisure milieux. Failure to recognise this fact also led commentators to overestimate the media's influence during the riots. Indeed, they saw the news media as a sort of surrogate agitator, urging teenagers to join in and stage-directing their actions. As we shall see, however, the question of media impact is rather more complex.

Questions of impact: confused terms, confined debates

The public debate on the media's influence on the riots began in earnest on Saturday 11 July when Mrs Mary Whitehouse sent a telegram to the editors of BBC and ITN news asking them to 'Please consider whether the current massive television coverage of acts of vandalism and violence is contributing to the spread of riots'. The text appeared on the bulletins of both channels the same day, together with statements from the two editors partly conceding the case. ITN's David Nicholas agreed that 'media coverage of the disturbances has probably had some "copycat" effect', while Peter Woon of the BBC admitted that 'it would be foolish to pretend that there has been no "copycat" effect'.

This idea of a simple copycat effect was taken up by several papers the following Monday. *The Times* carried a headline 'Copycat mobs in petrol bomb attacks on police', while the *Star*'s front page feature on the weekend's disturbances had a quote from the Tunbridge Wells police (where a group of youths had smashed shop windows in the High Street) claiming that 'the kids are just trying to copy the havoc that's happening elsewhere'. It also featured prominently in Lord Scarman's later criticisms of the media. He thought it 'likely that there was a substantial "copycat" element in many of the disorders which occurred during the summer' (Scarman, 2.30), and went on to say that 'the media, particularly the broadcasting media, do in my view bear a responsibility for the escalation of the disorders (including the looting) in Brixton on Saturday 11 April and for their continuation the following day, and for the imitative element in the later disorders elsewhere' (Scarman, 6.39). In making these criticisms, Lord Scarman is backed by a long tradition of popular commentary and academic research purporting to demonstrate a direct causal link between exposure to images of violence and subsequent imitative behaviour, particularly among young people. Even at its most sophisticated, this position is open to a number of criticisms,[24] but by working with the ill-defined notion of 'copycat' effects, Lord Scarman simplifies it still further. By focusing exclusively on the *actions* of rioters and looters, he effectively rules out any discussion of the media's role in shaping the *reactions* of the police, politicians and the general public.

Moreover, because he does not separate the different kinds of influence covered by the notion of 'copycat effects', his analysis is inadequate even in its own terms. Take, for example, the central idea of 'contagion'—the notion that the media coverage spread the 'disease' of rioting in much the same way as germs spread physical epidemics.

Contagious behaviour

Once again, this is not a new idea. People have worried that audiences would be tempted to imitate what they had seen on the stage ever since entertainments featuring crime and violence became popular, but the rise of a mass commercial press brought the added fear that crime reporting would spread these imitation effects over a much larger geographical area. As the French critic Gabriel Tarde put it in 1890: 'infectious epidemics spread with the air or the wind; epidemics of crime follow the line of the telegraph'.[25]

Almost a hundred years on, Richard Clutterbuck is still making the same point and claiming that the 'thirty-eight separate riots' which occurred in the five days following the news coverage of Toxteth of 6 July 'can have no possible explanation other than the copycat phenomenon'.[26] This argument looks convincing, but like Tarde, Clutterbuck mistakes correlation for causality. The fact that events occur together in time does not mean that one is directly 'caused' by the other. This problem besets even the most sophisticated versions of the contagion thesis, such as Seymour Spilerman's study of the pattern of rioting in America in the 1960s. He found that a well-reported riot in a large city tended to be followed by a rash of riots elsewhere. He also discovered that the severity of the rioting did not appear to be related to social conditions in the area, and he therefore concluded that national television news coverage was 'responsible in a most essential way for the outbreaks' and 'provided an essential mechanism for riot contagion'.[27] Unfortunately, he forgot to include police behaviour or the quality of police–community relations in his list of 'relevant' social conditions, even though all the evidence suggested that they were crucial.[28] Once policing is included, a more complex pattern emerges and we are faced with two processes rather than one. The possibility that the coverage of rioting in one area sparks off incidents elsewhere remains. But there is also the possibility that the resentment occasioned by reactive policing comes to a head more or less simultaneously in several places, producing independent riots.[29] This caveat does not mean that the news coverage plays no part in spreading riots, but it does suggest that the interaction between media imagery and situational dynamics is more complicated than allowed for by the simple notion of 'contagion'. The same is true of the relation between reporting and local rumour.

'Tooling up for trouble': reports and rumours

After the weekend of rioting in Brixton, the *Daily Mirror*'s front page for 13 April carried the headline 'THE SHAPE OF THINGS TO COME', with a large picture of a confrontation between police with riot shields and black and white youths throwing stones. In the top left-hand corner of the page was a quotation from Haringey's community relations officer predicting that 'the next riots will take place in Birmingham and Manchester'. Some observers have argued that this kind of coverage raised the consciousness of inner city youth and increased their readiness to take on the police. This is a possibility, but the coverage also had lessons for the police. It primed them to expect trouble in the major cities and strengthened their resolve to crack down on it early by stepping up their activities in inner city areas. This in turn cemented youth resentment at police behaviour and fed local rumours that a riot was imminent. As a result, both sides 'tooled up' for trouble, so that eventually it only took a minor incident on the streets to trigger a confrontation.

According to the 'copycat' thesis, however, once a riot is under way news coverage replaces rumour and personal contact as the major source of young people's information and encourages them on to the streets, thereby escalating it still further. Howard Tumber dismisses this argument totally, claiming that television is a minor information source, and that most participants first hear about the riots through the local grapevine,[30] but his evidence is too thin to support his case convincingly.

Somewhat better evidence comes from Peter Southgate's study of rioting in the Handsworth area of Birmingham, the weekend after Toxteth. 'Copying other areas' was the second most popular reason chosen by the sample of local men, aged between 16 and 34, who were interviewed for the study. Fifty per cent said they had first been informed of the disturbances through the mass media, 31 per cent via television. Southgate found that while teenagers were more likely to find out about the riot through the grapevine, 20 per cent of the 16- to 19-year-olds still first heard about it via television.[31] Moreover, because of the way the questions were asked, he may have underestimated the significance of television as an information source since American riot studies suggest that many of those who told other people that a riot was going on got their original information from television news reports.[32] Unfortunately there is no comparable evidence for the Brixton riots of 1981, but once again we can see that it is more productive to explore the *interaction* between reporting and the riots, rather than to pose the question of media influence in 'either/or' terms.

The 'lessons' of Northern Ireland:
petrol bombs and CS gas

The other central theme of the 'copycat' thesis concerns the media's role in disseminating the actual techniques of rioting: 'the question of whether young people grasp the specific tactics of social disruption shown on television and at some future opportune time and place decide to put these tactics to use'.[33] Several commentators were in no doubt at all that the extensive news coverage of riots involving petrol bombs in Northern Ireland had encouraged the rioters in Brixton and Liverpool 8 to use petrol bombs for the first time in England.[34] This argument was outlined by Milton Schulman in a *Standard* article on 16 July headed: 'Programming of the petrol bombers', taken up by Eric Moonman in his well-publicised pamphlet *Copycat Hooligans*, and confirmed by Lord Scarman's judgement that the use of petrol bombs was 'no doubt, copied from the disturbances in Northern Ireland' (Scarman, 1.2). The argument cannot be dismissed out of hand, though there is very little firm evidence to support it,[35] but it can be criticised for its one-sidedness. If the rioters learned 'lessons' from the news coverage of Northern Ireland, so did the police, as the use of CS gas for crowd control for the first time on the British mainland indicates. This example also points to a dimension of media influence that is totally ignored by supporters of the 'copycat' thesis: its impact on police policy, political debate and public opinion.

News reporting and 'law and order' politics

The dominant news image of Toxteth—as an exceptional threat to law and order requiring an exceptional response—played an important role in setting the agenda for the political discussions which followed, and in making support for the immediate issue of new riot equipment the touchstone of political responsibility. As a result the Parliamentary debates followed the pattern already established by the news coverage, downgrading alternative perspectives and constantly returning to the issue of how best to maintain police control of the streets and prevent further rioting.[36]

But it was not only Conservative politicians who endorsed this 'law and order' response to events. Opinion polls taken soon after the riots showed a significant groundswell of genuine popular support for tough measures. Only 8 per cent of those questioned in August thought the police handling of the riots had been too tough, and 67 per cent supported the creation of special anti-riot units to deal with future disturbances.[37] Another poll, a month later, showed 80 per cent support for using water cannon against rioters, though only 46 per cent agreed with the use of CS gas.[38]

Once it was firmly established in political debate and popular consciousness, this 'law and order' perspective proved remarkably resilient, and as John Clare points out in his earlier chapter, even Lord Scarman succumbed to the dominant images. He began his report with a 'purple' description of the temporary collapse of law and order which drew heavily on the popular press for its imagery and style, and he went on to support the calls for tough measures to prevent it happening again. He agreed that 'there will be circumstances in which the use of "hard" policing methods, including the deployment of the Special Patrol Group, is appropriate, even essential' (Scarman, 8.38). He accepted that there may be scope for the adoption by the police of 'a more positive, interventionist role in quelling disorder in order to speed dispersal' (Scarman, 5.73) and he supported the use of water cannon, CS gas and plastic bullets in situations where the chief officer of police judged that there was a real possibility of loss of life (Scarman, 5.74). However, he added that 'it would be tragic' if these changes in 'the manner of policing disorder' undermined his central proposals for bringing 'the police and the public closer together' (Scarman, 5.74) by tackling the causes of public distrust. These included: making consultation with local communities a statutory obligation; dismissing any officer found guilty of racially prejudiced behaviour, and introducing an independent element into the procedure for investigating complaints against the police.

These points were mentioned in the news coverage of the Report, but once again they were set within the dominant 'law and order' framework already established. The reporting was illustrated with riot scenes from Brixton and Toxteth which worked against the critical thrust of the Report and pulled attention back to the problem of how to keep order on the 'dangerous' streets of Brixton and Britain's other inner cities.[39] The Report's criticisms of police performance were taken up in current affairs programmes, documentaries and in the 'quality' press and weekly journals of opinion, but this coverage did not reach a mass audience. However, by publicising the views of authoritative critics of 'hard' policing, it did increase the pressure on the Government to implement the Report's main proposals. In response, the police, and particularly the Metropolitan Police (who had been Scarman's main concern), set out to strengthen popular support for their views by feeding selected stories to the popular press.

'The Yard fights back'

This policy of fostering active co-operation with the news media was developed by Sir Robert Mark in 1973, on the assumption that 'given the opportunity the press . . . (would) give a great deal of support to the Force',[40] and subsequent events have largely proved him right. However, as the *Daily Mail*'s chief crime reporter, Peter Burden points out, 'handing out information that the police want publicised can dull what should be a media man's sharply enquiring mind'.[41] Enquiry was certainly dulled in the press reporting of the 1981 'mugging' figures which were organised to support the argument that the exceptional level of violent street crime by black youth in Brixton could only be dealt with by tough policing.[42]

The campaign was launched by Peter Burden in the *Daily Mail* for 21 January 1982, with a story headed: 'More and more muggings but the Yard fights back', reporting that 'muggings' had broken all records in 1981 and that 'case files show that in some areas, most attacks are carried out by young blacks'.

The image of black youth as a predatory horde preying on defenceless pensioners was confirmed on 5 March 1982 with a double page story in the *Daily Mail* headed 'Prisoners behind the net curtains', which centred on an elderly widow's dramatic account of being robbed on a council estate in Brixton.

> About four weeks ago, at 9 in the morning, I saw my front door was open. I thought, 'That's funny', because I always close it, and I knew I had put the security latches on.
>
> Then I saw him. He was standing right in the doorway. He didn't say a word. He was black and tall. He knocked me down and then kicked me. He walked over me and took the money.

Four days later the *Daily Express* consolidated this image of Brixton with a double page spread on Railton Road headed 'On Britain's most brutal streets'. It carried a large photograph of three black youths walking down the street flanked by a picture of an elderly white woman sitting on a bench in the shopping precinct, captioned 'A moment's peace . . . but the old rarely venture out alone.' The story reinforced this theme and deftly linked the problem of 'mugging' and street crime to the issue of riots, by concentrating on locations specifically associated with violent confrontations between black youths and police—Lewisham, Southall and Notting Hill:

> The new crime figures for this black arc of racial disharmony that sweeps south from the Thames through Brixton and Lewisham and Southall [*sic*] and north to Notting Hill Gate and Stoke Newington will be published this week and the police call them 'terrifying'. It adds up to a mugging every half-hour in London.

In contrast to this barrage of coverage, the popular press paid comparatively little attention to the mounting evidence of racist attacks by whites. The result was a very partial definition of the 'problem' of street violence which linked it firmly to the threat posed by black youth. Having established this perspective on the situation, the popular press mobilised it to the full when the figures for robbery and other violent theft were finally released on 10 March 1982.

The *Daily Mail*'s front page for 11 March was headed 'BLACK CRIME: THE ALARMING FIGURES'. The coverage reported that the 1981 total of 18,763 robberies was 34 per cent up on the 1980 figure and that in 55.42 per cent of the cases the assailants were identified as 'coloured', and went on to say that the 'overwhelming majority' of the victims 'are white and are women. All too often elderly women.'

Popular press coverage as a whole, condensed the central themes of the 'law and order' perspective into a single dramatic image of threat. By drawing on established stereotypes of predatory adolescence and black youth it offered audiences an immediately intelligible perspective. At the same time, it excluded any sustained analysis of the supporting evidence. In the first place, the figures included robberies from business premises and non-violent snatches from bags, leaving only 5889 cases (31 per cent) that could be classified as 'street robberies', and even these need not involve injuries to the victim. Some papers, like the *Daily Mail*, did mention these distinctions, but others reported the total as referring entirely to 'muggings'. Under its headline 'MUGGERS GO ON THE RAMPAGE' for example, the *Daily Star* referred to 'the total of nearly 19,000 muggings'. There were also considerable problems with the claims that more than half the muggings in London were carried out by black assailants, and that the great majority of victims were women, and often elderly. Because the figures only record incidents reported to the police they rely heavily on people's recollections of what happened and on their willingness to make a report to the police, and these factors present two problems. Firstly, a number of victims could not describe their attacker, and even where they could, the term 'coloured' is used to record any reference to an assailant who did not look obviously Caucasian. Consequently it cannot be used as a synonym for black. Secondly, attacks may go unreported because the victims do not consider them serious enough to bother about or because they prefer not to go to the police. But even leaving these possibilities aside, the available evidence goes against the press stereotypes of 'muggers' and their victims.

Malcolm Ramsay's analysis of 'muggings' in Merseyside, Greater Manchester and the West Midlands in the first half of 1981 for example revealed that most victims were young, only 14 per cent were pensioners, and except for the East Midlands, more attackers were white than non-white.[43] The explanation for this, however, is demographic. Since 'mugging' is a mainly adolescent crime, the racial composition of assailants will be strongly related to the structure of the youth population as a whole. Michael Pratt's study of London in the early 1970s produced similar results.[44] The great majority of victims were male and only a fifth were over 50. The majority of attackers (58 per cent) were identified as black, though here again the figures have to be related to the structure of the youth population before it can be argued that black youth are more likely to be 'muggers'.

By and large, however, the popular press ignored these caveats and worked entirely within the framework established by the original riot coverage—of an exceptional threat requiring an exceptional response.

'The iron hand' and media influence

This framework was employed again later in the year when the Metropolitan Police's new Immediate Response Units were called into Railton Road on 1 November 1982 to help repossess eight houses scheduled for demolition. The resulting operation was greeted as a triumph for the new anti-riot tactics derived from Ulster. Under the front page headline 'POLICE ROUT BRIXTON MOB', the *Daily Mail* proclaimed that:

> The iron hand of Scotland Yard's new Commissioner, Sir Kenneth Newman, was demonstrated for the first time last night in Brixton, south London—and a potential riot was firmly squashed. . . . The action had all the hallmarks of the success achieved by Sir Kenneth in his tactics against terrorists and sectarian mobs in Belfast when he was Chief Constable of the Royal Ulster Constabulary.

Similarly, the *Daily Star*'s front page story under the headline 'BATON CHARGE', was a positive celebration of new reactive tactics and control equipment.

> Eighty police armed with batons last night charged a rioting mob in Brixton.

> The burly officers—wearing black flameproof combat uniforms—banged their 6 ft riot shields on the ground.

> Then they roared 'Charge' and stormed through the hordes of black youths who had tried to block off Railton Road.

In these descriptions, what was previously seen as an *exceptional* response now appears as a *normal and necessary* part of policing the inner cities, an essential back-up to the bobby on the beat. By creating a resilient but limited perspective on these issues, the reporting of the 1981 riots may well have helped to make this 'militarisation' of policing acceptable to the majority of the population. This is not the issue most critics have in mind when they talk about media influence, but in the long run it may turn out to be the most significant.

Notes

1. Michael Bruce MacKuen, 'Social communication and the mass policy agenda', in M. B. MacKuen and S. L. Coombs, *More Than News: Media Power in Public Affairs*, Sage Publications, 1981, pp. 19–144.
2. See Colin Sumner, ' "Political hooliganism" and "rampaging mobs": the national press coverage of the Toxteth "riots" ', in C Sumner (Ed.), *Crime Justice and the Mass Media*, University of Cambridge Institute of Criminology, 1982, p. 29.
3. For a further analysis of the television news coverage, see: Justin Wren-Lewis, 'The story of a riot: the television coverage of civil unrest in 1981', *Screen Education*, Autumn/Winter, 1981/2, No. 40, p. 26.
4. See, for example, Rob Rohrer, 'The deadly power of the ferret', *New Statesman*, 18 June 1982, pp. 6–7.
5. See Justin Wren-Lewis, *op. cit.*
6. Howard Tumber, *Television and the Riots*, British Film Institute, 1982, p. 38.
7. Anders Hansen, 'Press coverage of the summer 1981 riots', unpublished M.A. dissertation, University of Leicester, Centre for Mass Communication Research, 1982.
8. These terms are borrowed from Richard Hoggart's foreword to the Glasgow University Media Group's *Bad News*, Routledge & Kegan Paul, 1976.

9. See Tumber, *op. cit.*, p. 13.
10. *Ibid.*, p. 20.
11. See Graham Murdock, 'Disorderly images: television's presentation of crime and policing', in C. Sumner (Ed.), *op. cit.*, pp. 108–109.
12. See Ed Barber, 'Hard news', *Ten. 8 Photographic Journal*, No. 7/8, p. 9.
13. See particularly the *New Statesman* for 17 July 1981. The photograph is featured on the cover of D. Cowell, T. Jones and J. Young, *Policing the Riots*, Junction Books, 1982.
14. Of the mainstream dailies, only the *Financial Times* began its front page coverage with a description of the original incident that had sparked off the disturbances.
15. John Humphrys, 'Duty to inform—in pictures', *Television: the Journal of the Royal Television Society*, September/October 1981, p. 15.
16. C. McKay, *Memoirs of Extraordinary Popular Delusions of the Madness of Crowds*, preface to the edition of 1852, reprinted by George Harrap & Co, 1956, p. xx.
17. G. Le Bon, *The Crowd: A Study of the Popular Mind*, Viking Press edition, 1960, p. 32.
18. *News of the World*, 21 October 1900, p. 2.
19. *The Times*, Monday 4 August 1919, p. 8.
20. For a fuller discussion of the press coverage of this incident, see Patricia Holland, 'The New Cross fire and the popular press', *Multiracial Education*, Summer 1981, pp. 61–80.
21. This point is well made in Martin Kettle and Lucy Hodges, *Uprising! The Police, the People and the Riots in Britain's Cities*, Pan Books, 1982, pp. 20–21.
22. *Punch*, 20 February 1886, p. 93.
23. *The Times*, Wednesday 6 August 1919, p. 10.
24. See Graham Murdock, 'Mass communication and social violence: a critical review of recent research trends', in Peter March and Anne Campbell (Eds.), *Aggression and Violence*, Basil Blackwell, 1982, pp. 62–90.
25. Gabriel Tarde, *Penal Philosophy*, William Heinemann edition, 1912, pp. 340–341.
26. Richard Clutterbuck, 'Terrorism and urban violence, *Proceedings of the Academy of Political Science*, Vol. 34, No. 4, 1982, p. 170.
27. Seymour Spilerman, 'Structural characteristics of cities and the severity of racial disorders', *American Sociological Review*, October 1976, p. 790.
28. See especially the National Advisory Commission on Civil Disorders (The Kerner Commission) *Report*, Bantam Books, 1968.
29. Manus Midlarsky, 'Analysing diffusion and contagion effects: the urban disorders of the 1960s', *American Political Science Review*, September 1976, pp. 996–1008.
30. Howard Tumber, *op. cit.*, p. 46.
31. Peter Southgate, 'The disturbances of July 1981 in Handsworth, Birmingham', in Simon Field and Peter Southgate, *Public Disorder*, Home Office Research Study No. 72, pp. 41–70.
32. See Benjamin Singer, 'Mass media and communication processes in the Detroit riot of 1967,' *Public Opinion Quarterly*, Vol. 34, 1970, pp. 236–245.
33. William Belson, letter to *The Guardian*, 10 April 1982, p. 8.
34. Richard Clutterbuck, *The Media and Political Violence*, 2nd edition, Macmillan, 1983, p. xxvii.
35. The most widely quoted evidence comes from Eric Moonman's pamphlet *Copycat Hooligans*, published by the Centre for Contemporary Studies in November 1981, and based on street interviews with fifteen youths in Toxteth and an unspecified number in south London.
36. See Michael Ignatieff, 'It's a riot', *London Review of Books*, 20 August–2 September 1981, pp. 19–20.
37. *Daily Star*, Monday 31 August 1981, p. 4, based on a MORI poll of 1090 adults.
38. *The Observer*, Sunday 15 November 1981, based on an NOP survey of 1038 adults.
39. See Justin Wren-Lewis and Alan Clarke, 'Rioting on the media', *Marxism Today*, March 1982, pp. 32–33.
40. Quoted in Steve Chibnall, *Law and Order News*, Tavistock Publications, 1977, p. 174.
41. Peter Burden, 'The business of crime reporting: problems and dilemmas', in Colin Sumner (Ed.), *op. cit.*, p. 4.

42. The Metropolitan Police had put a similar argument to Lord Scarman to justify the Swamp '81 operation which was widely seen as having sparked off the riot. On this, see Louis Blom-Cooper and Richard Drabble, 'Police perceptions of crime: Brixton and the operational response', in *The British Journal of Criminology*, April 1982, pp. 184–187.
43. Malcolm Ramsay, 'Mugging: fears and facts', *New Society*, 25 March 1982, pp. 467–468.
44. Michael Pratt, *Mugging as a Social Problem*, Routledge & Kegan Paul, 1980, chapter 5.

PART 3

The Policing Issues

CHAPTER 8

The policing issues

JOHN BENYON

Lord Scarman's Inquiry was established under section 32 of the Police Act 1964, and by far the greatest part of his report is devoted to the policing issues raised by the riots.

He found that a gulf existed between the police and significant sections of the Lambeth public. Many young people 'had become indignant and resentful against the police, suspicious of everything they did' (Scarman, 4.1), and 'the worst construction was invariably put upon the police action' (Scarman, 4.3).

> Whatever the reason for this loss of confidence, and whether the police were to blame for it or not, it produced the attitudes and beliefs which underlay the disturbances, providing the tinder ready to blaze into violence on the least provocation, fancied or real, offered by the police (Scarman, 4.1).

Prevention and discretion

Unlike many countries, Britain does not have a national police force under one unified command—although many people fear that there is a remorseless trend towards this structure. Before 1964 there were 126 constabularies in England and Wales; now there are 43.

The first proposals to establish professional policing in England met with stiff resistance. Maintenance of law and order was seen as a local matter, rooted in frankpledge and watch and ward. There was a strong antipathy to standing armies, manifest after the 1780 Gordon Riots when Burke decried the use of the military to put them down, and Fox made the declaration that he would 'much rather be governed by a mob than a standing army'.[1]*

A bill to create a London police force was presented to Parliament in 1785, but, like further attempts during the subsequent 40 years, it met with a storm of protest. According to E. P. Thompson, the hostility to proposals,

---

* Superscript numbers refer to Notes at end of chapter.

such as Bentham's in 1817 for a Ministry of Police, was based on 'a curious blend of parochial defensiveness, Whig theory and popular resistance'.

> Tories feared the over-ruling of parochial and chartered rights, and of the powers of local J.P.s; Whigs feared an increase in the powers of Crown or of Government; . . . the radical populace until Chartist times saw in any police an engine of oppression.[2]

Nonetheless, the Irish Constabulary had been founded in 1786 and fourteen years later a police force began in Glasgow. Eventually, in 1829 Robert Peel's Act established a professional police force in the capital city, brought about principally, according to Sir Cyril Philips, for the purpose of 'ensuring public order in the streets . . . and containing violent threats to the social and political status quo'—rather than containing crime in general.[3]

The emphasis of the first Metropolitan Police Commissioners, Charles Rowan and Richard Mayne, was on the *prevention* of crime. They claimed that prevention rather than detection and punishment would better effect 'the security of person and property, the preservation of public tranquillity . . .'.[4] Lord Scarman elaborated upon these points, stressing that the first duty of a police officer is to maintain 'the Queen's peace'. When there is a deviation from normality, he must correct it by enforcing the law but 'his priorities are clear: the maintenance of public tranquillity comes first' (Scarman, 4.57). If a conflict arises between law enforcement and the maintenance of order, in the last resort the latter must be given priority, but the conflict can often be resolved by 'the constant and common-sense exercise of police discretion' (Scarman, 4.58).

This approach to policing, espoused by the first Metropolitan Police Commissioners and reiterated by Lord Scarman, appears to have been misunderstood by some commentators both within and outside the police service. As Lord Scarman pointed out, it does not entail one law for some and another law for others: the sort of crass argument put forward in some newspaper articles. It does recognise 'that successful policing depends on the exercise of discretion in how the law is enforced' (Scarman, 4.58). Police officers must frequently make judgements about how the law is to be applied and these decisions may sometimes be very difficult. Ill-considered actions, such as those by the young police constables outside the S & M Car Hire Office (Scarman, 3.78–3.79), can have drastic consequences.

A tale of failure

Lord Scarman came to the view that 'the history of relations between the police and the people of Brixton during recent years has been a tale of failure' (Scarman, 4.43), and he found that both the police and the local leaders 'must accept a share of the blame' (Scarman, 4.46). He considered that while the direction and policies of the police are not racist, some officers are occasionally guilty of racially prejudiced behaviour, and their actions cause incalculable harm. This behaviour 'goes far towards the creation of the image of a hostile police force, which was the myth which led the young people into these disorders' (Scarman, 4.64).

Scarman also found that harassment occurs (Scarman, 4.65–4.68). Furthermore, he identified a lack of flexibility in policing methods in Brixton—'a serious flaw' (Scarman, 4.70). An example of this inflexibility was the infamous operation known within the police as Swamp '81. The purpose of this operation was to detect and arrest burglars and robbers on the streets of Lambeth. One hundred and twelve local officers were involved and the strategy was 'to flood' areas of the Borough making extensive use of the stop and search power provided by section 66 of the Metropolitan Police Act 1839. (The Police and Criminal Evidence Bill, which failed when Parliament was dissolved in May 1983, included provisions to extend this power to all police officers outside London.) During the course of Operation Swamp, from 6 April to 11 April, 943 'stops' were made. Just over half of those stopped were black and over two-thirds were under 21. One hundred and eighteen people were arrested and 75 charges resulted, but these included only one for robbery, one for attempted burglary and 20 charges of theft or attempted theft (Scarman, 4.37–4.40). As critics have pointed out, judged by its own aims ('to arrest burglars and robbers') the operation was not very successful and resulted in over 850 innocent people being inconvenienced and irritated. Lord Scarman concluded that it 'was a serious mistake' and it was remarkable that the opinions of the local home beat officers had not been sought (Scarman, 4.75–4.80).

The Report gave attention to three other criticisms made of the police and concluded that in general the police did not over-react in the handling of the riots, that indeed the disorders revealed an inability by the police to react firmly and quickly enough, and finally that insufficient resources were available to prevent the looting which occurred (Scarman, 4.81–4.96). In general, Lord Scarman was critical of the police in the build-up to the riots, also blaming community leaders for the atmosphere of distrust which developed. But these failures 'neither justify nor excuse the disorders or the terrifying lawlessness of the crowds'. In general, he rejected criticisms of police behaviour on the streets during the riots and indeed he stressed

> the courage and dedication which was displayed by members of the police and emergency services in Brixton over that terrible weekend. They stood between our society and a total collapse of law and order in the streets of an important part of the capital. For that, they deserve, and must receive, the praise and thanks of all sections of our community (Scarman, 4.98).

The Brixton disorders and those in Toxteth, Moss Side, and elsewhere during the summer raised a number of questions about the role and behaviour of police officers, and Lord Scarman considered these problems in parts V and VII of his report.

Recruitment, racial prejudice and training

As Kenneth Oxford points out in his contribution to this book, in recent years there have been many developments to which the police have had to respond. Factors such as rising crime figures, increasingly sophisticated criminals, terrorism, and changes in social values, as well as the lack of adequate manpower, have led the police down paths which they may not otherwise have chosen.

> They are now professionals with a highly specialised set of skills and behavioural codes of their own. They run the risk of becoming, by reason of their professionalism, a 'corps d'élite' set apart from the rest of the community (Scarman, 5.3).

During the mid and late 1970s the real value of police salaries was eroded so that by 1977 the pay for a constable was some 20 per cent below average male industrial earnings. This had a significant impact on recruitment and on wastage from the ranks which reached its highest figure in 1977—over 9000 resignations in England and Wales. Since the Edmund-Davies' Committee's proposals[5] police pay has risen dramatically and a police constable at the top of the scale in September 1982 was paid nearly £10,000, to which a generous housing allowance should be added. In addition, police officers can retire much earlier than many other employees, on half pay after 25 years or two-thirds pay after 30 years.

The table opposite shows the salaries paid to various grades for selected recent years.

The pay rises, and the prospect of a secure job at a time of rising unemployment, have led to a substantial increase in applications. In 1980 the Chief Inspector of Constabulary was able to point out: 'Some of the large metropolitan forces, which had experienced great difficulty in the past in attracting and retaining suitable recruits . . . were able to operate at full strength for the first time.'[6]

Despite the rise in applications the police service remains largely a white male preserve. By 1980 some 19 per cent of recruits were women, but 'the police world retains a strongly masculine ethos',[7] and it does seem apparent from a number of studies that the risk pointed out by Lord Scarman—of the police becoming set apart from the community—is a real one.[8] Robert Reiner has characterised the general social outlook of policemen as 'hard-boiled, pessimistic, at best tragic, at worst cynical and bitter, conservative in

Annual Salaries of Police Officers

Rank	1977		1979		1982	
	Min	Max	Min	Max	Min	Max
Constable	2,775	3,918	4,086	6,471	6,189	9,798
Sergeant	3,918	4,563	6,186	7,095	9,369	10,749
Inspector	4,563	5,538	7,095	8,445	10,749	12,789
Chief Inspector	5,295	6,282	8,058	9,348	12,204	14,160
Superintendent	7,074	7,953	11,124	12,156	16,848	18,411
Chief Superintendent	8,049	8,874	12,258	13,365	18,564	20,241
Assistant Chief Constable	8,350	9,676	14,188		21,069	
Deputy Chief Constable	8,476	10,808	15,072	18,615	21,621	25,143
Chief Constable	8,731	14,410	18,840	23,268	25,419	31,107
Senior officers in the Metropolitan Police:						
Commander	8,740	9,172	14,442		21,429	
Deputy Asst Commissioner	9,783	10,891	17,592		23,913	
Assistant Commissioner	13,297		21,990		29,442	
Deputy Commissioner	14,653		24,192		32,388	

Source: House of Commons Official Report (*Hansard*), Vol. 35, No. 43, 24 January 1983. Written answers. Columns 269–270.

the broad moral sense (and probably the narrow political sense, too)'.[9] Many policemen are doubtless quite unlike this description, but if such an approach were to predominate within the police service, a deepening rift between the police and the community may result.

Lord Scarman's prime concern with recruitment was to increase the number of black and brown police officers. He found that on 6 October 1981 there were only 132 black officers in the Metropolitan Police, representing one half of 1 per cent of the total; a year later the figure had risen slightly to 162. In the whole of England and Wales the October 1981 figure was 326 black offcers (0.3 per cent) and this had risen to 401 by late 1982. If the ethnic minorities were to be proportionately represented in the police, at least a fourteen-fold increase would be needed.

The Report rejected quotas and a lowering of entrance standards, but recommended positive action to increase the recruits from ethnic minorities. The Chief Constable of Derbyshire, Mr Alf Parrish, introduced a new scheme on 1 January 1983, modelled on Lord Scarman's suggestion that special tuition could be provided to enable black entrants to achieve the required academic standard (Scarman, 5.9). However, the scheme received a mixed reception.

Lord Scarman also proposed that special efforts should be made to ensure that racially prejudiced recruits are not selected (Scarman, 5.14–5.15). Furthermore, he recommended that racially prejudiced or discriminatory behaviour should become a specific offence in the Police Discipline Code, the normal punishment for which should be dismissal (Scarman,

5.41–5.42). For reasons which are difficult to understand, the police organisations argued fiercely against this recommendation, and in November 1982 Mr Whitelaw, the Home Secretary, told the House of Commons that it would not be implemented. A typical view was that of the West Midlands Chief Constable, Sir Philip Knights, who said that racialist police officers existed, but probably no more than in the community as a whole.[10] But as Lord Scarman stressed, 'we cannot rest on the cynical proposition, which I have heard, that, since the police will necessarily reflect social attitudes, racially prejudiced people are bound to be found in their ranks' (Scarman, 5.15).

Training of police officers is considered by both Kenneth Oxford and Basil Griffiths in the chapters which follow. Among Lord Scarman's suggestions (Scarman, 5.16–5.26) was a recommendation for an increase in the length of initial recruit training to 6 months from the existing 15 weeks in the Metropolitan Police and 10 weeks elsewhere. Scarman also proposed improvements in the curriculum and he commended proposals for the introduction of human awareness training.

Many of these changes have now been put into effect, although the training period in the Metropolitan Police is still a month shorter than Lord Scarman advocated, and shorter still elsewhere. Human awareness training is intended to enable recruits to explore and understand their prejudices, and video recordings and simulation exercises are used to help them improve their dealing with members of the public. The Police Training Council published a report on 23 March 1983 which criticised the provision of training in community and race relations in a number of forces.[11] As a result of this study additional training for new recruits and for serving officers will be introduced.

Handling public disorders

Lord Scarman also made recommendations on in-service training and training in the handling of disorders (Scarman, 5.27–5.32). It is clear that his proposals have been taken very seriously within the service and a number of changes have been introduced. Improvements in the training of policemen to handle public disorders have received a high priority and by Spring 1982 it was reported that hundreds of police officers were involved. It is intended to train at least 10 per cent of police officers in each force in anti-riot strategies. The favoured tactic is the use of five-man 'snatch squads', fully equipped to withstand violent attacks. As their name suggests, the 'snatch squads' work as a team to arrest key targets in a riot; the idea is to remove leaders and disorient the rioters. One senior officer was quoted as saying: 'The training is extremely tough. The squads are highly disciplined units—moving together on a single command. But they are not a permanent riot squad.'[12]

Fears that Britain would develop a French-style riot police have been expressed for a number of years. The TUC General Secretary, Mr Len Murray, made this point in May 1979 when he gave the Joseph Simpson Lecture at the Metropolitan Police Cadet School, Hendon. He criticised the role of the Special Patrol Group (SPG), saying it is 'alien to the tradition in this country of leaving policing to a local constabulary with knowledge of and sympathy with the local community'.[13] Lord Scarman exonerated the SPG of criticisms levelled at it (Scarman, 5.53), and senior policemen seem well aware of the dangers of creating 'a force within a force', for officers may only serve in the SPG and similar special units for a few years.[14] Nevertheless, the SPG has been singled out as the worst kind of hostile policing with a 'burgeoning reputation as an elite, aggressive, unaccountable squad'.[15] Lord Scarman quoted the description in the Final Report of the Working Party into Community/Police Relations in Lambeth, January 1981, of 'attacks by the SPG on the people of Lambeth' (Scarman, 4.32).

The sorts of criticism which he heard led Lord Scarman to emphasise the importance of supervision and monitoring (Scarman, 5.36–5.40). The high proportion of young constables—36 per cent were between $18\frac{1}{2}$ years and 25 years in 1980—necessitates proper supervision by sergeants and inspectors to eliminate discourteous, abrasive and racially prejudiced conduct. He advocated increased training in management techniques to achieve better results and this is perhaps one of the least discussed but most challenging recommendations in the Report, for improved supervision and monitoring are key ways of eradicating misconduct by constables on the streets (Scarman, 5.33–5.35).

Another issue which Lord Scarman considered is the provision of special equipment for riot control. During the riots in Liverpool 8, in July 1981, CS gas was used for the first time on the British mainland for crowd control, and the Liverpool City Council asked for soldiers to be placed on readiness. Since then plastic bullets—or baton rounds as they are more euphemistically called—have been obtained by many police forces. Water cannon, too, are ready for use if needed.

The British police service is renowned for being one of the very few forces throughout the world which is unarmed, although, in London alone, it is estimated that some 215 armed policemen are on the streets at any one time, most of them protecting diplomats and dignitaries. Public concern about the use of guns by police was voiced after the shooting in Kensington of Mr Stephen Waldorf in January 1983. In answer to questions on the subject, Mr Whitelaw gave MPs wrong information which was corrected in written answers in Feburary.[16] According to reporters investigating the matter, 'the confusion over exactly how often firearms were used illustrates the problems involved in trying to keep a close control over the London police's gun policy'.[17]

The controversy over whether the police should use weapons such as plastic bullets, CS gas and guns is likely to continue to be a feature of the debate about policing issues.

Accountability, consultation and policing methods

Lord Scarman stated that policing is too complex to be divided simplistically into 'hard' and 'soft' styles, and he accepted that the use of special units, such as the SPG, will be needed in some circumstances (Scarman, 5.44–5.47). He particularly stressed the importance of policing by consent and he drew attention to the crucial role of the home beat officer. The status of the beat officer must be raised, for all too often he is regarded as 'outside the mainstream of operational policing' (known by other police officers by nicknames such as 'hobby bobby'). More foot patrols are needed and the high turnover of officers, moving from one police district to another, should be reduced (Scarman, 5.48–5.54).

Many of these suggestions have been introduced by police forces throughout the country. Indeed, John Alderson in Devon and Cornwall and David Webb in Handsworth, to name the two best known examples, had introduced 'community policing' well before the urban disorders occurred.[18] Lord Scarman defined community policing as 'policing with the active consent and support of the community' (Scarman, 5.46)—and few could surely disagree with this as the ideal approach. Unfortunately though, it is easier to use it as some sort of slogan than to practise it effectively. Kettle and Hodges quote Alexei Sayle, the unorthodox comedian: 'Round his way, he says, they've now got community policing. You're walking along the street, a police van pulls up, a squad of coppers leap out, pin you to the ground and tell you the time.'[19]

Indeed, the predecessors to the Metropolitan Police, the watchmen, were referred to as 'these perambulating horologists, these hourbawlers'.[20] As Lord Scarman pointed out, a major problem which the police service must overcome is the low status afforded to foot patrols by colleagues within the force. The police officer on the beat is arguably the most important person in the service but this is not the way police officers see it. Kenneth Oxford, Chief Constable of Merseyside, has stressed the importance and the difficulty of overcoming this problem.

> We must not debase the value of the officer on the beat; for too long he has been regarded as a lower-class officer. Everyone wants to be in the mounted section, on motorcycle patrol, or in the CID. The status of the beat policeman has got to be enhanced, and I am having to tell men in

some departments, 'You have the experience I need on the streets.' I will promise such officers that their promotion prospects will not be harmed.[21]

The new Commissioner of the Metropolitan Police, Sir Kenneth Newman, made similar points during his first press conference in October 1982. Maintaining harmony in the community should be rewarded, as well as solving crime. However, chief police officers such as Oxford and Newman will have to work hard to allay policemen's fears that their promotion prospects will not be affected. Research such as that by Jones shows that arrest-statistics, rather than the far less quantifiable preventative role, largely determine promotion.[22]

Lord Scarman laid particular stress on the importance of policing by consent, and he saw consultation and accountability as two ways of realising it. He recommended that statutory provision should be made to require local consultation between the police and the community (Scarman, 5.65–5.66). Clause 67 of the Police and Criminal Evidence Bill, which was being considered in the House of Commons (in early 1983) provided for consultative 'arrangements' to be made, but the provision was rather vague and was described by the National Council for Civil Liberties as 'wholly inadequate'. The Bill failed when Parliament was dissolved on 13 May 1983.

Equally important, said Scarman, is proper accountability which should be linked with consultation.

Accountability is the constitutional mechanism which can provide the backing: for it renders the police answerable for what they do. Thereby it prevents them from slipping into an enclosed fortress of inward thinking and social isolation which would in the long term result in a siege mentality—the police in their fortress (happy as long as it is secure) and the rest of us outside, unhappy, uncertain and insecure (for we do not know what they will do, or how they will do it) (Scarman, 5.58).

The Report found that the arrangements which exist are generally satisfactory although many police authorities are unclear of their role and 'do not always exercise the firmness which the statute envisages as necessary to the discharge of their awesome responsibility' (Scarman, 5.62). In the capital, Lord Scarman considered that the Home Secretary should remain the police authority to whom the Metropolitan Police are accountable (Scarman, 5.67–5.68).

This section of the Report provoked considerable opposition. Many argued that statutory consultation would interfere with police operations and independence, while many others considered that London should have a police authority modelled on those in the rest of the country.

Much of the discussion of police independence seems to rest on a fallacy of police autonomy. The various Acts have made it quite clear that the police should be accountable to their police authority which will maintain 'an adequate and efficient police force'. Lord Scarman discussed this question (Scarman, 4.59–4.60 and 5.56) and concluded that 'community in-volvement in the policy and *operations* of policing is perfectly feasible without undermining the independence of the police . . .' (Scarman, 5.56; italics added). However, his view that no one 'may tell the police what decisions to take or *what methods to employ* . . .' (Scarman, 4.59; italics added) is surely questionable. Some police authorities have certainly told their chief constables what methods *not* to employ. And Mr George Cunningham, MP for Islington South and Finsbury until 1983, went further. Writing in the Police Federation journal, he stated 'the notion that in all "operational" matters the police should be free to do as they please cannot be accepted'.[23]

Many of those arguing in favour of police independence really appear to be concerned to ensure the *impartiality* of the police. Before 1964, some watch committees were accused of direct interference in police activities and this charge was frequently levelled at the Liverpool Watch. However, in a detailed study, Brogden shows that while on occasions the Watch 'disputed aspects of the police function', there was little direct intervention.[24]

Roy Hattersley, Shadow Home Secretary, has made the point that the old watch committees seem to have been more effective in ensuring ac-countability. Chief constables 'are, as far as most decisions are concerned, answerable to nobody'. Hattersley accepted that in London the Home Secretary must be responsible for some special policing matters such as the protection of diplomats and counter-espionage. But in general, he argued, the Metropolitan Police should be accountable to a democratically elected police authority and he committed a future Labour government to establish this structure. Hattersley stated:

> I am absolutely certain that, had the Metropolitan Police been in-fluenced over the past 10 years by elected representatives from all or any of the parties, many of the mistakes would have been avoided and its reputation would stand far higher than it stands today. The Metropolitan Police would have been closer to the people.[25]

Investigating allegations of misconduct

In his contribution to this book, Alan Goodson considers the questions of accountability and consultation and also the issue of police complaints. Lord Scarman found 'a widespread and dangerous lack of public confidence in the existing system' (Scarman, 5.43) and he considered that 'any solution falling short of a system of independent investigation available for all complaints (other than the frivolous) which are not withdrawn, is unlikely to be successful. Any such system should include a "conciliation process" ' (Scarman, 7.21).

The police complaints system has been criticised for many years and the arguments are well-rehearsed. An effective system is clearly vital if police discipline is to be properly enforced, and if the rights of individual citizens are to be safeguarded. It is equally important though that the accused police officer should be protected from malicious complaints.

The Police Complaints Board was set up by the Police Act 1976 to provide an independent element in the process, but criticisms of the procedure continued (see Scarman, 7.14–7.17). Opposition to a fully independent system centres on the cost and on practical difficulties such as who would staff the independent agency, and how they would ensure co-operation from within the police service.

Another factor has been the so-called 'double jeopardy' rule. This has meant that in those cases where the Director of Public Prosecutions has decided there is insufficient evidence to prosecute an accused officer, the Police Complaints Board has been precluded from bringing disciplinary charges. This Home Office interpretation of 'double jeopardy' was clearly illogical and nonsensical from the outset, but was only overturned by the Divisional Court in December 1982.

The Police Federation and a number of chief constables now support fundamental changes in the system. The Federation believes that accused officers should have legal representation and rights before an independent investigation. The present system certainly appears unfair and lacks credibility, for an amazingly small number of complaints are substantiated. According to a Home Office report, complaints against the Metropolitan Police rose to 8786 in 1979. Just 3.1 per cent of those by whites and a mere 1.3 per cent of those by blacks and Asians were substantiated.[26] In England and Wales in 1980, 31,009 complaints were made of which 1288 (4.2 per cent) were substantiated; 77 cases resulted in proceedings and 149 in disciplinary charges. By contrast, in 1977 the police received 23,020 letters of appreciation, thanking 33,652 officers for their work and help.[27]

During the Scarman Inquiry allegations of misconduct and the use of unlawful weapons by the police were made. Lord Scarman stated 'these allegations must be most carefully examined by the Commissioner and if verified, stringent action must, in my view, be taken against those concerned' (Scarman, 4.83). One case became well known after a photograph of a police constable carrying a pickaxe handle was published in *The Sunday Times*. After the Director of Public Prosecutions decided not to start criminal proceedings, the police constable pleaded guilty to a charge of discreditable conduct, and a sergeant and a detective inspector pleaded guilty to charges of neglect of duty. All received reprimands. One of the complainants, Archdeacon Wood of the Diocese of Southwark, said: 'If the reprimand means that their police careers can proceed as normal, it does not augur well for policing in this country'.[28]

The Police and Criminal Evidence Bill 1982–1983 did not provide the fundamental changes which Lord Scarman advocated. The proposals were in minor cases to introduce conciliation by a senior police officer and to hand supervision of the most serious cases to the Police Complaints Board. The proposals satisfied neither the critics of the system, such as the National Council for Civil Liberties, nor the Police Federation which believed that the proposed three-tier system was worse than the existing one—and there was still no mention of the policeman's rights.

One of Lord Scarman's proposals which has been implemented is the suggestion to allow lay visitors to police stations. On 11 March 1983 the Greater Manchester Police Authority, fully supported by Chief Constable James Anderton, decided to go ahead with lay visitors from May. The visitors are members of the police committee and visit police stations without notice, having access to prisoners by consent. Similar schemes are being introduced elsewhere in the country.

'Unfailing patience and courtesy'

It is clear that the police service has responded positively and energetically to Lord Scarman's recommendations. But it is equally clear that rigorous action is needed if the unacceptable face of policing—the harassment, 'the discourtesies' and 'the bullying',[29] which Lord Scarman found—is to be removed.

Unfortunately, prevalent images of the police seem to be based on the fatuous American and British television fictions of handsome young men rushing around in fast cars.

It has been claimed by several authorities that many young policemen perceive their role in this way. Reiner has stated that increasingly officers are attracted by

> the glamour, excitement and challenge of the crime-fighting aspects of the work, the 'machismo syndrome', the pull of 'big white cars and flashing blue lights'. . . . The orientations of policemen before they join up and the culture of the work bolster and reinforce each other to produce an action and crime-fighting perspective, with training producing only a temporary and short-lived liberalising antidote. . . .[30]

It is surely not surprising that offcers who are imbued with the *Starsky and Hutch* image should encounter adverse reactions from members of the public. Those policemen like Leslie Curtis, Chairman of the Police Federation, who have what has been called 'a profound nostalgia for Dock

Green'[31] have an up-hill battle. It is essential that the efforts of the many quiet, unassuming police officers on the beat are properly recognised, and all policemen should be constantly reminded of the first Metropolitan Police Commissioners' emphasis on the *prevention* of crime and the preservation of public tranquility. Perhaps Rowan's and Mayne's original words should be engraved inside each police station:

> Every member of the force must remember that his duty is to protect and help members of the public no less than to apprehend guilty persons. Consequently, while prompt to prevent crime and to arrest criminals, he must look upon himself as a servant and guardian of the general public and treat all law-abiding citizens, irrespective of their social position, with unfailing patience and courtesy.[32]

In the chapters which follow, these policing dilemmas and issues are explored from different viewpoints. Unfortunately much of the discussion in the media and in Parliament seems to take place from entrenched positions—as Michael Zander puts it, 'most people who engage in the debate tend to be in one of two opposing camps'.[33] A polarised debate, with each side seeking to stereotype the other, does not further a sensible discussion of these crucial issues. Just as it is easy for some to fail to stress the excellent work done in difficult circumstances by the majority of policemen, so too others find it more comfortable to ignore or gloss over the unacceptable behaviour of a minority of officers.

In the next chapter, Kenneth Oxford considers some of these issues, looking particularly at the methods of policing, new equipment and technology, and training. He stresses two key factors which set the context for modern policing; first, the importance of consent and community relations, and second, the increasing levels of crime.

Basil Griffiths offers a Police Federation view in Chapter 10. He too considers policing methods, equipment and training and in addition he looks at discipline and complaints. He argues fiercely for the traditional principles of the British approach and in favour of one-tier policing.

Margaret Simey considers the relationship between police and the community which they serve. She highlights the problems inherent in democratic scrutiny of professional organisations, and argues that we must seek partnership policing which requires a change of heart by both police and public.

In Chapter 12, Alan Goodson also concentrates on the police and the public. He considers accountability and consultation and also looks at the complaints system and recruitment to the service. He welcomes the debate on these issues which has followed the Scarman Report and he calls for increased efforts to ensure that the relationship between police and public remains cemented.

Finally in this section, Paul Boateng considers how the relationships between the police and the public in inner city areas can be strengthened. He argues that greater accountability is the key to better understanding and trust and he calls for radical changes particularly in the way the Metropolitan Police are held to account.

Although the authors in this section address common problems, they do not reach the same conclusions. But hopefully increased debate about professional policing in our changing society will bring about the reforms—in structures, approaches but most of all attitudes—which seem to be needed.

Notes

1. Quoted in E. P. Thompson, *The Making of the English Working Class*, Pelican, 1970, p. 78.
2. *Ibid.*, p. 89.
3. Sir Cyril Philips, 'Politics in the making of the English police', in *The Home Office*, RIPA, 1983, p. 37.
4. Quoted in B. Whitaker, *The Police in Society*, Sinclair Browne, 1982, p. 40.
5. Committee of Inquiry on the Police, *Reports on Negotiating Machinery and Pay* (Chairman: Lord Edmund-Davies), HMSO, 1978 (Cmnd 7283).
6. *Report of Her Majesty's Chief Inspector of Constabulary 1980* (HC 409), p. 6.
7. R. Reiner, 'Who are the police?', *The Political Quarterly*, Vol. 53, No. 2, April–June 1982, p. 170.
8. See, for example, C. J. Vick, 'Explaining police pessimism', and R. C. Adlam, 'The police personality', in D. W. Pope and N. L. Weiner (Eds.), *Modern Policing*, Croom Helm, 1981; R. Reiner, *The Blue-Coated Worker*, Cambridge University Press, 1978; A. N. Colman and L. P. Gorman, 'Conservatism, dogmatism and authoritarianism in British police officers', *Sociology*, 1982.
9. Reiner, 'Who are the police?', *loc. cit.*, p. 178.
10. Reported in the *Coventry Evening Telegraph*, 26 November 1981.
11. Police Training Council, *Community and Race Relations Training for the Police*, Home Office, March 1983.
12. M. Bilton, 'Police train "snatch squads" ', *The Sunday Times*, 28 March 1982.
13. J. Weeks, ' "Flying riot police" worry Len Murray', *The Daily Telegraph*, 23 May 1979.
14. See House of Commons Official Report (*Hansard*), Vol. 980, 10 March 1980; written answers, cols. 395–396.
15. M. Kettle and L. Hodges, *Uprising!*, Pan, 1982, p. 93.
16. House of Commons Official Report (*Hansard*), 2 February 1983, written answers, col. 109. Mr Whitelaw revealed that two people were injured by police shooting in 1980, one in 1981, three in 1982.
17. D. Leigh and P. Lashmar, 'Whitelaw figures wrong on gun use by London police', *The Observer*, 23 January 1983.
18. See, for example, J. Alderson, *Policing Freedom*, Macdonald & Evans, 1979; C. Moore and J. Brown, *Community versus Crime*, Bedford Square, 1981.
19. Kettle and Hodges, *op. cit.*, p. 241.
20. Sir Cyril Philips, 'Politics in the making of the English police', *loc. cit.*, p. 39.
21. Quoted in C. Bedford, *Weep for the City*, Lion, 1982, pp. 78–79.
22. J. M. Jones, *Organisational Aspects of Police Behaviour*, Gower, 1980.
23. *Police*, April 1982.
24. M. Brogden, *The Police: Autonomy and Consent*, Academic Press, 1982. See especially Chapter 2, pp. 39–73.
25. Mr Roy Hattersley speaking to the South Gloucestershire Constituency Labour Party in Yate, 19 February 1982.

26. Reported in *The Guardian*, 11 March 1982.
27. B. Whitaker, *op. cit.*, p. 251.
28. Reported in *The Guardian*, 20 January 1983.
29. In February 1982 Lord Scarman told the annual meeting of the Legal Action Group that a build-up of 'discourtesies and roughness' had left youngsters in Brixton, and their parents, with a growing feeling of injustice and resentment. 'They were being bullied', he said.
30. Reiner, 'Who are the police?', *loc. cit.*, p. 178.
31. 'A force that has to move along, please', *The Guardian*, 20 November 1982.
32. Quoted in B. Whitaker, *op. cit.*, pp. 40–41.
33. M. Zander, 'Police powers', *The Political Quarterly*, Vol. 53, No. 2, April–June 1982, p. 128.

CHAPTER 9

Policing by consent

KENNETH OXFORD

The traditional system of policing in this country is firmly established on the principle of policing by consent, rather than coercion: police forces are not an arm of the state but servants of the community whose confidence they must secure. Success in this depends upon police officers understanding the fears and apprehensions of all groups of people within the community, including ethnic minorities, and doing whatever is necessary to enable all citizens to go about their lawful business.

This approach was underlined by Lord Scarman who stressed that if the police are to secure the confidence and assent of the community they must strike a balance between the measures to enforce the law and the maintenance of the peace (Scarman, 4.56–4.60).

Policing methods in a changing society

Within these traditions it is undeniable that systems and methods of policing must vary from place to place. We would not expect a rural county area to be policed in the same way as an inner city area. It is also true that systems of policing change in the same area whenever there is a need to deal with a particular contingency such as outbreaks of disorder or high levels of a particular crime.

In normal times the integral relationship between the traditional constable and society will not change, but policing of serious public disorder is very different from day-to-day policework. These violent outbreaks require a very high professional understanding of the responsibilities involved by all officers, particularly by those in senior positions. These incidents must be seen to be dealt with for what they are—a threat to individuals and to society as a whole.

Our policing methods today reflect the changes in our society and it is all very well to call for community policing as the panacea for all problems with which we are faced, when it is obvious that is not the case. I only wish that it were. Incidentally, I have yet to find out the definition of 'community policing' and what people mean by it. It seems to mean all things to all men.

The past twenty years have seen rapid changes in methods of policing with the increased use of vehicles, technology and specialised squads. Almost all these developments have been criticised by some group or organisation for moving away from our traditional role towards what they describe as a so-called 'police state'. These critics are not supported by the majority of the public who, during all that time, have continued to show more confidence in the police service than any other organisation in the country.[1]* That does not mean that the police service turns a deaf ear to such criticisms or dismisses them as ill-founded. Indeed, quite the reverse—they are all considered and adopted, amended or dismissed on their merits.

Let us examine some of the changes in our society in the past two decades which have forced changes on the police service. In 1960, the national annual crime figures were just under three-quarters of a million, and by 1970 they had reach one-and-a-half million. New accounting rules were introduced at the beginning of 1980 and in that year notifiable offences reached two-and-a-half million. The most recent figures are for 1981, and these show a 10 per cent increase on the previous year: the number of offences recorded has now reached 2,794,000.[2] I have little doubt that the figures for 1982 will top the three million mark.

The prevention and detection of crime is at the heart of society's expectations of the police service, and such increases pose a real challenge to all police officers, and will continue to do so as long as the number of crimes doubles every 10 years.

Much criticism has been levelled at the use of mobile police patrols rather than foot patrol officers, and nowhere has this criticism been more vociferous than over the use of 'panda cars'. I use this example to show that the service does react to such criticism, because the use of these vehicles is being phased out or reduced and deployed in different situations in almost every police force in the country. That does not mean to say they were not effective when they were first brought into use in the early 1960s. At that time, police manpower was in short supply, whilst the calls upon police time were increasing dramatically. In effect, the financial and economic climate forced the use of these vehicles on to the service because they were cheaper than recruiting the extra number of officers which would have been required. To some extent their continued use has been the result of the financial strictures placed on the police service, as on other public services. The poor rates of police pay in the mid-1970s[3] meant we could not recruit suitable people into the service, and we could not keep many of the experienced officers we already possessed. They left for better paid employment, most of them never to return. This is one of the primary

---

* Superscript numbers refer to Notes at end of chapter.

reasons why we have such a young and relatively inexperienced service at the moment. Despite its critics, the panda car did provide the public with a very quick response to their calls, far quicker than had been the case before their inception. This latter fact was highlighted in the Scarman Report, together with the need for a speedy and effective response to emergencies (Scarman, 5.50).

Retaining public confidence

The Scarman Report also looked at the methods of policing adopted within Brixton and, by implication, other similar inner city areas (Scarman, 5.44–5.54). At its most simplistic, the Report highlights the dichotomy of the so-called 'hard' and 'soft' policing.

Lord Scarman stresses that a system of 'hard' policing is often necessary, particularly when there is a requirement to act firmly against crime (Scarman, 5.46). Although I feel that policing is far too complex a subject to categorise, 'hard' policing is the description given to police saturation of an area and the exercise of laws such as 'stop and search' in an attempt to diminish certain types of crime or outbreaks of disorder.

Most people are now aware of the debate on the increase of recorded crime throughout the country, and in particular the serious increases in so-called street crime. In the main, these violent attacks are perpetrated on victims who are least likely to be able to defend themselves, such as women and the elderly.

If the police are to retain the confidence of the public it is essential that positive action is taken against such offences, and it is inevitable that the police response is fairly hard line. It is likely that extra officers will be deployed in the areas with the highest incidence of such offences to supplement the regular officers. Some of the officers will be in plain clothes, although most will be in uniform and on foot with mobile support. The tactics will depend on the circumstances, but when attacks take place, it is likely that members of the public will be stopped and questioned whenever necessary. The use of extra officers and associated techniques has resulted in some criticism, especially when the extra officers are drawn from our mobile reserves. In London and the other major cities calls have been made to disband these reserves, such as the Special Patrol Group or Task Forces, or whatever they may be called. Much of the criticism, that such groups are élitist, highly trained, paramilitary officers, is both emotive and inaccurate (see Scarman, 5.53). The truth is that the members of these reserves are ordinary uniformed officers experienced in foot patrol duties and working together as a team. They are not given special equipment, other than personnel carriers and similar vehicles to move them from place to place as a group, and they are very small in number in relation to forces' strengths.

They are deployed in any area, at the request of the divisional commander of that area, and usually work on foot in concert with the regular officers of the area. Apart from such crime prevention and detection exercises, these officers are used on search operations for missing persons and in the investigation of serious crimes such as murder, rape and sexual offences, when they provide an invaluable service on general enquiries for which they are trained and organised.

Such reserves are a very necessary and integral part of the service, providing a viable and practical method of policing of large urban conurbations when additional patrols are required. Their actions are properly supervised and scrutinised, and the members remain within the departments for relatively short periods—two or three years—to prevent a build-up of élitist attitudes.

At the opposite end of the policing spectrum, at least by definition, is the low profile approach of community policing which, contrary to reports in the press, is not the exclusive property of a minority of 'enlightened chief officers'. This approach has been utilised by all forces over many years. Merseyside, for example, has operated specialist officers with responsibility for juveniles for over 30 years, and with responsibility for community liaison for 15 years, although if you delve into the history of the development of those particular forces, they were the subject of much criticism of that day of the police service involving itself far too much with social services. But the wheel has turned full circle. We are now told that we should be very much more involved with social and local amenities.

These types of officers, which Lord Scarman refers to as Home Beat Officers, are deployed in every force in the country, albeit with different titles (Scarman, 5.48–5.51). They provide an ideal and essential means for the dissemination of information between the police and the community and they have the facility for bringing forward ideas and suggestions to the highest levels of the community and the police service in order to attain a speedy and appropriate response to community requirements.

The second, but most important, factor in the use of 'soft' policing is the increase in the numbers and deployment of that avuncular 'bobby on the beat'. As I pointed out earlier, the determining factors on the levels of foot patrols in the past were largely out of the hands of senior police officers, but since the improvement in police pay and police recruitment, the position has improved considerably.[4] There are now more officers on the beat than has ever been the case in the past, but as it is a relatively recent phenomenon we have not yet seen the maximum benefit in terms of police–public relationships this increase will bring about.

The systems of community policing require a degree of consultation between the police and their communities, and it is appropriate to look at Lord Scarman's recommendations on this subject. His main proposals are that statutory liaison committees, or something similar, should be established at police divisional or sub-divisional level (Scarman, 5.55–5.71). On the face of it, such a suggestion would appear to be beneficial to both groups, as it would allow our senior police officers to discuss matters of policing policy openly and responsibly with the community, and help to gain, or improve, the support of the community. Such a practice has always existed prior to Scarman, but there has been an increase in the use of such meetings since the disorders of 1981. There are, however, practical difficulties which were not considered, or at least commented on, by Lord Scarman.

In my force, the divisional and sub-divisional commanders meet with all manner of community groups and individuals, including elected representatives, church leaders and residents' associations. In some cases these meetings have proved useful, the matters discussed have been of a local or parochial nature and capable of resolution, and opportunities have been provided for the dissemination of mutual information. In other cases such meetings have been less than helpful. The influence of party politics can and does create confusion when one considers that a police authority with a statutory responsibility for the police may be of a different political complexion from a district or parish council within the same area, and their views on policing may conflict. Equally, the views of certain community groups are directly opposed to others in the same area, and there are some groups who refuse to meet with the police or other groups because of the differing views, and there is little that can be done to overcome this problem, other than by persuasion.

New equipment and technology

The increasing use of technology and new equipment started to gain momentum in the police service about 20 years ago with the advent of personal radios and the 'panda car', but it is only in the last 2 years that additional equipment has been acquired for use in the control of public disorder. Police officers are now protected with suitable headgear designed to prevent serious injury from missiles and minimise the risk of facial burns from petrol bombs, because we have a new dimension in the public order field, within the experience of anyone serving in the police service today. Fireproof clothing and portable fire fighting equipment has been designed for similar contingencies, and the Government has made available CS gas, baton rounds and water cannon should they be required, as a last resort (Scarman, 5.74). Such equipment has, in some quarters, been condemned as repressive and an over-reaction, but although we all hope it will never have to be used, we must protect our officers and the public at large from the staggering number of injuries that were inflicted in 1981. Three hundred police officers were injured in Liverpool on one night in July 1981, and 230 of them required hospital treatment. It is all very well to criticise the police, but we have to recruit our new officers from our communities and they expect—no, they *demand*—and deserve protection. They cannot understand the double standards, the hypocrisy, the ambivalence, which are applied by some of our critics.

Lord Scarman was right when he deplored the actions of the rioters and said there was no justification for attacks on the police in the street, or arson or riot, and those engaged in violence against the police were guilty of grave criminal offences which society cannot condone (Scarman, 4.97–4.99). I mentioned earlier that policing of public disorder requires different methods from normal routine duties, but I am confident the police service can, if necessary, use the strategies and equipment needed for such events and still return to the more traditional role after the culmination of events.

I would like to refer again to the debate on the continuing increase in the levels of crime. It has been suggested that additional police manpower particularly on the beat is the primary hope for the reversal of these trends, when all our experience suggests this is not the case. The short palliative answer is not more policemen, but more community involvement and responsibility. Much more research will have to be undertaken into the fundamental causes of crime before the position is improved, but the numbers and the changing nature of crime and criminals require an increasing use of technological equipment to prevent the position becoming unmanageable. Let me look at the police use of computers, which epitomises the conflict between law enforcement by the police and policing by consent.

Computers and crime

The Police National Computer (PNC) has been used by all forces for a number of years now, and originally contained the details of owners of motor vehicles and of stolen and found vehicles. Such a facility represented a tremendous saving of time and effort in relation to the police and other agencies. It also provided a much more efficient service to those members of the public who are the victims of auto-theft. Considering that a motor vehicle represents the second most expensive item, after a house, that most people possess, the theft of a car is of considerable importance to them.

Additional information has now been added to this system including an index of wanted persons, disqualified drivers and missing persons, and presently fingerprint records are being made available through the PNC. The result of such facilities is a great potential for improving efficiency in crime prevention and detection, particularly when you consider the many hours spent at present to identify one set of fingerprints by manual search.

The use of PNC facilities is governed by a very strict code of practice which is constantly under review and designed to safeguard the privacy of the individual and security of the information under storage.[5]

There are now many other areas where the police service makes use of such technology and one of the most recent innovations is a system called command and control. This is a system designed to allow police managers to make the most effective use of their valuable resources—manpower and vehicles. It will ensure that the correct priorities can be assessed in the coverage of beats or areas and that police response to any given incident or situation is improved, and more importantly, controlled. The potential for controlling police resources will provide the public with a more efficient service and will prevent over-reaction to many incidents, a much criticised area of policing methods.

It is, however, the use of crime-reporting and crime-intelligence computers which is subject to the most intense and concentrated criticism, and so it should be. Such computers are the most recent technological acquisitions to be utilised in the fight against crime, and indeed they are still in the experimental stages. Potentially they offer the police service a great opportunity to maintain our present commitment to the investigation and detection of crime, a commitment which, in the light of present trends and without the use of such computers, would inevitably be reduced.

Let me give you an example of the problems faced by the current increases in crime. In Merseyside during 1980 and 1981 the number of burglaries increased by 10,500, and the sheer volume of that increase needs to be carefully considered. It means 10,500 extra files and complainants to visit by one or more officers, and has the effect of lessening the amount of attention to each case, and consequently a lower rate of detection. All this has taken place when increases in the numbers of detective officers are minimal or at a standstill. This type of position is common throughout the country.

Consider the criticisms made of police use of computers. Information stored on computer banks may be inaccurate and cannot be checked by the individual; the rapid search of indices can predict patterns of crime or can identify suspects on the basis of inaccurate information; the privacy of the individual is under threat; or the information could be used in the future by some less than democratic government operating a police state. In truth, all the information which may be stored on these machines had already been stored in written form—but even this point is attacked because the computer can utilise this information much faster than was previously possible. This is of course true, but such facilities also provide the opportunity to remove erroneous material which could never be successfully undertaken by manual means. There is no value in recording inaccurate information, quite the reverse, so adequate safeguards must be provided. The police service is aware of such misgivings, and has developed strict codes of practice as to the use of computers, effectively to weed out information on a regular basis, and ensure that no unauthorised access can be gained to the records. In order to ensure that the freedom of the individual is not compromised, the police service must actively seek to maintain a balance between the need to retain information to help in the fight against crime and the traditional liberties of the public.

In the end it is the public who will decide what kind of police force it wants because its police force will reflect the nature of the society in which it operates. The public must decide whether there should be unrestricted freedom for the individual with all that this implies, or whether liberty should be exercised with a responsibility to the whole community where people can live in their homes in safety or walk the streets of our inner cities without fear of personal attack.

Training and the police service

In his report Lord Scarman places great emphasis on the need to increase and improve the levels of police training, in all ranks, but particularly in the areas of community relations and handling public disorder, and in the initial training of our recruits (Scarman, 5.16–5.32). This general view is supported by a consensus within the police service, and it is something that we have been saying for a long time in any event.

In respect of initial training he recommends that the present 10-week course (15 weeks in the Metropolitan Police) be replaced as a matter of urgency by 6 months of training, although he appreciates the difficulties such a change would create (Scarman, 5.18–5.23). In the past economic restraints have again been an important factor in deciding the length of such courses, and it is difficult to see where the finance will be found at the present time to implement the recommendations. In order to process the present numbers of recruits there would have to be a threefold increase in resources, buildings, teaching staff, equipment and cash. In my view the cost would be prohibitive, and the alternative—reducing the number of recruits—would have a disastrous effect on the efficiency of the service and possibly our role in society.

In the light of the current debate on the police service one could be forgiven for thinking that training of police officers was at worst almost non-existent or at best ineffective or inappropriate. This is not the case. In the past 20 years overall training of police officers has increased and changed out of all recognition at national, regional and local level. Training is given for every aspect of police work and for all ranks from constable to chief constable.

Training in community relations is included in all general courses held in my force including refresher courses, local procedure courses, and those for

CID and newly promoted sergeants and inspectors. Similar courses are held in every force in the country. The current training package on community relations presented to new recruits during their initial training includes instruction in the following topics: the development of the police in modern society, human behaviour of groups and individuals, barriers to communication, interview techniques and police attitudes, common social problems, prejudice, community and race relations, and many others designed to provide a firm foundation for any young officer to act with confidence and understanding in public.

In Merseyside constables, sergeants and inspectors attend a special public relations course designed to influence police attitudes and increase understanding and knowledge about ethnic minorities and their fears, problems and aspirations.

At a national level community and race relations courses and seminars are held at police training centres and some university and other academic establishments. The inputs at these levels are of the highest standards and the speakers include representatives of interested parties, community and race relations experts, church leaders, politicians and police officers.

The Police College at Bramshill which caters for police managers and supervisors, from sergeant to chief officer, includes community relations in its curriculum for all courses as well as conducting specific courses and seminars at regular intervals.

I have laboured this point to show that the police service does not sit back and ignore society's problems but takes deliberate and positive action to improve our knowledge and understanding of the difficulties which can affect all of us. I very much doubt if there is any other organisation which expends so much time and effort in this direction even if there is still a need for improvement. It is important and obvious to remember that all additional training means a reduction of police officers available for operational duties, and at times when increases in manpower are unlikely, very careful consideration has to be given to the requirements of these two factors.

Let me move on to the training of police officers to respond to outbreaks of public disorder and the recommendations of Lord Scarman (Scarman, 5.29–5.30) which in the main have been implemented or are under consideration.

With the benefit of hindsight (and we all know that hindsight is an exact science), it is apparent that the police were not properly trained or equipped to deal with the scale of disorder which beset this country in 1981. The number of police casualties would support that fact, but the situation is well on the way to being put right. I might add that prior to these disorders the police service had been reluctant to equip itself for such contingencies because of the possible adverse effect such a course of action would have on the traditional image of the British police officer. It is only in the past 10 years, with the increase in violent public protest, that police officers have been issued with shields and protective helmets.

Training now takes account of our experiences of 1981, and has been formulated at national level. All police officers who might be called to police outbreaks of disorder are now trained in the techniques of the use of riot shields singly and in groups and formations. They are instructed in the new tactics designed to remove the initiative from rioters and give the police service a much more flexible approach than has ever been the case in the past.

Previously it had been the conventional practice to contain rioters by lines of police officers behind riot shields and then try to divide them into smaller groups and eventually disperse them. This approach together with the only offensive tactic open to us—the use of a baton charge—proved to be completely and utterly ineffective in the face of the tactics adopted by the protagonists in 1981.

National guidelines are now in force in relation to such training and all senior officers up to and including assistant chief constable have received training, commensurate with their rank and responsibility, on the strategy and tactics for handling disorder and have been made aware of the latest developments.

Let me conclude with a quotation:

> When that time arrives—we will say next year, or at most, the year after—this 'public opinion' of ours will be quite ready to begin again to devour with gusto and credulity another 'shocking police scandal' and vehemently demand 'reform'.
>
> The truth is that most people have no real knowledge of a policeman's life.
>
> Consequently, no sooner does some person with an axe to grind, or a grievance to air, stir up mud against the police than every one of us pricks up his ears, and is ready to take seriously the most absurd lies and swallow the shallowest slander without a grain of salt. This is a very unsatisfactory state of things—unfair to the police and dangerous to the public.
>
> The public cannot expect to be served as it would wish by men who know that, whether they do well or ill, at the first breath of calumny the very people to whom they give their best, are ready to believe almost anything that detractors, however ignorant or 'interested', choose to allege against them.[6]

These words are from *The Times* of 1908, and they are as true today as they were 75 years ago.

Notes

1. An opinion poll in *The Times* in September 1980 showed that 71 per cent rated the police 'good', 26 per cent 'reasonable' and only 3 per cent 'bad'. After the riots, 75 per cent of respondents reported no decrease in their confidence in the police: see *The Observer*, 15 November 1981. A ranking of the public's view of different groups is given in B. Whitaker, *The Police in Society*, Sinclair Browne, 1982, p. 212;

Percentage expressing a great deal
of confidence in the management of:

Police	71
Medicine	67
The Military	60
Law courts	42
Education	39
Civil service	26
The press	24
Parliament	19
Trade unions	18

2. Home Office, *Criminal Statistics (England and Wales) 1981*, HMSO, October 1982 (Cmnd 8668).
3. 'By 1977, a constable's pay had fallen to 20 per cent below the average male earnings in industry, though the Willink Royal Commission had said it should stand 4 per cent above.' B. Whitaker, *The Police in Society*, Sinclair Browne, 1982, p. 226.
4. Police pay was considerably raised as a result of the Lord Edmund-Davies' recommendations: Committee of Inquiry on the Police, *Reports on Negotiating Machinery and Pay*, HMSO, July 1978 (Cmnd 7283).
5. The issues raised by information privacy and computers have been considered by the Younger Committee which reported in 1972 and in the White Paper, *Computers and Privacy*, HMSO, December 1975 (Cmnd 6353). The Committee on Data Protection (Chairman: Sir Norman Lindop) also considered these matters in great detail and its report (Cmnd 7341) was published in December 1978. In May 1981 the United Kingdom signed the Council of Europe Data Protection Convention and the subsequent Data Protection Bill received its second reading in the House of Lords on 20 January 1983, but failed to pass into law when Parliament was dissolved in May 1983. The proposals have been re-introduced and are expected to become law during 1984.
6. *The Times*, 1908, commenting on the Report of the Royal Commission into the duties of the Metropolitan Police, Cmnd 4156.

CHAPTER 10

One-tier policing

BASIL GRIFFITHS

A famous Victorian *Punch* cartoon aptly reflects the way in which the Police Federation[1]* reacted to the publication of the Scarman Report. The cartoon depicted a young curate taking tea with one of his lady parishioners, who asked 'How do you like the egg?' His reply was, 'It's all right madam—it's good in parts.' It was with similar sentiments that the Report was welcomed as a constructive contribution to the seemingly never-ending debate upon the quality and nature of the police service. It has to be regarded as one man's view (albeit an eminent and informed man) of the problems currently besetting the police and their relationships with the community—but there is no reason to accept it as other than that.

It is perhaps possible to criticise the Report as having set out to be all things to all people, and certainly the temptation is to pluck from the Report those parts which sustain a particular point of view and to ignore that which is converse. To a large extent the media, in presenting the Report for public consumption, tended to be selectively negative, representing it as being highly critical of the police—which (as anyone who has actually read the full Report will know) is simply not the case. Indeed, although it gave the Police Federation little satisfaction, many of Lord Scarman's recommendations, particularly in the fields of training and operational methods, accord with policies and warnings voiced by the Police Federation over many years.

Principles of British policing

The origins of the British police system and the establishment of a paid professional police force are generally credited to the Home Secretary of the day, Sir Robert Peel.[2] Yet it can be argued that whilst the London Metropolitan Police Force was established during his Home Secretaryship, that creation rather than being an inspiration was really the hallmark of his failure. The first professional paid police system, in what was then one

---

* Superscript numbers refer to Notes at end of chapter.

united country, had some years earlier been established in the form of the Royal Irish Constabulary—a force which Peel as Secretary for Ireland during the years 1812 to 1818 had used to contain order in that ever-troubled island. It might also be seen as significant that Peel vehemently defended the 'Peterloo massacre' of 1819—a use of the military against the civil population and an incident which ironically gave force to the argument for the establishment of a proper police system on mainland Britain.

The Royal Irish Constabulary was a para-military organisation and a countrywide police system under the direct control of a government minister. It was a model which Parliament found repugnant if applied to the rest of the United Kingdom. This fear of a politically controlled repressive force, on the Napoleonic model, resulted in a compromise embodying safeguards which effectively exist to the present day. The result was an organised force of constables, each one individually responsible at law for his actions and directed, as were his unpaid predecessors, by the magistracy. To this day the Commissioner of the Metropolitan Police is a Justice of the Peace and directives to arrest offenders are given in the form of warrants issued by magistrates. An arrest by a police officer, other than with the authority of a warrant, is entirely the responsibility of that individual officer. Unlike his continental counterpart he cannot be ordered to make an arrest by a superior or claim excuse at law for such direction should he act unlawfully. It is interesting to note that the British colonial police forces were set up on the Irish rather than the English model, and even after independence many such forces have retained that structure even to the nomenclature of ranks.

In contrast the London Metropolitan constable wore a uniform which was no more than the normal civilian dress of the day, which emphasised his non-military character. His operational accountability was, as now, not to any political or elected authority, but to the law itself.

Accountability and control

How then can such a body of constables be directed—how can a centralised policy be imposed? There are no simple answers to these questions—their complexity can only be illustrated by example.

The Scarman Report details the occasion when the Leader of Lambeth Borough Council asked Commander Fairbairn, the officer in charge at Brixton, to renounce the use of the mis-named 'sus' law (Scarman, 4.34–4.35). Yet the Commander had no more power to suspend the law of the land than he could prevent an individual constable from exercising the powers conferred upon him by that law.

A further illustration of this independency of action involved a Member of Parliament who was arrested while driving a motor car under the influence of drink. The chief constable of the force concerned decided not to proceed with the prosecution, but the arresting officer, feeling strongly that justice had not prevailed, proceeded in his own right as a constable to a conviction.

During the controversial 1969 tour of the South African rugby football team, when demonstrators against apartheid invaded the pitches, chief constables were 'advised' by the Home Secretary of the day that police officers should not interfere when such incidents took place on private football grounds. The 'advice' was firmly ignored on the grounds that the preservation of the peace is a primary duty of the police,[3] and it is established in English law that it is the duty of a constable to enter upon and act within private premises to prevent a breach of that peace.[4]

Policy directives within the police service must thus be limited to the maintenance of the rule of law by the most effective means available. Chief constables have every discretionary power to issue orders to their subordinates to concentrate on those matters which they regard as requiring priority in any area—for example street crime—but nevertheless the responsibility at law still remains with the individual constable. But some offences are by their nature more controversial than others. Determining action for such offences as the misuse of drugs, sexual offences, pornography and public order is difficult and requires an especially nice judgement which can only be conditioned by community opinion and the attitude of the courts towards offenders.

Much is made within the Scarman Report of the need for senior police officers when making such decisions to consult local representatives within the community. Yet such judgements, whether made by a constable exercising his discretion or by a chief officer making a major policy decision, must inevitably be influenced by public expectations. It would be a foolish chief constable who failed to explain fully his policies to his police committee, and at divisional level local councillors should always have access to divisional commanders. The efforts in this respect made by the district commander at Brixton as detailed in the Report (Scarman, 4.5–4.46) illustrate the point. But there are those who go further, claiming that locally elected politicians should actually assume operational control of the local police. It is questionable if all those who propound this point of view have really thought this question through: those with political objectives in mind may well have done, but the words of Lord Russell of Liverpool, the British Nuremburg judge, when speaking of the Hitler régime are apt on this issue. He said: 'That which epitomized the Nazi system of government was the total subservience of the rule of law to political expediency.' It is worth remembering that Nazis were elected to power in Germany and those who advance the notion of police accountability as a libertarian cause might ponder that there are those in British politics who show a taste for totalitarianism.

The police and public support

Throughout Lord Scarman's Report the basic precept of British policing is stressed: that without the consent of the general public the system simply will not work. All British policemen would support this view, for as practical police operatives their whole existence sustains it, and it is notable that Lord Scarman took the point (Scarman, 4.53) that the majority of the Brixton community support the police operations to reduce street crime.

Yet it is quite unreasonable to suppose that the police could enjoy total public support at all times—or indeed that they should seek it. Perhaps in this respect the service has become the victim of an unreal middle-class expectation of the universally benevolent policeman—an expectation impossible to sustain.

Policy and methods of policing will not ultimately be determined by the adoption of recommendations in a report. They will instead be determined by the nature of the community to be policed and the resources available to carry out that task. It may be very difficult for some people to accept that there exists and has existed since the days of the industrial revolution hard core urban areas where a positive hatred is maintained towards the police by a sizable minority of the people who live there. And this hatred is matched by a belligerence displayed towards any form of authority. It is amongst such people—unemployed even in times of full employment—that crime and violence is a way of life. It may be that the simple explanation for the wave of rioting was that those criminal elements discovered, possibly inspired by the tactics of their Ulster counterparts, that by the use of the petrol bomb their arch enemies—the police—could for the first time be shown as impotent to prevent widespread crime and disorder.

It is in these inner city areas that the respectable, the old and the weak suffer most as victims of the criminality of the minority. It is this majority, perhaps the one at Brixton to which Scarman refers, who look to the police as their only means of protection. A partial failure on the part of the police to fulfill that task, as evinced by the level of crime and violence in such areas, may be laid at the door of decades of neglect of policing needs.

The methods of policing

The neglect of the needs of our police service is to be found in the policies of successive governments who, while showing a ready acquiescence to the demands of the 'civil rights' lobbyists, have at the same time been prepared to introduce economies which have removed the policeman from his role as the traditional pedestrian police-beat constable. Poor pay, restrictions upon recruiting and a refusal to increase unrealistic establishments were coupled with the increased demands upon limited police resources as a result of the crime explosion which occurred in the affluent and permissive 1960s. The result was the removal of the policeman from the public to perform retro-active and fire brigade policing in the panda car. The appalling effects on both the morale and the efficiency of the police service will take a decade of good leadership, training and selective recruiting to remedy.

The reaction against this style of policing has come, ironically enough, from the very politicians who were responsible for its creation. In its place there are those who advocate what has fast become the 'cult of community policing', and even within the police service itself there are those who are foolish enough to appear to be lining up on either side of a fence dividing what is becoming known as 'hard' and 'soft' policing. On this question Scarman recognises what has certainly been obvious to the experienced operational policeman for a very long time. His answer is clearly spelled out in the Report: 'The solution lies, I suggest, in an approach to policing . . . which marries the work of Home Beat and operational police officers . . . in a single policing style based on small beats regularly patrolled by officers normally operating on foot' (Scarman, 5.51).

And so the argument turns full circle. The call is now for a return to traditional policing or, more simply, to the system which operated prior to the introduction of the panda car. Such a return would of necessity mean a considerable increase in establishments with a massive retraining pro-gramme, and hence a great deal more money. But the danger of the cheaper alternative proposed, should the notion of community policing prevail, is that selected policemen showing particular qualities would become the community policemen—providing the 'acceptable face' of the police service—leaving the residual majority to form the special patrol groups to deal with the public order situations. In other words, there would be established the framework of a two tier policing system—a *gendarmerie* and a *corps urbane*, the former simply carrying out the directives of authority and ultimately losing their constable status. Thus the Napoleonic police system, despised and rejected in 1829, could be realised before the end of the twentieth century.

Riot equipment

A police officer now nearing the end of his service would have been the recruit of 30 years ago. At that time he, like members of the public, would have found it inconceivable that police officers in this country would ever face rioting mobs hurling Molotov cocktails. Similarly, it would have seemed incredible that British policemen would be issued with fireproof uniforms, riot helmets and plastic shields, or that the availability of water cannon, rubber bullets and CS gas would be a matter for serious consideration. In 1980 the Police Federation and the other police representative bodies were adamant that the image of the traditional policeman should be maintained at all costs. By the following year those same bodies were making demands, more in sorrow than in anger, for the issue of proper riot equipment. Those demands were made in the face of 2000 police officers injured in rioting in the space of just one fortnight.

It is simply not a question of the police force going over to the offensive. No one would wish to see such things as water cannon, gas or rubber bullets becoming regular features of police operations, but events have clearly shown that 'in the last resort' they must now be available to protect the police as well as the public. It is in the nature of any society that anarchy must not be allowed to prevail, and should the legitimate and accountable arm of the state fail to suppress such disorder (whether because of a lack of equipment or for any other reason) then that authority will inevitably be replaced by an authority without accountability or legitimacy.

Discipline and complaints

The Police Discipline Code[5] must be the most stringent applied to any public body in the country. There cannot be any other police force in the world that holds its individual members more accountable. British police officers are subject to both the civil and the criminal law for any action they may take, and they are unable to claim as an excuse that such action was taken on the orders of a superior officer. Furthermore, policemen are subject to a complaints system involving an investigation and disciplinary hearing which largely denies them the basic rights afforded to every other citizen. The whole system of complaints is overseen by an independent complaints board and by the Director of Public Prosecutions in respect of criminal allegations. The police officer, ever conscious in his day-to-day operational duties of the peril of making a wrong decision, is very often bitter and certainly puzzled by the furore which is constantly evoked by the question of complaints against the police by members of the public. It does not seem to him that the average man in the street is particularly concerned, whilst some politicians, media people and those purporting to speak on behalf of minority interests seem obsessed with the issue.

It does not seem likely that there can be many police forces elsewhere in the world who actually hand out pamphlets telling people how to complain or have so many very senior officers investigating complaints against policemen. Nevertheless, whatever the efforts made on the part of the police themselves, the chorus of dissatisfaction continues. The bitterness is compounded in that the ordinary policeman's dissatisfaction with this oppressive system is largely ignored. The police officers' representatives have long campaigned against the injustice that rules of evidence can be ignored at whim at a disciplinary hearing. The accused policeman does not even enjoy the basic right of legal representation, and he can suffer suspension from duty, often for months at a time, awaiting the outcome of an investigation with all it may mean to both his morale and, worse still, to his family. At the same time the service in which he takes pride suffers a constant barrage of accusation and innuendo, and cases of unsubstantiated police malpractice become the *causes célèbres* of many ambitious politicians. After each major campaign of this nature Home Secretaries busily set up working parties and promise fresh legislation, adding new and burdensome legislation to an already over-complicated machine.

It is widely known that the Police Federation opposed any change which might involve the investigation of complaints by an outside investigatory body. The objection was not based on a fear that such an investigation might more effectively reveal the guilt of an accused officer—this is unlikely; the problem lay rather in suggesting who might have sufficient investigatory expertise and impartiality to be entrusted with this task. However, the Police Federation reversed its position when it was realised that while there were no proposals to bring in an independent authority, both of investigation and of hearing, there were positive moves towards change. The fear is that these changes are merely cosmetic, and do nothing to bring a greater sense of justice to either the policeman or the complainant. These changes which have now been openly described both in the 1982 Queen's Speech and by the Government are simply a way of paying the Danegeld to those who will persist even more vociferously in using the complaints controversy to denigrate the police.

The main proposals, both contained within the Scarman Report (Scarman, 7.11–7.29), call for an initial system of conciliation in minor complaints and an independent assessor to oversee the investigation of complaints which will continue to be investigated by senior police officers. The latter proposal is simply a duplication of the work of the Police Complaints Board who already have the power to call for further investigation if in any particular case they are dissatisfied. Since there appears to be a total absence of any intention to meet the demands of the policeman for fair play in these matters, the new measures are unlikely to change attitudes or lead to a lessening of further demands for reform.

The disciplinary offence of racial discrimination

From the policeman's point of view the most unacceptable of all the Report's recommendations is the proposal that there should be a special offence written into the Discipline Code to deal with racial discrimination, and that policemen found guilty of such an offence should face automatic dismissal (Scarman, 5.41 and 5.42).

This conclusion and the proposed Draconian punishment seem a little at odds with the main text of the Report which concludes that a penchant for using discriminatory action on racial grounds is rare among police officers. It does seem particularly unfair that policemen should be placed in jeopardy in this way when the same complaint is so often levelled against members of other public bodies. In addition the Report recognises that the existing offence of 'discreditable conduct'[6] covers such behaviour and it is open to any chief officer to increase the penalty for that offence should racially prejudiced or discriminatory behaviour be involved. That view has since been unanimously accepted by the Police Advisory Board[7] representing local authorities, the Home Office and police representative bodies.

Police training

The inadequacy of training for recruits into the police service is fully described in the Report (Scarman, 5.16–5.26), which recognises what can justifiably be described as a scandalous state of affairs.

In this country a mere *ten weeks* has been provided for a recruit's full-time centralised training (only recently but minimally increased in some forces) in contrast to one or two *years* in other European countries. At the same time we place individual responsibilities for decision-making on the shoulders of these young people at a level which would be unheard of in those countries. In these circumstances it is testimony to the personal qualities of our young police officers, and to their credit, that they acquit themselves so well without many incidents of conflict arising between themselves and members of the public.

The sophistication of modern society makes unparalleled demands on the professionalism of today's policeman. Yet his training has not substantially changed from that which a policeman received 30 years ago, and this was a training designed to fit a young officer with the knowledge required to police a community of comparative tranquillity. Public houses, even in the inner cities, tended to close their doors at 10.00 pm, as did most other places of public entertainment. Late night restaurants were a rarity and outside the centre of London licensed clubs were non-existent. To be walking the street after midnight almost amounted to a criminal offence in itself and would almost always receive the attention of a patrolling policeman! A motor car driven at night was rare enough to justify police enquiry and a driver under the age of 30 was suspicious in itself: ordinary young men could rarely afford such a possession. Known serious crime was one fifth of the 1982 level. The comparative difficulty experienced by the young police officer of today patrolling our inner city areas must be recognised. The lack of comprehensive training to equip him to deal with the complex problems with which he will be confronted does both the policeman and the community he serves a great injustice.

The Police Training Council[8] is currently reviewing the future training needs of the recruit, and already the parties involved appear to be looking for ways to avoid grasping the nettle of Scarman's recommendations. Only the Police Federation maintains the essential concept of six months' full-time centralised training, as advocated in the Report (Scarman, 5.19). Others talk of maintaining the present system supplemented by 'on the job' or localised training, but they fail (or refuse on grounds of economy) to realise that such supplementary training should be *additional* to, and not instead of, the recommended six months.

Middle and higher management within the police service has also been neglected. A post-war report on police training[9] recommended that sergeants prior to promotion to inspector should undergo a six-month course at the Police Staff College at Bramshill to equip them for the responsibilities of that rank. The course initially set up in accordance with the recommendation was subsequently changed to allow only for those who had achieved the rank of inspector to receive such training; subsequent economies resulted in only selected inspectors undergoing the course, and recently such training has been relegated to a mere four weeks' training organised on a local basis away from the Staff College. Yet these are the very ranks, sergeants and inspectors, who are responsible for the practical training of recruits.

Industry regards the training of its personnel as a capital investment for the future, and to neglect it in the police service is to put at risk not only that service but the community it serves. Whatever merits may be contained in the Scarman Report, whatever reforms in policy making or other innovations may be brought into being within the police service, and whatever rules and regulations may be introduced to control the conduct of police officers—all will be to no avail without the capital investment of proper training.

Society may get the sort of police service it deserves, but it will certainly not get the one it *needs* unless it is prepared to pay for it.

Notes

1. The Police Federation of England and Wales is a statutory body representing those ranks of the police service up to and including that of chief inspector. The Federation is charged with the making of representations on all matters affecting the welfare and efficiency of the police service.
2. Sir Robert Peel (1788–1850) was Tory Home Secretary 1822–1827 and 1828–1830. His Act brought the London Metropolitan Police into being on 29 September 1829. Dublin had a force as early as 1786 while Glasgow raised her force in 1800.

3. This point is emphasised by Lord Scarman in his Report (Scarman, 4.55–4.58).
4. See *Thomas* vs. *Sawkins*.
5. The Police Discipline Code forms part of the 'Police Regulations' which take the form of subordinate legislation made by the Home Secretary under the authority of the Police Acts. Offences against the Regulations are dealt with by the chief constable of the force concerned, who has the power to award punishments ranging from a caution or a fine to dismissal from the force.
6. See schedule 2 of the Police (Discipline) Regulations 1977—SI 1977, No. 580.
7. The Police Advisory Board is composed of representatives of the Police Federation, the Police Superintendents' Association, the Association of Chief Police Officers, the Association of Metropolitan Authorities, the Association of County Councils and the Home Office. It is a consultative body set up to advise the Home Secretary on matters affecting the police service.
8. The Police Training Council, which is constituted in a similar manner to the Police Advisory Board, advises on all matters connected with police training.
9. *Report of the Committee on Police Conditions of Service:* The Oaksey Committee, 1949 (Cmnd 7831).

CHAPTER 11

Partnership policing

MARGARET SIMEY[1]*

The police and politics

In the current flurry of interest in what caused the public disorders of 1981 and where blame can be laid, the real villain of the piece has escaped attention. It was 'government' and not the police which failed and continues to fail the people of Toxteth. Yet both Scarman and Hytner[2] specifically excluded politics from their considerations and their example is followed in most utterances on the subject, whether they come from Devon or Sparkbrook. Utterances there have certainly been in plenty; the taboo on public discussion of policing has at last been broken. The police struggle to keep their heads above the waters of a welter of debate and criticism. Whole books are written on the once-forbidden topic of the relationship between the police and racial minorities. Only the embargo on comment which links policing with politics still holds fast, if anything strengthened by the backlash against any attempt to introduce change or reform.

This should be cause for anxiety because it is precisely in this—the relationship between police and people—that the nub of the whole windy law-and-order argument is to be found. The gist of the evidence placed before the Merseyside Police Authority as we struggled to get to grips with the catastrophe which had befallen us was all to this one effect. To quote our *Interim Report*:

> The sheer weight of adverse comment alone compels us to recognise that a gulf exists between the police and certain sections of the public in Liverpool 8.

Abandoning the blame game, we had to accept that the force for which we were responsible was seen by too many people as a body apart: a service imposed from outside in which local people had no say, instruments of the Government rather than servants of the people. And as the dust settled, our

---

* Superscript numbers refer to Notes at end of chapter.

own share as politicians in permitting such a situation to develop became all too painfully evident.

Open hostility against the police has dramatised the situation in unmistakeable terms. On the one hand there are the professionals—the organised and disciplined cohorts of the force, with a powerful commitment to the standards and ethics of their calling. On the other hand there is the largely disorganised mass of the consumers of the service—the so-called community—who use and pay for that service, but whose only common sentiment is the feeling that whether they are satisfied or not, there is very little they can do about it. And between the two there is the Police Authority whose sole reason for existence is to ensure that a force is provided which shall 'adequately and efficiently' meet the policing needs of the area. What ever power they may have exercised in their previous existence as the Watch Committee, the Police Authority's present situation is not a happy one. During the past couple of decades, the growing professional power of the police has been matched by a reverse trend so far as elected members are concerned. The apparent apathy of the Police Authority of today reflects the process of social and economic disintegration which has undermined the effectiveness of local government generally.

Thus left to their own devices, the police have taken over an increasing share of the decision-making responsibility which should properly fall to the politicians. Almost unobserved, they have acquired an astonishingly comprehensive control over every aspect of the service. Recruitment and training, deployment of manpower and resources, even the extent to which they shall be accountable for what they do: all this falls within their purview under the general heading of matters 'operational'.

The conclusion to be drawn is clear. The political dimension of policing as a public service has been taken over by the professionals and with it has gone all possibility of effective democratic scrutiny. So long as this basic imbalance of power between police and policed continues to exist, it must constitute a source of grave danger to the very concept of policing by consent.

The central dilemma of government

This imbalance of power is not of course specific to the police: it is in fact the central dilemma of democratic government in our times. The need to delegate responsibility is imposed by the sheer size of the urban community. But how can the people exercise their ultimate right to have the final say in the sort of service they receive—and pay for—without the improper exercise of that authority for partisan and selfish ends? Curiously, improper interference is always assumed to be politically motivated. Yet undue influence can be just as much a cause for alarm when it is prompted by an organised group of those engaged in the service for their own ends.

The growth of the challenge to political control by the providers of the public services is a comparatively recent feature of the government scene. The police are perhaps the latest comers. It is a feature which is gathering strength, and if ways and means of accommodating it are not devised—and quickly—it may well be that the future will see the confrontation between providers and politicians replacing that between political parties, where splintering is rapidly obliterating the traditional lines of demarcation. The implications for policing in particular call for thought if we are to avoid the disastrous consequences of polarisation as demonstrated by events in Toxteth and elsewhere.

How should we tackle this situation? The wearisome arguments over 'control' conceal what those with practical experience of political life quickly realise, though few will admit to it: that there is no future in struggles as to who shall be top dog. Gone are the days when the Town Clerk of Liverpool was reputed to report daily to a brewery to receive the instructions of the Leader of the Council. In practice, the reality is that any administrator worth his salt can, should he choose, make rings around even an experienced member. His control over the information made available, his expertise in running a massive and complex undertaking, the time and the resources at his command, compared with the paltry assistance available to the party member, ensure that the dice are loaded in his favour before the struggle for power even begins.

Attempts to impose some sort of balance between the conflicting parties by means of legislation are of equally limited value. Certainly legislation is needed to clarify and amend the deficiencies of the 1964 Police Act. But it is futile to attempt to decide definitively, by law, the respective areas of responsibility as between the operational and the political, for the simple reason that the indefinable grey area between the two is so extensive as to be pretty well all-encompassing. Strict demarcation between the two is simply not possible. Legislative control is too blunt an instrument to apply to the infinite variety of individual circumstances.

To say this is not to yield one jot of the basic principle that *ultimate control of any public service must remain vested in the people.* From that dictum not even the police can be excused. Much misunderstanding stems from the reverse assumption that somehow the police enjoy total autonomy as if by divine right, and that those who dare to challenge this encroach on sacred territory where they have no right to tread. On the contrary, it cannot be too strongly emphasised that not even the necessity of ensuring the impartial enforcement of the law relieves a democratic society of the ultimate responsibility for all that is done in its name—above all where the liberty of the individual is at stake.

Nonetheless, the fact must be faced that no principle, however fundamental, can escape the harsh test of reality. To talk of 'control' and 'policing by consent' is claptrap unless steps are taken to ensure that the principle is capable of translation into practice. It was because the gap between the expectations which were commonly held, and the reality of the practice to which people were subjected, became so wide as to be no longer tolerable that Toxteth went up in flames of protest. The stark truth is that government by consent, regarding policing above all else, is no longer a reality to many in Britain today. Loyalty to the principle of ultimate public control stands fast. How to relate it to reality is the task we must confront.

The social contract

Instead, therefore, of arguing on about who shall 'control' whom, we would be better occupied if we turned our attention to the practical problems of putting our principles into practice. Given that in a mass society authority must necessarily be delegated in a big way, the key question must surely be the nature of the social contract under which we are prepared to sign away control over our own affairs. The theory that policing should be based on the consent of the policed is the pride and joy of the British tradition, but it is meaningless unless the terms on which that consent is given are clearly understood, generally acceptable, and constantly revised to ensure their relevance to changing circumstances.

The bones of the contract are clear enough. The public for their part voluntarily consent to the delegation of certain authority to those of our members nominated for that purpose. They in return undertake to hold themselves accountable for the way in which that authority is exercised; but what does that add up to in practice?

The law-and-order school would have us leave it all to the police, gladly endowing them with all the additional powers and resources they see fit to demand. Such an abrogation of responsibility is bred out of fear. That way, to quote Scarman, 'is a staging post to the police state' (Scarman, 4.60). An equally popular panacea is to talk of 'community policing'. This has a nostalgic appeal, but examined more closely it adds up to no more than a demand for the police to take up the burden left behind by the departure from the urban scene in particular of many of those who stood for 'government': the clergy, the teachers and doctors, local shopkeepers and the rest. There is no hope for the future in such backward glances.

Scarman shows a better grasp of reality. 'There has to be some way', he asserts, 'in which to secure that the independent judgement of the police can not only operate within the law but with the support of the community' (Scarman, 4.60). He fails though to follow the logic of his argument to its conclusion, perhaps sensing that by so doing he might open the lid of a Pandora's box, with consequences he is reluctant to face. Nevertheless, the intricate balancing act which he sees as essential to the relationship between police and public implies a fundamental review of existing practice. The tenor of the case he makes is to the effect that though each has a separate and distinct role to play, they are inextricably linked in practice. The contribution of neither can be dispensed with. Such a balance cannot be achieved by confrontation: it is essentially the product of a two-way process of co-operation between partners who are equal but different, united by their joint responsibility to the society of which they are a part.

This is an unpalatable thought to many on either side. Neither police nor politicians take kindly to the thought of sharing such power as they have acquired with each other or with the public at large. Nevertheless, we have no other choice if we are to progress towards a new and more relevant style of government under which consent is a reality. Either we come to terms with the fact of our dependence on the professionals, or we resign ourselves to existence under a system of imposed government.

Partnership policing: the police

The implications for the police of their claim to professional status have so far escaped attention, other than the considerable unease provoked by the assertion of their right to the power and privileges of an autonomous calling. Hence the criticism of the complaints system and the demand for more effective accountability. Though desirable in themselves, reforms directed to these specific ends in the legislation currently being considered will not reach the heart of the matter. The essence of the present imbalance lies in the assumption of power by the professionals without an adequate appreciation of the obligations which alone can justify it. Scarman talks of accountability as the proper corrective (Scarman, 5.55–5.71), but more fundamental measures are required if the position is to be radically altered. It is the reluctance of the police to recognise this fact which is the major obstacle to either their own progress as a profession or that of policing as a public service.

The basic premise on which all else depends is of course the extreme reluctance of the police to face up to the implications of their status as public servants.

Partnership with society means greater professional acceptance of political authority and the rights of government to determine priorities and to fix the basic terms of the professional work.[3]

Once this hurdle is overcome the whole perspective changes. It would enable the police to

> ... face the responsibilities which follow from such a position— responsibilities in resources use, in the furthering of publicly agreed priorities even if they generate little enthusiasm in the profession, in accepting the legitimacy of management action to set boundaries to the extent of professional freedom.[4]

Viewed in this light Scarman's proposals for public consultation acquire added significance as providing opportunities to demonstrate the intention to make professional accountability a reality. The regeneration of Police Authorities would be welcome for the same reason, instead of arousing resentment as improper political interference. Again, since the hallmark of the professional is the assumption of responsibility for the maintenance of standards, the police should play a leading part in seeking the reform of the system of complaints and the redress of grievances. The promotion of improvements in the system of recruitment and training would similarly be assumed to be vital professional responsibilities. The protection of the rights of the individual as against those of society is essentially a professional responsibility; it is one to which little consideration is ever given.

Finally it is essential that the disparate voices of the various sectional groups (ACPO and the like[5]) should be brought together in the interests of the profession rather than the defence of pay and conditions of employment. Some form of Professional Review Council is urgently needed to ensure that the professional input into policing is relevant, coherent and not self-seeking. The mere obstinate assertion of privilege is an insufficient justification for the claim to professional status.

Talk of what ought to be is the stuff of day-dreams. Given the authoritarian reaction to the violent and rebellious climate of our times, all the indications are that the police will be called upon to secure the peace by the increasing use of violence. Nevertheless, the evident shift of attitude which can be observed amongst the more open minded, in the force and outside it, suggests that a breeze if not a wind of change is beginning to stir. Given encouragement, it is not wholly impossible that the dream can become a reality. The police are more willing than they used to be to abandon something of their defensive stances in favour of a more co-operative attitude towards the public. The mixed reaction to Scarman indicates that there are at least some who are willing to move towards a new relationship. The developing programme for civilianisation, the lack of opposition to the proposal for lay visitors to police stations, the increasing use of outsiders in training (though not yet in recruitment and selection) and the campaign for the enrolment of 'specials' as reservists, are all cracks in a hitherto impregnable front.

Partnership policing: the public

All this will make heavy demands on the police, requiring of them no less than a change of heart: no easy task! But even that of itself will not be enough. Little recognition is paid to the fact that to impose such a demand will be to ask the impossible unless it is accompanied by an equally far-reaching revision of the contribution to be made to policing by the public. It is indicative of all that is wrong about the policing of our society today that, for all the zest with which we endeavour to set the service to rights, any reference to this vital omission goes unremarked. The police are almost alone in reminding us, even if only tentatively, of the injunction of the early Metropolitan Commissioners that the police are the public and the public are the police.

It would be easy enough to pursue the point in literal terms. Scarman's proposals offer an opportunity for the public to be involved in day-to-day policing far beyond mere critical consumerism. The task of persuading people to take up this invitation will not be an easy one because long years of exclusion from the exercise of civic responsibility has bred apathy and hostility. This will only be overcome by dogged perseverance. The lessons to be learned from the various experiments in 'community policing' are relevant and there is in addition the urgent need for a far-reaching review of the ramshackle machinery for the administration of the service. If accountability is to mean anything, every cog must be made to work in effective co-ordination with all the rest, be they Home Office, Police Authority, County Council, college governors, or whatever. The lack of tools for measuring cost effectiveness and the inadequate use of the budget for this purpose is lamentable.

But behind and beyond all this lies a much more serious issue which is fundamental to the working of policing by consent and to the partnership on which it must be founded. *The purpose of the social contract is to govern the delegation of power*. It is extraordinary that so little attempt is ever made to define the precise extent of the authority so delegated. Nowhere is it laid down other than in the broadest of terms what it is that we want our police to do. What are they to be accountable for? Hence Barry Pain's comment on retiring from the presidency of the Association of Chief Police Officers—that no-one had ever told him what was expected of him as a chief constable—so he had virtually done as he pleased. Merseyside was perhaps the only authority where the majority party on taking office in May 1981 did so, on the basis of a detailed manifesto stating its aims and objectives. The Association of Metropolitan Authorities has followed suit with its comprehensive *Policies for the Police Service*, but the practice is by no means universal. It is regrettable that the proposed new legislation will do nothing to clarify this situation.

Quite unexpectedly the issue has surfaced, and with some urgency, as the outcome of early Scarman consultative meetings. Though regard for the police still stands high, the level of dissatisfaction with the services rendered indicates a worrying disparity between public expectation and practical possibility. Perhaps because officers on the beat are visible symbols of security, an increase in their numbers is seen as the remedy for all ills. Children out of control, old people in need for friendly support, youth clubs lacking virile leadership, as well as a raft of unspecified anxieties bred by the fear of violence and insecurity, are all held to require the presence of more police, preferably on foot. Even when it is recognised that these problems are evidence of a disturbed and disintegrating society—where the growing assertion of individual freedom as against social discipline has resulted in a breakdown of respect for law and order and a challenge to the authority of those who administer it—the cry is still the same.

Responsibility for public tranquillity on such a vast scale cannot and must not be off-loaded on to the police. Policing by consent can only operate in the context of a law-abiding and stable society. Without that, it is no longer a viable proposition. Nostalgic yearnings after village policemen will get us nowhere in the 1980s. Nor can we acquiesce in the imposition of order by force after the demonstration on our own doorsteps of the disastrous consequences which flow from such a policy. The onus is inescapably on us to see that the police are only asked to undertake that which is within their capacity; the rest is for us to do. It was our failure as a society to set about the conditions in the inner cities which led to the breakdown of social order in the 1980s. Let us not be found wanting twice. The responsibility is ours, and it is one we cannot delegate to the police.

Notes

1. I have had an abiding interest in the mechanics of how democracy works ever since, as a suffragette, I realised the potential of the vote. Twenty years' experience as an elected member for the Granby ward, in the heart of Toxteth, convinces me that our only hope for the future lies in 'politeracy': the skill of managing our common affairs. I am now on the Merseyside County Council, and serve as Chairman of the Merseyside Police Authority.
2. *Report of the Moss Side Enquiry Panel to the Leader of the Greater Manchester Council* (Chairman, Mr Benet Hytner, QC), 1981.
3. Paul Wilding, *Socialism and Professionalism*, Fabian Tract 473, 1981, p. 18. See also Paul Wilding, *Professional Power and Social Welfare*, Routledge & Kegan Paul, 1982.
4. Paul Wilding, *Socialism and Professionalism, op. cit.,* p. 18.
5. There are three groups within the police service representing different sections of the force: the Association of Chief Police Officers (ACPO), to which officers above the rank of chief superintendent in England, Wales and Northern Ireland belong—a total of some 200 policemen; the Police Superintendents Association (PSA) and the Police Federation. All officers in England and Wales up to the rank of chief inspector automatically belong to the Police Federation.

CHAPTER 12

Police and the public

ALAN GOODSON

Of course the Scarman Report was a product of the extreme violence generated within the community during the summer of 1981, and the dark shadow of the riots hangs over most of its pages. But aside from this central theme, many matters outside the narrow concept of public order are raised and the document serves as a timely catalyst for reappraisal of some issues which are central to the general philosophy of policing in this country. Indeed the fundamental problem of the relationship between police and public and the appropriate balance between control and independence of the police have been highlighted in the public debate that has followed the publication of the Report.

Accountability

Much has been said recently about the need for the police generally, and chief constables in particular, to be more accountable to the public they serve. This means for some people a greater control over what they are permitted to do. Lord Scarman, while recognising that much good work had been done by police forces to foster good relations with the community (Scarman, 5.55), saw a greater need to involve the community in the operations of policing 'without undermining the independence of the police or destroying the secrecy of those operations against crime which have to be kept private' (Scarman, 5.56). Traditionally, operational decisions have been held to be inappropriate topics for community consultation. Indeed the current public debate surrounding the powers of chief constables stems from their obsession with the need for operational independence. And tiresome as this may be for some people, it is the rock upon which they stand. There is no doubt that it is the declared objective of some politicians to hand over operational control to the politicians—and this must not happen!

An example of this philosophy can be found in the expressed views of an experienced Member of Parliament, Mr Alexander Lyon, who said:

However, in the way that we are policed, how the police react to us, and how we react to the police, there should be a focus of control, determined by the public and not by an independent official, however prestigious, so that if the people do not like the way things are going, they can get rid of the decision makers and put in someone else. That is the answer on the GLC and its contemporary leadership. If people do not like Ken Livingstone, then they can get rid of him at the next election. If people do not like Sir Kenneth Newman, they cannot get rid of him by an election. Surely, this is what democracy is all about.[1]*

It is obvious that times change and in recent years the police service has moved very much to the centre of the political stage. It has been argued that the police service does not exist in isolation; it is part of that democratic process known as 'politics' and must be answerable to the community. The police operate by consent within communities and society, and cannot be exempt from being responsible to that society. In that sense it is said the police service cannot avoid being involved politically. I agree that chief constables must respond to the views of the community about general policing arrangements. The existing arrangements for debating and discussing problems are quite adequate and there is no doubt that they can be exploited to considerably more effect than they have in the past (Scarman, 5.62–5.64). But there is a feeling among some people about the arrogance of the chief constable. They think he is too powerful and are not really sure what legal controls can be exercised over him. Politicians today, too, seem anxious to have greater power over public officials generally, and make them more accountable to those who are in office by dint of the democratic vote. The political emphasis therefore in some places has been to curb the powers of the chief constable.

Well, chief constables consult today more than ever before, they listen to the views of the community through a variety of channels and where appropriate revise their objectives in the light of what they hear. But we must be clear that the chief constable is, and must remain, independent in his enforcement of the law: he and he alone has this responsibility. He has the legal duty and not even the courts can intervene. And we are not just talking about the prosecution of individuals. The policing of industrial disputes for instance, or the dilemma of banning a political march, are good examples of the need for this operational independence from politicians. In these situations a chief constable would find it absolutely intolerable to police the occasion in accordance with the dictates of any politician. And so after all the consultation has taken place, and after the deepest consideration by the chief constable of all the views of the community, at the end of the day

---

* Superscript numbers refer to Notes at end of chapter.

he alone will decide upon the operational enforcement of the law—and untrammelled by the advice of any committee of politicians. To do otherwise would change the impartiality of the law enforcement process and alter the fundamental basis upon which the British police system operates.

Lord Scarman was satisfied that there was no need for a change in the formal powers or duties of Police Authorities but that chief constables should take their Authorities fully into their confidence and should co-operate in establishing consultative arrangements in their police areas (Scarman, 5.64–5.65). As I have already indicated *providing there is an absolute safeguard to their operational independence* I agree that chief constables should pursue a policy of open discussion with their Authority and should heed advice given to them. And I believe that the existing constitution and role of the Authority should be maintained. Indeed, whatever the ultimate arrangements for consultation may be, the Police Authority should be at the centre of them, have a direct link with the consultation machinery, and be responsible for it. Their own constitutional position should not be undermined by any new arrangements.

Consultation

Lord Scarman favours legislation to impose a duty on the Police Authority to require the establishment of consultative machinery at police divisional or sub-divisional level (Scarman, 5.66–5.69). Such a declaratory provision would make Authorities act more vigorously, would clearly be seen to be part of their mandatory responsibilities, and in the crisis situation—where discussion was in danger of breaking down—there would be an obligation to consult which would make it happen. So runs the argument in favour of statutory consultation, but I do not take this view. I prefer to see a system which will build upon the existing arrangements which in many places are already comprehensive. Consultation arrangements should be seen to relate to actual problems and should not be cosmetic and I do not believe that the law is a suitable instrument to persuade people to get round a table and talk. A law might well be concerned with prescribing detail, and the last thing that is required is the concept of a committee more concerned with the process and the whole paraphernalia of minutes, voting and so on. Rather than impose a statutory system from above I would prefer to see the consultation grow up from the community. Who will be the members of the consultation group and who will appoint them is a problem. The nature of the consultation will vary enormously from place to place. What would be appropriate for Melton Mowbray would not suit Brixton. I have no doubt that practised 'committee men' will be falling over themselves to get on these committees. But are they the people we want? Certainly in the inner cities the problem is acute. The ethnic minorities do not want the politicians and the Community Relations Councils to talk for them. They want to do it themselves, but they shy away from any formalised committee structure. The need is for the young black people and the police constables to talk. This process must be taken out of the political arena and be seen to be operating with working policemen; and in some way the chief constable himself must get down to what is actually happening on the ground. There is a great danger that the participants will expect as a right the instant result, and if it does not materialise they will become disillusioned; and so the system must be seen to be effective. *The real consultation must take place at grass roots level:* the role of the Police Authority will be to see that such consultation in fact does go on; they cannot possibly do all the consultation themselves.

In many places existing arrangements will suffice. In others, particularly inner city areas, I see some structure being given to the existing informal links that have been forged between police and public, using this as a base to build up more meaningful consultation. Much of the discussion itself will not be formalised in nature, although it will form part of a developed liaison system. The results must flow up to the chief constable and the Police Authority.

In terms, therefore, of accountability and consultation, I do not believe that the existing provisions are unsuitable. There is a need for a close relationship between police, public and Police Authorities and an understanding and trust between them. There will of course be some people who will set out to see that this does not happen. But hopefully commonsense among the majority will prevail and benefits for all will result.

The Police and Criminal Evidence Bill[2] which failed when Parliament was dissolved on 13 May 1983 proposed that there would be a duty of consultation on Police Authorities generally in co-operation with chief constables in England and Wales, and upon the commissioners of the Metropolis and the City of London in co-operation with Boroughs and Districts and the Common Council in London. These provisions were drawn in sufficiently wide terms to allow each area to draw up arrangements appropriate to its needs and it is important that this flexibility should be allowed in any new Police Act passed by Parliament.

Complaints

Members of the police service, particularly those at the sharp end of the business where the action is, have a healthy scepticism of the public debate that has gone on for some years about the unfairness of the system for investigating complaints against police. All recognise the need for a proper procedure to enable the genuine complainant to make his complaint and to have it properly investigated impartially. But they look with a wry smile at the existing top heavy structure that has been erected with its safeguards and the hierarchy of individuals carrying a responsibility: the superintendent; the deputy chief constable; HM Inspector of Constabulary; the Complaints Board; the Director of Public Prosecutions; the chief constable; and the Police Authority, at least four of whom may be regarded as independent. They may be forgiven for thinking that the public will never be satisfied; and indeed they may be right. Even Lord Scarman identified the difficulty of satisfying the complainant where there is a direct conflict of evidence without any third element present which would objectively resolve the conflict and where the complaint is therefore held to be unsubstantiated (Scarman, 7.17). This is unlikely to satisfy anyone and it suggests that whatever the system for considering complaints none is going to satisfy all complainants or silence all critics. Reinforced by the observations of the Police Complaints Board in their *Triennial Review Report* that 'in the vast majority of cases which come before them, a thorough and fair investigation has been made by the police into the complainant's allegations'[3] (Scarman, 7.20), the police service does not believe that any real improvement on the current system will be achieved.

Lord Scarman heard much evidence that the existing complaints procedure does not command the confidence of the public. He says that he received a clear indication that the arrangements set up in 1976 for an additional independent element have failed to stem criticism of the existing procedure, and that there is a lack of confidence in the impartiality and fairness of the procedure among the community generally (Scarman, 7.14). While I respect this view, I do not believe that the existing procedures will be improved although I accept that the perception of some of the public is one of concern. It also seems that much of the criticism comes from certain small and articulate groups whose access to the media creates a misleading impression of the strength of this concern. But what should be done about it?

Lord Scarman does not believe that the critics will be silenced unless an independent service for the investigation of all complaints against the police is established (Scarman, 7.21 and 7.28). He sets out the difficulties, and appreciates the cost (at least £9 million a year), but he believes that if public confidence in the complaints procedure is to be achieved any solution falling short of a system of independent investigation available for all complaints is unlikely to be successful (Scarman, 7.21). Well that may be so, but I do not believe that such a system would be effective or a practicable proposition, and the cost would be prohibitive. The notion that some new bureaucratic team of investigators would do a better job than the professionals is a totally misplaced theory: inevitably they would be second class. And furthermore, the present critics would not be satisfied because I am certain that the independent investigation would produce at best the same results as those under existing procedures, and at worst would not get anywhere near the truth.

Lord Scarman recommends a form of conciliation in the handling of minor complaints (Scarman, 7.24–7.26). I agree that anything that can be done to take the trivia out of the cumbersome formal procedure is to be welcomed. But I sense that success will largely depend upon the policeman apologising: and that will not often happen! The idea that all the complainant really wants is for a senior officer to have a word with the policeman presupposes that the policeman is in some way in the wrong. In the big debate about complaints, emphasis is always placed on the need to safeguard the interests of the complainant: but of course the policeman is a unit of the equation too and where he believes he has acted properly he will not conciliate. And why should he? Further, a successful conciliator needs to be an expert in the process of conciliation and this will be a new quality required of senior police officers. But I agree with Lord Scarman that an attempt should be made to explore this possibility, if only to clear the system of the complaints which, though they may be minor, do tie down a large proportion of the investigating senior officers' time and add reams to the mountain of paper that is generated.

Lord Scarman would no longer refer minor criminal complaints to the Director of Public Prosecutions, although they would continue to be referred to the Complaints Board (Scarman, 7.26). If the chief constable is then to take the decision subject to the review by the Board, I would agree. But the decision should not rest with the Board. He would also have a more flexible approach to the concept of 'double jeopardy' and I agree with this.

He would also like to see an independent supervisor—he suggests the chairman of the Police Complaints Board or his representative—involved in the investigation process (Scarman, 7.23). He would be a member of the investigation team, and would keep regularly in touch with the progress of the investigation and should be able to offer guidance and to influence its conduct. If there is to be an injection of a further independent element in the investigation process, then in my view it should be the Director of Public Prosecutions and not the chairman of the Complaints Board. The Director already acts impartially and independently in considering reports upon, and if necessary making further enquiries into, whether criminal proceedings should be instituted against police officers. This would be a logical extension of his independent role and would avoid the risk of conflict between another independent element and the Director, each of whose roles would overlap in investigating such cases. Moreover the Director is not only a high legal authority in whom the public should have every confidence, but himself is accountable to the Attorney General who is in turn accountable to Parliament. Those who will not accept the impartiality of the Director will not accept the impartiality of anyone, unless of course he is prepared to find the policeman guilty.

My own view, therefore, is that a new system will not in fact improve the propriety or the depth of an investigation, nor will it change the result of an enquiry. But for presentation purposes and hopefully to secure a greater public confidence in the system, some change is necessary. A greater publicity of the arrangements should be made. I too would try a conciliation process for minor complaints. I would continue the present system for the middle range of complaints. For the very serious complaints, I would make it mandatory for the deputy chief constable to call in an investigating officer from another force, and I would give the Director of Public Prosecutions a responsibility for a much closer scrutiny of the investigating process.

The Police and Criminal Evidence Bill proposed a three-tier system. Conciliation and an informal procedure for minor complaints were to be introduced, while the middle range of complaints would be investigated as they have been in the past and referred to the Director of Public Prosecutions or the Police Complaints Board, except that complaints involving crime would no longer be automatically referred to the Director of Public Prosecutions. Instead the chief constable would have discretion to proceed either criminally or, with the consent of the Police Complaints Board, by way of discipline. The most serious complaints were to be investigated under the supervision of an independent assessor.

When a further Police Bill is introduced to the new Parliament no doubt these proposals will be argued out at great length. But I personally fear that it will not satisfy the vehement critics of the present system and will by no means be the end of public debate over this issue.

Recruitment

Lord Scarman's concern about the under-representation in the police of ethnic minorities (Scarman, 5.6, 5.12 and 5.13) is one that is shared by the police service. It is well recognised that the service needs to be broadly representative of the people it serves and any imbalance needs to be remedied where possible. For some years now efforts have been made to attract more black recruits, but without much success. Only a small number have come forward, and many of these have not been able to get through the selection process. Moreover it is a fact that very few young black people offer themselves for consideration.

Why this should be so goes beyond a mere lack of interest or lower general standards within the ethnic minority. Lord Scarman identified a strong undercurrent of hostility towards the police among many West Indians, coupled with a fear of being alienated from family and friends, and of being

ostracised because of colour prejudice within the service (Scarman, 5.6).
The solution to this fundamental hostility will not be found over-night and
only a long-term programme designed to change ingrained attitudes will be
sufficient (Scarman, 5.12).

But what can done in the immediate future? Lord Scarman quite properly
in my view rejected lowered standards and quotas (Scarman, 5.7–5.8). He
advocated special additional training for would-be black entrants to the
police to assist them to meet at least the academic standard required for
entry (Scarman, 5.9). That would be a task for the educationalists and not
the police.[4] But the applicant would have to be assured of entry if he
subsequently made the academic grade, and so would need to go
successfully through the other selection procedures—physical tests and
interviews—before launching himself on the academic brush-up. He would
need to understand too that during his two-year probationary period he
must make the grade or he would have to go. I fear that this arrangement
might well raise the expectations of some sub-standard recruits, only to have
their hopes dashed at a later stage, and I personally doubt if this suggestion
would make any appreciable difference to the numbers of black police
officers.

But we do need to attract the better qualified black recruit and the service
is committed to this course of action. We have tried in the past with little
success, but we are renewing our efforts using all the publicity and personal
contacts we have. The cadet system has proved useful but alas in many
places this entry is being run down for financial and other reasons. The
Special Constabulary is also a source of recruitment and renewed efforts are
being made in this direction. But it will all take time, will require a change in
the attitude of many black people to the police and will require the support
of responsible black leaders. We in the police will certainly do our part!

Lord Scarman also emphasised the need to ensure that racially prejudiced
people are not selected as police officers (Scarman, 5.14–5.15). Easier said
than done! Very comprehensive enquiries are already made into the
background of applicants prior to their recruitment, with checks on their
activities to date, interviews, and close monitoring of their progress during
their first two years of probation. Any sign of racial prejudice would be
grounds for termination of service. However, research is currently being
pursued in the Metropolitan Police and in the Central Planning Unit for the
country, with a view to the inclusion of a bias test as part of the recruiting
procedure and using improved methods of measuring attitudes. Further,
'human awareness' training programmes are being developed to help
officers recognise and identify their own prejudices, weaknesses and
strengths, and to train them to a high level of sensitivity towards the needs of
all members of the public.[5]

The future

The classical philosophy of British policing has been founded upon the support of the public. That has to be earned, and more so today in a multicultural society than ever before. Lord Scarman has broadly pointed the way he thinks we should go in the 1980s. We would all of us do well to reflect upon his views and work together to see that the relationship between police and public remains cemented to withstand the considerable strains placed upon it by our modern complex society. We in the police service will do our bit. Genuine effort from the community is also required. Failure will change the face of the British police service, and not for the better.

Notes

1. See *Hansard*, 5 April 1982, p. 804.
2. The Police and Criminal Evidence Bill was ordered to be printed on 17 November 1982. It was officially described as 'A bill to make further provision in relation to the powers and duties of the police, criminal evidence and complaints against the police; to provide for arrangements for obtaining the views of the community on policing and for a rank of deputy chief constable; to amend the law relating to the Police Federations and Police Forces and Police Cadets in Scotland; and for connected purposes' (1982–1983, HCB 16). The new Government formed in June 1983 is expected to propose further legislation.
3. Police Complaints Board, *Triennial Review Report* (Cmnd 7966), HMSO, 1980, paragraph 62.
4. *Editor's note:* it was announced that on 1 January 1983 eleven black and eleven white entrants began training as police cadets in Derbyshire, although none had the usual academic entrance standards. Derbyshire Chief Constable, Mr Alf Parrish, stressed that the recruits would need to pass the normal entry examination into the regular police force and Derbyshire Education Committee would send a teacher to help the cadets develop their academic work to a sufficiently high standard (reported in *The Guardian*, 20 December 1982).
5. *Editor's note:* in a poll, commissioned by London Weekend Television in October 1982, 33 per cent of the sample stated that they did not believe that policemen are racially prejudiced. More worryingly, 44 per cent believed that the average policeman is 'unconsciously racially prejudiced' (*The Observer*, 24 October 1982). In response to these sorts of findings and Lord Scarman's strictures the Metropolitan Police Training School in north London has introduced a number of innovations. The 'human awareness' training is based on the premise that greater self-awareness will increase recruits' abilities to understand how members of ethnic minorities feel and to analyse how police officers treat them. According to Chief Inspector Ian McKenzie, who runs the human awareness training, 'we concentrate on encouraging people to explore their attitudes and to get the behaviour right. If the behaviour is right, the good attitudes should eventually follow. Deep-rooted racial prejudice probably takes about five years of psychotherapy to dispel' (*The Guardian*, 13 January 1983).

CHAPTER 13

The police, the community and accountability

PAUL BOATENG

The police are an integral part of the life of any democratic community and they owe their responsibilities to the community which they are employed to serve. Increasingly, however, in recent years the police forces of this country have assumed a life of their own. They have become bigger, and they no longer relate to the local government structures in the way that they did. There is no effective control of the police forces exercised either by the electorate or by those who are elected. Each city, town and street has its own problems and needs, but the recent history of insensitive policing under the remote control of a super policeman known as a chief constable or a commissioner of police has resulted in a breakdown of confidence, a failure in communications, a build-up of resentment and a decline in efficiency which is alarming. This applies particularly in the inner areas of our major cities and most particularly in Greater London, where there is not even a semblance of local control through a police authority composed at least in part of locally elected councillors.

Accountability in its broadest sense

It is undeniable that crime detection depends almost entirely upon public support and information, and when the police do not receive the full-hearted co-operation of the public, they cannot succeed in their task of catching criminals or preventing crime. An ideal police service has its roots in the community from which it recruits its members, and it is responsive to the needs of the area in which it works. Moreover, it is accountable to the public which pays the costs of its operations, and its composition reflects the community which it serves.

None of these conditions exist at the present time. As a result the reported crime rate is increasing, the clear-up rate of crime is decreasing, and the codes of conduct are being ignored by individual police officers who are seemingly not under sufficient control or discipline to prevent abuse of their undoubted power. The police pundits, the political chief constables and the

Police Federation cry out for more power—a cry in which they are joined by the Government and its supporters. Any suggestions that increased police powers may be counter-productive, that there need to be stricter rules of behaviour by police officers, or that expressions of racialism should be disciplined, create a response that the critics are anarchists, 'anti-police', 'anti-law and order' and in favour of criminals and criminal behaviour.

It must be understood from the start of any debate about 'the police, the community and accountability' that only by radical changes in the present structure of policing can public peace and tranquillity be achieved. At present we live in a democracy where only the police are perceived to be immune from democratic control. In the implementation of criminal investigation procedures, the police must be subject to the checks and balances that have been introduced from time to time into criminal law. Civil liberties are central to the image and reality of this country, and civil liberties can be secured only by the protection of the rights of the individual to be treated as innocent until proven guilty, to be free to move without fear of stops and searches, malicious harassment, racial abuse or pressured interrogations designed to produce confession, not truth. It is a myth to think of the policeman as merely a civilian in uniform. His powers and his uniform and the respect to which he is entitled provide scope for good, but also potential for harm. We must all be accountable to the law—and this must include the police. Furthermore, it is essential to see accountability in its broadest sense. We have to examine the issues of recruitment and training, and we must ensure that complaints against the police are independently investigated so that the findings are above dispute. Only in this way can the police regain the respect which it is claimed they used to have and, more importantly, only in this way can they become an effective and modest part of the social and community services which any society needs.

Recruitment and selection of police officers

Lord Scarman spends some time on the question of recruitment (Scarman, 5.6–5.15) and rightly so, for it is surely alarming the increasing extent to which those people who are called upon to police the inner cities are actually drawn from other areas. In the Metropolitan Police some 80 per cent of police recruits (and cadets) come from outside London, and although there are 25,000 uniformed police, in 1983 only 183 of them came from the black or Asian communities. When ever the officers go off duty, they go out of the inner city into suburban areas, where they experience a very different lifestyle from that of the people they are called upon to police. This is something that we have to recognise, for we must achieve not only greater recruitment from the inner cities themselves, but we must also ensure that more of our officers live in the communities which they serve, so that they and the community form part of the same group (see Scarman, 5.3).

One must recognise that the police service reflects many of the attitudes and ideas that exist within the wider society, and therefore one should not be surprised when one finds within the police force a degree of racism (Scarman, 5.15). After all, police recruits have come through the educational system like everyone else. Because we live in a society which still has racism firmly entrenched within its institutions as well as its individuals, it should not surprise us when we find racism within the police force. But this is a matter of particular concern because the police, by virtue of their responsibilities, are equipped with a greater degree of power than ordinary individuals. And as the police very much reflect the attitudes and the mores that exist within society as a whole, it is no use arguing that if there were more blacks in the police force, this would solve the problems of the relationship between the police and the black communities in the inner cities. Nothing could be further from the truth (see Scarman, 5.12).

It is clear that there are unlikely to be significantly more black policemen until such time as the service shows quite clearly that it is willing and able to put its own house in order—in terms of its attitude towards the black community. Therefore to spend vast sums of money on recruitment campaigns that are aimed specifically at black people is a waste of time and money, and those sums of money would be much better spent on training, and on strengthening the means of selection of recruits to the police force. While blacks continue to perceive, and with cause, the police force as an oppressive institution—as an institution which has not come to grips with the racism that exists within it—they are not, regardless of advertising campaigns, going to flock to join the police in any large or appreciable numbers. In the aftermath of Scarman, we must look for a greater willingness by the Home Office, the Police Federation and the police associations, to take on board the issue of selection in recruitment. This requires the development of psychological profiles for applicants to the police force, not simply to weed out people who have a tendency towards racist attitudes (Scarman, 5.14–5.15), but also to remove those people who have a tendency toward authoritarian and oppressive attitudes in general. This is something that needs to be done as a matter of urgency, and it is on this issue that attention should be focused when considering the question of recruitment.

The need for real accountability

One cannot discuss the prospect of bringing the police and the community closer together without looking at the central issue of accountability. Similarly, this question is an important factor in realising

Lord Scarman's stress on the need to see law enforcement as a concern for the community as a whole, rather than simply for the police. But when one looks at the structures that exist for police accountability today, they are found wanting. We cannot accept a situation in which the Police Act, 1964 (or indeed the Police Act expected in 1984) is used as a means of effectively restricting the ability of police authorities adequately to supervise, let alone control, the activities of the forces as they operate within their particular area. We need to see a recognition by chief officers that it is perfectly legitimate for police authorities to concern themselves with matters of policing policy, that it is positively desirable if police and community are going to be better able to work together (see Scarman, 5.55–5.66).

The Police Bill introduced at the end of 1982 confirmed the worst fears expressed by many people in the aftermath of the riots and Lord Scarman's Report. The Government in preparing the new legislation fell into the trap of believing that increased powers, more discretion for police officers, less safeguards for the public, and an absence of statutory control by local authorities over the policies and operations of the police, would all lead to better policing. In fact the opposite is the case. Accountability is central to the issue of good policing and in my view can only be achieved through the establishment of a statutory responsibility for every local authority for the policing of its streets. *We need a Police Act which enshrines clearly the right of police authorities to concern themselves with matters of operational policy.* Such an act should embody the right of police authorities to concern themselves with appointments of the rank of chief superintendent and above, and it should also clarify and strengthen the role of police authorities in connection with complaints generally.

This is the absolute *sine qua non* of our making any advance in this area at all. But we are not simply talking about the need for reform of existing institutions; we must also look at the question of creating *new* institutions, whereby we can strengthen links between police and community, and the degree of control which exists in relation to the police force. It must be recognised in so doing that it is not enough just to leave it to the police authorities, and to believe that this will necessarily improve the relationship between police and public. We need to consider the whole question of how police authorities relate to their forces at all levels, and here the Scarman proposal of Borough or District liaison committees is of value (Scarman, 5.65, 5.69 and 5.71). We need to recognise that lay people have a role to play in bringing about genuine democratic accountability of the police, and it is important to involve black groups, trades councils, representatives of the chambers of commerce, representatives of tenants' associations, and others, at a local level in this machinery of accountability. But one has to understand that any machinery is negated unless it exists on the one hand within a statutory framework, and on the other hand is linked with a police authority which is empowered to exercise a real element of control and supervision over the police. That is why the Report is fatally flawed in its proposals for London (Scarman, 5.67–5.68).

We have a situation in London in which there is no forum for the elected representatives of the ratepayers to have any influence at all over policing policy, or even over police budgetary matters. Lord Scarman, in my view, has got it wrong in acquiescing to the position in which the Home Secretary remains the police authority for London. Unless the sort of consultative machinery at a local level that he envisages is linked with a police authority that has a degree of power, the goal of accountability and the improvements in policing that would go with it will remain unrealised.

Restoring public confidence in the complaints system

It is also important to look at other aspects of police accountability, and primarily at the existing police complaints system, which one cannot pretend by any stretch of the imagination commands public confidence (see Scarman, 7.11 and 7.14). Indeed, there has been a growing recognition on the part of all and sundry that nothing less than a radical reform of police complaints procedures will suffice.

We cannot duck the central issue which is the need to restore public confidence in the police complaints system by the institution of a wholly independent investigatory body. And we cannot simply believe that by grafting on a lay person who is responsible for the general oversight of complaints, or even by grafting on a local ombudsman, that we are going to be able effectively to ensure that public confidence in the complaints system is restored.

Recently, these proposals for an independent investigatory system have been countered by another argument (an argument that is brought up now about almost any proposal for reform or change), and that is that it would cost too much. But this factor by itself must not deter us from pursuing the reforms. For one thing, we do not even have a proper assessment of the cost of the existing complaints procedures, let alone the cost of any proposed alterations in these procedures by the introduction of a wholly independent process. And when one looks at the question of cost, one must bear in mind the costs of the crisis of confidence which the present arrangements have generated. Lord Scarman found that 'unless there is a strengthening of the independent "non-police" element in the system, public confidence will continue to be lacking' (Scarman, 5.43). We have to see the cost of the 1981 riots as being an indication of the sort of cost that we are going to have to bear in the future, unless we are prepared to grasp the nettle, and launch a wholesale root and branch reform of the existing police complaints procedure.

Community policing and accountability

We have to bear in mind the context in which this debate is taking place—a context in which there is not only a crisis of confidence between the police and some of the public, but a context also in which there is a rising rate of recorded crime (and I use those words advisedly), accompanied by a fall in the rate of detection. There seems to be a crisis in the efficiency of the police, and those people who cling rigidly to existing practice must be prepared themselves to answer some very hard questions as to whether or not they are satisfied with the existing performance of the police. Are the police satisfied with their own detection rate; are they satisfied that they are coming to grips with the problem of crime? It is of course all too easy for us to get lured by the publication of crime statistics, in the way that they have been published, down a path that says we must give our police more powers, and very often it is put in those crude and unspecific terms. This is the path down which the Police and Criminal Evidence Bill which failed in May 1983 was seeking to take us and we go down this road with a real degree of risk and hazard to civil liberties, and indeed to the democratic system.

We must recognise that it is essential, if the police are to be accountable for their powers, that there are rules of procedure and codes of conduct that make the police answerable effectively to the law for how they go about the business of investigating crime. The Judges Rules, as they are presently constituted, or the proposed Codes of Conduct, do not fulfil that task. The recommendations of the Royal Commission on Criminal Procedure 1981 (Command 8092) if implemented will create real problems in terms of the accountability of the police in the investigative process: this is another important aspect of the issue.

Another important feature of the notion of police accountability is the debate that has been taking place about community policing (see Scarman, 5.44–5.51). 'Community policing' is one of those phrases that means all things to all people, and when we hear the Home Secretary referring frequently to our community police, and the Commissioner of the Metropolitan Police telling us that in the metropolis we already have community policing—well, that is news to the community! We have got to be prepared to be much more rigorous in our examination of policing philosophy, and we have got to avoid the use of words like 'community' without in fact making it very clear what we mean.

Community policing—by whatever definition—cannot be achieved when specialist groups of the police, such as the Special Patrol Group and other squads of riot police comparable to the French CRS, descend on an area and use heavy-handed confrontational methods and then are suddenly expected to revert a few days later to the friendly bobby on the beat, knowing and loving his neighbours. These two types of policing are contradictory in theory and disastrous in practice. Quite rightly, Lord Scarman criticised the impact of Operation Swamp which created hostility among the population of the area, and was singularly unsuccessful in apprehending criminals (Scarman, 4.76–4.80). Community policing by its every implication means *involving the community in the policing decisions.* If the community is to be consulted and then have its advice rejected by the police, then community policing is a nonsense.

In the spirit of the community policing espoused by John Alderson in Devon and Cornwall, community policing means a greater degree of intervention on the part of the police in the social services, in education, in planning, in areas that have been the preserve of local government and local authorities. If this concept is to be adopted then we have to be quite clear what we are supporting, and what the implications are for accountability. If one has a situation in which officers are espousing community policing, but at the same time refusing to accept the proper role of the police authority and refusing to accept a degree of supervision and control over their activities, then it seems to me that there are very real dangers to civil liberties. This could lead all too easily to a police state, in which the proper professional distinctions between the roles of social workers, probation officers, local government workers, teachers and policemen, become confused.

We have to be aware of these dangers when we are talking about community policing, for it can only be a solution when it is linked to structures that enable an effective degree of control over the police through elected police authorities. Community policing requires a greater degree of openness than exists generally at the moment, and it must involve the community as a whole in decision making and in monitoring what actually happens. If we are talking about policing and crime prevention being matters for the whole community (not just the elected representatives, but also the wealth of community groups—ethnic, social, commercial, religious and political), then we must be prepared to open up our institutions to enable that community to have a voice.

Adapting to a changed society

We must not conduct this debate on the basis that those who call for reform of our existing institutions are somehow subversive. It seems that anyone who calls for radical changes in the institutions and methods of policing is labelled 'anti-police' and regarded as someone who desires to let loose elements whose main aim it is to bring about the end of law and order and civilised behaviour as we know it. This is a dangerous myth, and chief constables should not engage in it—they at least should know better. We expect those people who represent the police in this debate to indicate that we all have a common interest in maintaining the position in which our institutions are capable of changing and altering and adapting to a society that is very different from the one which existed when they were instituted. We have to recognise that the debate must be couched in these terms, and not in the terms of polarisation that it sometimes is.

PART 4

Unemployment, Racial Disadvantage and the Cities

CHAPTER 14

Unemployment, racial disadvantage and the cities

JOHN BENYON

Social deprivation was frequently cited as a principal cause of the riots. As the selection of reactions in Chapter 1 shows, social and economic causes were highlighted by a variety of opinion leaders, such as trade unionists, church spokesmen, media commentators and particularly the Labour front bench.

Lord Scarman stressed the importance of the social context of the rioting:

> While good policing can help diminish tension and avoid disorder, it cannot remove the causes of social stress where these are to be found, as those in Brixton and elsewhere are, deeply embedded in fundamental economic and social conditions. Any attempt to resolve the circumstances from which the disorders ... sprang cannot therefore be limited to recommendations about policing but must embrace the wider social context (Scarman, 6.1).

However, Lord Scarman's Inquiry was established under section 32 of the Police Act 1964 and he felt inhibited from venturing far into a discussion of social policy: 'It would be inappropriate for me to make specific suggestions or proposals in the field of Government financial or economic policy' (Scarman, 6.2). Nevertheless, he did feel it proper to comment on aspects of government policy which affect policing in areas such as Brixton and Toxteth.

The Kerner Report

It is interesting to compare the official investigation into the 1967 riots in the United States with that conducted by Lord Scarman. The National Advisory Commission on Civil Disorders was established by President Johnson in 1967, and rather than a one-man inquiry it consisted of eleven people, including both Democrat and Republican politicians, a black civil rights campaigner, a police chief, an industrialist and a trade unionist. It had nearly 200 staff. The chairman was Governor Otto Kerner of Illinois, after whom the commission is known.

The American riots were different from the 1981 English disorders in a number of respects. The US disturbances were confrontations between black people and the police, unlike those in Britain which were not race riots (Scarman, 3.110) with the exception of that in Southall on 3 July 1981. Furthermore, the American riots in 1967 did not take place during an economic recession, although unemployment in many riot areas was high. The US disorders were also more extensive: the Kerner Commission investigated 23 riot-hit cities in which over 80 people had been killed during the disorders.

The Kerner Commission's Report[1]* was nearly four times longer than the Scarman Report and it paid considerable attention to economic and social deprivation. The Report included over 60 pages of recommendations dealing with issues such as employment, education, welfare and housing. By contrast, the Scarman Report's chapter on 'the disorders and social policy' is 13 pages in length.

Kerner drew a profile of the typical rioter. He was a black male under 24, slightly better educated than the average inner city Negro and likely to be partially employed in a menial or low status job. Contrary to expectations, the black rioters were not the *most* deprived members of the community.[2] Indeed, it appeared that whilst the black ghettos which experienced riots were amongst the most deprived areas, the poorest members of these areas were less likely to riot than those slightly better off.

What did appear to be significant were the *attitudes* of the young blacks who rioted. The participants tended to feel strongly that they deserved better jobs and were barred from obtaining them by racial discrimination. They were also likely to be hostile towards whites and middle class Negroes and resentful of perceived injustices and unfairness.[3]

Unemployment: the growing problem

The areas in which the American riots occurred were characterised by high levels of unemployment. The British riots, too, often took place in communities where a large number of people were out of work. Lord Scarman reported that in early 1981, while unemployment in the Brixton area was 13 per cent, unemployment amongst the ethnic minority was over 25 per cent. For black males under 19 the figure was an estimated 55 per cent (Scarman, 2.20). He found a similarly appalling story in Toxteth and

---

* Superscript numbers refer to Notes at end of chapter.

Moss Side. The 1981 census returns showed that 33.8 per cent of all men in the Granby (Liverpool 8) ward were out of work while the figure for Moss Side was 27.1 per cent.[4] In Toxteth, by June 1981 over 21,000 people were jobless and 'unemployment again appears particularly to have affected young people, and within that group, young black people' (Scarman, 2.27).

The unacceptably high level of youth unemployment was often seen as a principal factor by those politicians and commentators who argued that social deprivation was the fundamental cause of the riots. Roy Hattersley stressed this point in the House of Commons, and Eric Heffer, MP for Liverpool, Walton, singled out unemployment,[5] while the Prime Minister conceded, 'it may well be a factor, but I do not believe it is the principal factor'.[6] Figures published in 1982 showed that more than 4000 people were arrested during the disturbances in July and August 1981, of which some 66 per cent were under 21. About 50 per cent of all those arrested were unemployed.[7]

A study of the Handsworth/Soho area of Birmingham, where rioting occurred on 10–12 July 1981, supported the view that unemployment was an important factor. Interviews were carried out, in the autumn, to ascertain the views of local young men on the causes of the riots. The major cause was clearly felt to be unemployment, chosen by 43 per cent of the sample. The next two most popular choices were 'copying other areas' (23 per cent) and boredom (22 per cent). Of those in the sample who had left school, 32 per cent were out of work, whereas amongst those who admitted active participation in the riots and had left school, 63 per cent were unemployed.[8]

Of course, many areas which have large numbers of unemployed young people experienced no rioting. But Lord Scarman was in no doubt that unemployment was an important element in the Brixton disorders, and those in other parts of the country. Unemployment is

> an evil that touches all of the community. There can be no doubt that it was a major factor in the complex pattern of conditions which lies at the root of the disorders in Brixton and elsewhere. In a materialistic society, the relative . . . deprivation it entails is keenly felt, and idleness gives time for resentment and envy to grow. . . . The structural causes of unemployment . . . are deeper and more complex than the mere existence of the current recession. . . . In order to secure social stability, there will be a long term need to provide useful, gainful employment and suitable educational, recreational and leisure opportunities for young people, especially in the inner city (Scarman, 6.28–6.29).

Since 1981, unemployment has continued to rise month by month. The official figure for March 1983 was 3,172,000 but the Department of Employment admitted that a further 360,000 people were excluded because they were involved in special employment and training programmes. The regions with the highest unemployment were Northern Ireland (19.7 per cent), the North of England (16.7 per cent), Wales (16.2 per cent) and the West Midlands (15.8 per cent). In March 1982, Robin Pitt, leader of the Conservative-controlled Lambeth Council, announced that a staggering 78 per cent of black youths in Brixton between 16 and 19 years old were out of work. In the same month, figures showed that out of some 31,000 employees of Liverpool City Council, only 251 were black: well under 1 per cent.

In December 1982, the Government introduced a new basis of calculating the unemployment figures using a computer count at benefit offices, rather than the Job Centre registers. This reduced the total by 200,000, leading to accusations that the figures were being 'massaged' down. Many researchers believe that the official figures seriously underestimate the number of unemployed—which some studies have now put as high as five million.[9]

A number of new schemes have been introduced since the 1981 riots. These are under the auspices of the Manpower Services Commission, the spending of which will rise to some £2000 million by 1984. Priority is being given to the Youth Training Scheme (YTS) and the Community Programme which will provide 130,000 full and part-time temporary jobs for the long-term unemployed. The YTS is intended to cater for all school leavers by providing 460,000 year-long vocational courses at an annual cost of some £1100 million. It came into operation in September 1983. The scheme has attracted considerable criticism from trade unions and pressure groups who are concerned that it may be abused by employers, and at the end of the twelve months it is unlikely that many of the 17-year-olds will be offered a permanent job.[10] The Manpower Services Commission is unable to create the permanent jobs which are needed if the unemployment afflicting so many young people in the cities is to be reduced.

Lord Scarman found that unemployment has a particularly severe impact on members of the ethnic minorities. He supported suggestions, made by the Home Affairs Committee[11] and the Commission for Racial Equality, for improving support for ethnic minority businesses. He stated:

> I do urge the necessity for speedy action if we are to avoid the perpetuation in this country of an economically dispossessed black population. A weakness in British society is that there are too few people of West Indian origin in the business, entrepreneurial, and professional class (Scarman, 6.27).

Unfortunately, there is little evidence of the speedy response urged by Lord Scarman. Some monitoring has been carried out by the Government (Scarman, 6.30) and some extra money has been made available (Scarman, 6.33), but, as the following chapters in this book suggest, far more serious efforts are needed.

Racial disadvantage and positive action

There is now a great deal of evidence of the seriousness of racial disadvantage and discrimination in English cities.[12] As Lord Scarman made clear, this is partly locational—ethnic minorities often live in deprived areas—but it is also a result of discrimination and racialism.

> All the evidence I have received, both on the subject of racial disadvantage and more generally, suggests that racialism and discrimination against black people—often hidden, sometimes unconscious—remain a major source of social tension and conflict (Scarman, 6.35).

He called for a clear determination to enforce the law, and a positive lead by Government, employers, trade union leaders and others in positions of authority. The essays by Russell Profitt, Usha Prashar and Ken Young in this book emphasise the need for a concerted effort to wage war on racism and racial discrimination, but this part of the Scarman Report does not seem to have attracted sustained media attention.

Lord Scarman's call for positive action to redress the balance of racial disadvantage *did* provoke media coverage, which was generally critical. The chapter by Usha Prashar considers this question, and it has become clear that either certain newspapers failed to read and understand Lord Scarman's prescriptions or they wilfully misrepresented them. Positive action—not quotas or positive discrimination in the American sense—entails the institution of special programmes to tackle particular problems. Need must be the criterion and this principle has been recognised by sections 35, 37, 38 of the Race Relations Act, 1976 (Scarman, 6.32). Lord Scarman urges that the existing law be vigorously implemented.

Besides unemployment, Lord Scarman drew attention to two other areas of disadvantage which particularly affect members of the ethnic minorities living in inner city areas: housing and education. He found that housing provision in Brixton is under 'considerable stress' with at least 12,000 dwellings in the Borough of Lambeth defined as unfit, and a further 8250 lacking one or more basic amenities. This amounted to 20 per cent of the housing stock and a further 12 per cent needed major renovation (Scarman, 2.6–2.9).

Similar evidence of poor housing is to be found in Moss Side and Toxteth. Despite massive redevelopment, 6 per cent of households in Moss Side are overcrowded and 15 per cent lack exclusive use of all basic amenities (Scarman, 2.29). Liverpool 8, too, has experienced redevelopment with the consequent disruption of the community—it has been estimated that over 50,000 people have been moved out to the overspill estates of Cantril Farm, Netherley and Speke.[13]

It should be noted, of course, that people in many inner city areas suffer from substandard housing and overcrowding and only a few of these areas experienced serious disturbances. Acute housing stress was not identified as a *cause* of the disorders, but as one of the 'social *conditions* which create a predisposition towards violent protest' (Scarman, 2.38). It is hardly surprising that substandard provision and discrimination in housing allocation—of which there is a good deal of evidence[14]—leads to resentment and bitterness amongst those who suffer it.

Lord Scarman also drew attention to the dissatisfaction felt about schooling by many black and Asian parents. Among the criticisms voiced to him were concern at a lack of discipline in schools, an alleged failure to motivate children, and a 'lack of understanding by teachers of the cultural background of black pupils' (Scarman, 6.16). The under-achievement of Afro-Caribbean children was highlighted by the Rampton Report and the Select Committee on Home Affairs' Report,[15] and Scarman supported a number of their proposals, such as increased provision of under-fives education, improved training of teachers and a positive government initiative in ethnic minority education. He also supported education in the use of leisure and, more controversially, police involvement in schools (Scarman, 6.19–6.25).

The problems highlighted by Lord Scarman do not appear to have improved significantly, although there are a few encouraging signs. In May 1982 Mr Michael Heseltine, Environment Secretary, told a news conference that in parts of Liverpool only three out of every hundred mortgage applicants were black, compared with 53 per cent in Southall and 60 per cent in Kilburn. As a result of these figures, special efforts were to be made to encourage successful applicants. The Secretary of State also paid tribute to the efforts being made by the private sector in Liverpool 8 to regenerate the local economy.[16] A month later it was learned that the Government had not implemented a number of the Home Affairs Committee's recommendations to tackle racial disadvantage. Most notably, no Cabinet Committee had been established to co-ordinate different government departments' policies on racial discrimination and assaults.

The Government did though take action on the Select Committee's criticisms of section 11 aid—criticisms which were endorsed by Lord Scarman (Scarman, 6.33–6.34). Under section 11 of the Local Government Act 1966, local authorities may receive grants of 75 per cent of the cost of making special provisions for immigrants. Most appointments were for English language teaching. New guidelines were announced in November 1982 which widened the eligibility for section 11 aid, but did not go as far as many critics wished. As the Home Affairs Committee pointed out, this money, which totalled some £70 million in 1981–2, was the 'only Government finance earmarked directly and exclusively for combating racial disadvantage'.[17]

Ineffective urban programmes

According to Lord Scarman racial disadvantage is one of twin problems, the other being the inner city (Scarman, 6.4). He pointed to the failure of successive attempts to grapple with inner city decline: 'large sums have been spent to little apparent effect' (Scarman, 6.5) and he noted 'the lack of an effective co-ordinated approach' and the 'conflicting policies and priorities'. Local communities should be more fully involved in the planning and management of their areas and services and there should be greater private sector involvement in inner city regeneration. Finally, Lord Scarman argued for close liaison between the police, local services and voluntary agencies and greater involvement of the police in 'community redevelopment and planning' (Scarman, 6.6–6.9), a suggestion which provoked opposition.

Studies of inner city policies do indeed suggest a lack of co-ordination and a failure to avoid conflicting priorities.[18] A number of government policies seem to have exacerbated the decline of the cities. The new towns policy led to an exodus of skilled workers, and enticed investment away from the old cities. Massive redevelopment schemes swept away thousands of small businesses, which were either relocated on the urban fringes, or lost entirely as they could not afford higher rents and overheads. The loss of these small firms was disastrous for a number of redeveloped areas; thousands of labour-intensive and low-skilled jobs for school leavers disappeared.

Furthermore, redevelopment was often only half carried through. As the money ran out, derelict sites were all that remained of the terraced housing and small firms. Increasingly on view in many cities were rubble-strewn muddy plots, surrounded by decaying terraces—blighted by the threat of demolition—with high-rise flats in the distance. Further blighting was caused by grandiose plans for urban motorways, the threat of which dissuaded people from investing in houses or factories which were located on the projected routes.

Following Enoch Powell's notorious 'rivers of blood' speech, the Government began to try to arrest the decline of the cities. In May 1968 Harold Wilson announced the Urban Programme to provide relief for 'areas of special need'. According to Edwards and Batley, the approach was *ad hoc* and ill-defined:

> Because of its connection with the immigrant issue, the Programme was launched with a haste that militated against the development of any clear objectives or strategy. It was politically imperative to be doing something and to be seen to be doing it. . . .[19]

The Urban Programme was supposedly a Home Office responsibility, although it involved several other government departments. It seems that there was a lack of co-ordination and control: 'it remained without firm direction'.[20]

Further programmes to tackle urban problems were announced in the train of Harold Wilson's launch of the Urban Programme. The Community Development Project was inaugurated in 1969 to improve the quality of life in areas of multiple deprivation, and in the 1970s new schemes were introduced, including Housing Action Areas, The Six Cities 'Total Approach' Studies, Comprehensive Community Programmes and Recreation Priority Areas. Three of the 'Total Approach' studies focused on areas 'known to suffer from multiple deprivations'[21]—Liverpool 8, Birmingham Small Heath and the London Borough of Lambeth.

These Inner Area Studies found disturbing levels of neglect, deprivation and social breakdown. The Liverpool 8 study found discrimination *against* the area by local government and other agencies. 'There is not sufficient delegation or public involvement to allow expression of the needs and values of the inner city area in local authority services'.[22] In many respects, the Inner Area Studies highlighted the problems (such as ineffective use of resources, lack of co-ordination and a failure to involve local people) which Lord Scarman reiterated years later.

Following the publication of the 1977 White Paper,[23] the Inner Urban Areas Act, 1978, established Inner City Partnerships whereby local authorities and central government would act in tandem to assist economic regeneration. Lambeth, Birmingham and Liverpool were among the seven Partnerships which were established. But, as Lord Scarman pointed out, it is apparent that they 'are not the complete answer' (Scarman, 6.6). Although quite large sums of money have been allocated from the Urban Programme to finance the Partnerships—for example £78 million out of £165 million in 1979–80—much of this has been spent on capital schemes rather than revenue projects. It has been argued that while industrial investment and some educational and recreational benefits have resulted, there is little evidence of a redirection of spending to aid the most deprived areas.[24]

The Local Government, Planning and Land Act, 1980, made provision for yet another structure for urban regeneration. The Urban Development Corporations are intended to achieve this by 'encouraging the development of industry, creating an attractive environment and ensuring that housing and social facilities are available to encourage people to live and work in the area'.[25] Their powers and structure are similar to the New Town Development Corporations, which have been lauded for their achievements but also bitterly attacked for being undemocratic and remote. Two Urban Development Corporations have been established, one for the London Docklands and the other for Merseyside.

Another innovation, introduced in 1980 by the Conservative Government, are the Enterprise Zones. The aim of this scheme is to give businesses additional incentives to invest within designated areas. Special tax concessions, such as a 10-year exemption from rates and allowances on capital acquisitions, and reduced planning requirements are among the attractions offered to investors. Eleven Zones were designated in 1981, including areas such as Speke, the Isle of Dogs in London's Docklands and Salford, and others have been added subsequently. However, a number of researchers have criticised the usefulness of Enterprise Zones, and it seems unlikely that they will greatly aid inner city regeneration.[26]

The cities under stress

Despite these attempts by successive governments to tackle the problems of inner city areas, such as Lambeth, Granby, Moss Side and Handsworth, Lord Scarman was clearly not satisfied that a sufficiently 'co-ordinated and directed attack' had been mounted (Scarman, 6.6). Since the publication of his report there has been little evidence of improvements and indeed the Government seems to have persisted with the 'top down' approach (exemplified by the Urban Development Corporations) which was criticised in the Report (Scarman, 6.7).

A central feature of the inner city programme has been the inadequate provision of resources. While criticisms of the way money has been spent seem largely justified, it is essential that sufficient funding is available to deal effectively with the chronic problems. The economic recession and the consequent lack of private investment and the considerable reductions in local government expenditure have worsened still further the plight of many inner urban areas. Local authorities for these areas have tended to be worst affected by cut-backs in income, particularly that from central government. For the year 1981–2 the Association of Metropolitan Authorities estimated that inner city areas lost about £660 million in rate support and other grants—more than three times the entire value of the Urban Programme.[27]

Peter Jackson *et al.*[28] have produced considerable evidence to show the plight of the older cities which are suffering both a decline in their populations and a contraction in their local economies. Those who have left the cities tend to be the middle and high income earners, and many of those who remains are, in public expenditure terms, 'high cost citizens'. They conclude that

> Current policies are placing greater stress upon local governments already faced with mounting demands for expenditure increases. How this stress will be accommodated remains to be seen.[29]

Similar fears were voiced in April 1983 by the Inner London Consultative Employment Group, made up of Conservative and Labour councillors, the CBI, the London Chamber of Commerce and Industry and others. The

Group pointed out that the population of Inner London fell by 2.2 million (15 per cent) between 1971 and 1981 and the emigrants tended to be the better-off and skilled. Male unemployment in the area is 17 per cent and in some wards has reached 40 per cent. There should be a reform of the rate support grant arrangements, the Group argued, to reverse London's loss of central government funding and Inner City Partnership status should be given to the whole of Inner London. The report said

> Inner London is facing an economic and social crisis and desperately needs a substantial injection of public investment to avert disaster.[30]

Since the 1981 riots some extra resources have been forthcoming, particularly for the two worst affected areas—Brixton and Toxteth. Central government money has been made available for capital projects, and Lambeth's rate support grant was increased in 1982. A private sector campaign on the theme 'We're backing Brixton', together with Inner City Partnership money, resulted in environmental improvements which it is hoped will encourage more shoppers and private investment. However, unemployment remains appallingly high.

In Liverpool 8, the attention of the then Environment Secretary, Mr Michael Heseltine, led to the establishment of the Merseyside Task Force in an attempt to cut through red tape and co-ordinate the efforts of private and public bodies. The Financial Institutions Group, made up of private capital representatives, was also formed to harness public and private investment. One of this group's proposals led to the Urban Development Grants Scheme, announced in February 1983. The housing investment allocation for Liverpool was also increased after the riots, from £35 million in 1981–2 to £57 million in 1982–3.

But, as the contributions which follow make clear, the problems of unemployment, racial disadvantage and the cities are so intractable that far greater national resources are needed than are presently being made available.

In Chapter 15 Kenneth Roberts considers the problem of youth unemployment and its impact on those who experience it and in the following essay Devon Thomas outlines his personal experiences as a black person living in Brixton. He highlights the need for more self-generated economic activity and sees the central issue as one of power.

John Rex looks at inner city policy in Chapter 17 and finds it sadly wanting. Drawing on his research in Birmingham, he charts the failure of successive governments to tackle the real problems, particularly racial discrimination. These themes are taken up in the following essay by Russell Profitt, who stresses the problem of racialism in Britain. He believes that unless equal treatment and equal opportunities become the norm, riots are bound to recur.

In Chapter 19 Usha Prashar examines Lord Scarman's call for positive action and considers some of the ways in which racial disadvantage can be attacked. This call is taken up by Ken Young in the final chapter in this section, where he looks at the vital role that local government must play in overcoming racial disadvantage and discrimination.

The contributions to this section powerfully reinforce Lord Scarman's concluding remarks in his report. He stated that 'racial disadvantage is a fact of current British life' and 'urgent action is needed if it is not to become an endemic, ineradicable disease threatening the very survival of our society' (Scarman, 9.1). To this end 'the attack on racial disadvantage must be more direct than it has been' (Scarman, 9.4). The evidence suggests that so far this call has yet to be heeded.

Notes

1. O. Kerner *et al.*, *Report of the National Advisory Commission on Civil Disorders*, US Government Printing Office, 1968 (reprinted by Bantam Books).
2. *Ibid.*; see also C. McPhail, 'Civil disorder participation: a critical examination of recent research', *American Sociological Review*, **36**, 1971, pp. 1058–1073; R. M. Fogelson, *Violence as Protest: a Study of Riots and Ghettos*, Doubleday, 1971; N. S. Caplan and J. M. Paige, 'A study of ghetto rioters', *Scientific American*, **219**, 2, 1968, pp. 15–21; D. O. Sears and J. B. McConahay, *The Politics of Violence: the New Urban Blacks and the Watts Riot*, Houghton Miflin, 1973.
3. See the Kerner Report and other studies such as those in N. E. Cohen (Ed.), *The Los Angeles Riots: a Socio-psychological Study*, Praeger, 1970.
4. 1981 census figures quoted in *The Economist*, 'Britain's urban breakdown', Economist brief, 1982, p. 11.
5. House of Commons Official Report (*Hansard*), 6 July 1981, Vol. 8, No. 135, cols. 21–30.
6. *Ibid.*, col. 258.
7. Home Office Statistical Department, *Bulletin*, Autumn 1982.
8. S. Field and P. Southgate, *Public Disorders: a Review of Research and a Study of One Inner City Area*, Home Office Research Study No. 72, HMSO, 1982, pp. 41–73.
9. See, for example, Labour Research Department, *Labour Research*, December 1982.
10. Youthaid, *Bulletin*, December 1982.
11. House of Commons, *Racial Disadvantage: Fifth Report from the Home Affairs Committee, Session 1980–1981*, HC 424, HMSO, 1981.
12. *Ibid.*; see also J. Rex and S. Tomlinson, *Colonial Immigrants in a British City*, Routledge & Kegan Paul, 1979; W. W. Daniel, *Racial Discrimination in England*, Penguin, 1968; D. J. Smith, *The Facts of Racial Disadvantage*, Political and Economic Planning, February 1976 (P.E.P. Broadsheet No. 560); D. J. Smith, *Racial Disadvantage in Britain*, Penguin, 1977.
13. C. Bedford, *Weep for the City*, Lion, 1982, p. 19.
14. For example, R. Skellington, 'How blacks lose out in council housing', *New Society*, 29 January 1981; J. Rex and S. Tomlinson, *op. cit.*; A. Simpson, *Stacking the Decks: a Study of Race, Inequality and Council Housing in Nottingham*, Nottingham Community Relations Council, 1981.
15. *West Indian Children in Our Schools*: The Interim Report of the Committee of Inquiry into the Education of Children from Ethnic Minority Groups (Chairman: Mr A. Rampton, OBE), HMSO, 1981, Cmnd 8273; House of Commons, *Racial Disadvantage: Fifth Report from the Home Affairs Committee, Session 1980–81*, *op. cit.*
16. *The Guardian*, 25 May 1982.

17. House of Commons, *op. cit.*, para. 48ff; see also *Racial Disadvantage: The Government Reply to the Fifth Report from the Home Affairs Committee, Session 1980–1981*, HC 424, HMSO, January 1982, Cmnd 8476.
18. See, for example, J. Edwards and R. Batley, *The Politics of Positive Discrimination*, Tavistock, 1978; A. Blowers *et al.* (Eds.), *Urban Change and Conflict*, Harper & Row, 1982; P. Lawless, *Urban Deprivation and Government Initiative*, Faber, 1979; D. H. McKay and A. W. Cox, *The Politics of Urban Change*, Croom Helm, 1979; C. Cockburn, *The Local State: Management of Cities and People*, Pluto Press, 1977; M. Goldsmith, *Politics, Planning and the City*, Hutchinson, 1980.
19. Edwards and Batley, *op. cit.*, pp. 67–68.
20. *Ibid.*, p. 140.
21. P. Walker, 'A Conservative view', in M. Loney and M. Allen (Eds.), *The Crisis of the Inner City*, Macmillan, 1979, p. 11.
22. Department of the Environment, *Change or Decay: Final Report of the Liverpool Inner Area Study*, HMSO, 1977.
23. *Policy for the Inner Cities*, HMSO, 1977, Cmnd 6845.
24. For further discussion see P. Butler and R. H. Williams, 'Inner city partnerships and established policies', *Policy and Politics*, 1981, Vol. 9, No. 1.
25. *Local Government, Planning and Land Act, 1980*, para. 136.
26. M. Keating, 'Enterprise zones: from rhetoric to reality', *Municipal Journal*, 21 August 1981; S. Taylor, 'The politics of enterprise zones', *Public Administration*, Winter 1981.
27. Quoted in *The Guardian*, 12 April 1982, p. 3.
28. P. M. Jackson, J. Meadows and A. P. Taylor, 'Urban fiscal decay in UK cities', *Local Government Studies*, September/October 1982, pp. 23–43.
29. *Ibid.*, p. 42.
30. *The Guardian*, 6 April 1983: 'Tories join call for spending to rescue London'.

CHAPTER 15

Youth unemployment and urban unrest

KENNETH ROBERTS

Lord Scarman identified unemployment as 'a major factor in the complex pattern of conditions which lies at the root of disorders in Brixton and elsewhere' (Scarman, 6.28). His report, however, attempts little analysis of how unemployment is translated into urban unrest, or the solutions that are likely to work in the eyes of inner city youth, rather than in those of government ministers and officials. The following passages endeavour to supply some missing links.

No part of my argument suggests the 1981 summer riots were provoked directly or mainly by youth unemployment. The young people who took to the streets in 1981 were, above all else, expressing their feelings about the police. The riots were the direct result of crime, policing and police–community relations problems, and as the Report recognised (see Scarman, 8.8–8.42) the immediate response must be to tackle these issues. Nevertheless, I shall argue that whatever measures are taken to heal police–community relations in our Brixtons, Toxteths and Moss Sides, and however we try to achieve consent, assent or partnership, the initiatives will never stand a fair chance of success while youth unemployment remains at its current levels (see Scarman, 6.28–6.29). Unemployment was an important part of the context within which all the 1981 disturbances occurred, and to understand the significance of this context it is necessary, firstly, to explain what unemployment means in terms of prospects that await *all* school-leavers in our inner cities, and then to look at ethnic minority youth in particular.

School-leavers' prospects

National and even regional unemployments rates—'the bread-and-butter' of political debate—conceal as much as they reveal. In the years preceding 1981, youth unemployment in some areas in Brixton had risen towards 30 per cent.[1]* It is all too easy to imagine that this figure meant 70 per cent

* Superscript numbers refer to Notes at end of chapter.

175

of school-leavers in the relevant areas graduating from school to continuous employment. In practice, before youth unemployment has reached 20 per cent, the majority of the young people in the affected areas can expect a taste of life on the dole before their working lives are far advanced. Twenty per cent unemployment does not mean that four-fifths of school-leavers immediately find jobs in which they remain. Nor does it mean that all school-leavers spend 20 per cent of their early working lives unemployed— but this latter simplification is closer to the truth. School-leavers in Brixton's multi-racial areas, and in all the other inner city districts covered by my recent investigations, have faced typical early career histories of sub-employment (Scarman, 2.19 and 2.20).

The majority graduate from school to unemployment and then today (in most cases) on to schemes or projects, back to unemployment, and then maybe on to further schemes or 'real jobs'. These are almost certainly unskilled, and usually short-lived, either because the jobs themselves end, or because the incumbents soon grow dissatisfied with the routine work, the bosses or the (low) wages. For some years now, in our inner cities, the majority of young people have *not* been moving from school into secure, stable, progressive jobs, but into early working lives of sub-employment: short-lived jobs interspersed by schemes, and all separated by spells on the dole.

For some young people, unemployment has become long-term. In parts of Toxteth, by 1980, more than a third of all young people were becoming long-term unemployed.[2] As jobless levels have subsequently risen across the country, families and neighbourhoods which formerly experienced unemployment only as a newspaper problem have found their own children facing the sub-employed early career pattern. In areas where unemployment was already widespread, the proportions of young people who remain 'afloat' (in circulation, moving between jobs and schemes) have declined, and the proportions sinking into long-term joblessness have increased. This has been the direction of change in Brixton, Moss Side, and other districts with above-average unemployment rates since 1980. The long-term unemployed are sometimes described as 'hardcore'. Employment service staffs often confess that these clients' situations are hopeless. By age 19 or 20, with no substantial work experience, the 'hardcore' have nothing to commend them to employers against 'nice fresh school-leavers', and have often exhausted the repertoire of special measures.

Contemporary youth unemployment is essentially a job problem, not a youth problem. If jobs were available, our young people would take and hold them. If there were decent jobs, offering attractive pay and prospects, with training leading to skilled status, the young people would settle and exhibit the 'responsible' attitudes that employers claim to seek.[3] The current unemployment does not reflect imperfections in the quality of our school-leavers. The failure is in the labour market—on the jobs side. Today's school-leavers are better qualified in terms of paper certificates than any previous generation. Even in inner city neighbourhoods, including Brixton's high unemployment tracts, the majority now leave school with qualifications of some description.[4] Few possess A-levels. There are many more CSEs. But the majority of the young people who, in recent years, have left school to face unemployment, have studied, sat exams, and entered the labour market with recognised credentials. In schools, certificates and examinations are 'sold' as passports to jobs. Pupils are encouraged to enrol for examination courses, and to work diligently, by teachers who tell them, rightly, that qualifications enhance job chances. But qualifications carry no guarantee. When there are insufficient jobs, qualifications, whatever their level and character, cannot save some of their holders from unemployment. In these circumstances, their qualifications simply increase the young people's frustration. They feel, with justification, that they have been let down· and sold out, and they complain bitterly of broken promises. Educational 'solutions' sometimes aggravate young people's difficulties.

The young people's experiences

Many unemployed young people are extremely bitter. Some are broken: they abandon their former hopes and ambitions, and express a willingness to accept 'anything'—any job that pays anything above the dole. Others, in contrast, display greater persistence and resilience. They preserve their aspirations, and their 'standards'.

Discussing the young unemployeds' resilience requires careful wording. Those who 'cope' through spells of joblessness, and who protect their 'selves' from the stigma of unemployment, are not enjoying the time of their young lives. Young people invariably regard unemployment as a serious problem. Their first priority is jobs, preferably decent jobs. Anything else— schemes, courses or more generous social security benefits—are regarded as very much second-best. But it is not difficult to locate unemployed young people who will explain that they are *not* prepared to take absolutely any job, whatever the work, and however low the wages.

In most inner cities unemployment has become too common, and spells out-of-work are now too normal an experience, to isolate their victims. The young unemployed are not a small minority group. Among other age-groups, unemployment reduces social intercourse, whereas unemployed young people spend more time with their peers than when they are working.[5] Some teach one another not to regard their joblessness as a stigma. They confirm the wisdom of quitting 'trash jobs', despite the risks of unemployment, and support each other's determination not to 'sell out' as 'slave labour'.

Responses to unemployment are influenced by the jobs, schemes and courses that young people experience, or hear about from friends. No-one applauds unemployment. Young people, and adults, dislike the boredom and poverty. But many are even more vociferous in criticising the quality of jobs and schemes they have been invited to apply for, and/or sampled. Can young people be expected to feel grateful when the Youth Opportunities Programme leads back to unemployment? The wider society's solutions are among the young people's problems. The latter are not all enthusiastically awaiting the Youth Training Scheme offering £25 a week. Are the young people supposed to be impressed by the quality of jobs paying less than £40 per week offered under the Young Workers Scheme? These opportunities are obviously created for other people's children. Some of the intended beneficiaries are saying 'No thank you.' Governments' responses to youth unemployment have not alleviated, but have heightened, many young people's bitterness and frustration. An injection of entrepreneurial spirit breeding small businesses as a solution to unemployment finds favour in some quarters. Small businesses are good news for successful small businessmen, but for young people they usually mean, at best, more 'trash jobs'—insecure and low paid, in depressing premises.

Ethnic minorities

The areas covered in my own recent research, all high unemployment districts in Brixton, North and West London, Toxteth, Moss Side and Wolverhampton, were multi-racial, with people of Afro-Caribbean origin the main ethnic minority. All the relevant enquiries have underlined how powerfully race differentiates young people's prospects at the time of leaving school and entering labour markets.[6] All the young people from the districts covered by my enquiries were heavily and multiply disadvantaged by housing, often by family poverty, by attending low-achievement schools, and always by entering depressed labour markets. The prospects of all the young people, black and white, boys and girls, were poor, but tended to be worse for the blacks (Scarman, 6.26–6.29). The latter's unemployment rates ran approximately 40 per cent above their disadvantaged white neighbours. National rates of unemployment among young blacks run well above the level for whites. This is partly because Britain's ethnic minorities are concentrated in high unemployment areas, like inner Liverpool, Moss Side and Brixton. Then, within these high unemployment areas, black school-leavers are less successful in the competition for jobs than local whites from the same streets, who leave the same schools with identical qualifications.

There are additional differences between the circumstances of black and white youth in our inner cities which deserve attention. Firstly, according to my own research and all other relevant studies, it seems that within the areas where the majority live, young blacks are now leaving school better qualified than local whites.[7] Nationally there is no dispute that young blacks, though not Asians, under-achieve in school[8] (Scarman, 2.18). But within the inner city schools that the majority of young blacks attend, they not only equal but often surpass the (modest) levels of attainment of their white classmates. Few young blacks are leaving school with good A-levels and flooding into the universities, but this level of attainment is equally rare among local whites. In their schools, qualifications usually mean CSEs, sometimes O-levels, and ethnic minority youth are proving more capable of acquiring them, and then entering the labour market with these qualifications, than whites from multi-racial neighbourhoods.

Secondly, and not unrelated to the above, black young people leave school with slightly higher ambitions than their white contemporaries. This is not to say that the blacks are unrealistically ambitious: they are the better qualified. In any case, they are not all demanding jobs as airline pilots and brain surgeons. In general, the boys aspire to trades and training, while the girls seek jobs in offices as secretaries, telephonists and receptionists, in libraries, with children, and as social and community workers. There is no evidence to suggest that the school-leavers' aspirations are unrealistic relative to their own abilities, but more often than not these ambitions prove unrealisable in their local labour markets.

It is not difficult to explain the above ethnic differences once the composition of inner urban populations is examined. The white families who still inhabit our inner Liverpools and Manchesters tend to be those that have missed the exodus. In contrast, black families with all types and levels of ambition and talent are still concentrated in these areas. The young blacks currently leaving school are mostly 'second generation', the children of immigrants who came to Britain in the 1950s and 1960s, and many of them talented people, who were then underemployed in unskilled occupations, and, as result of various constraints, have generally remained at this level of employment, and still live in the same 'twilight' areas.[9] Many young blacks now growing up in our Brixtons and Moss Sides have supportive parents, who want their children to succeed, to realise the parents' frustrated dreams.[10] The young people, like middle-class whites, reflect their parents' ambitions. The parents are keen for their children to do well at school, and obtain qualifications that will lead to good jobs. Parents and young people who 'do not want to know' about examinations, and who are willing to accept any jobs, are more common among inner city whites. Black school-leavers are more likely to possess modest qualifications, and to be moderately ambitious. Hence the greater gap between young black school-leavers' aspirations and what actually awaits them. The blacks possess better qualifications, higher aspirations, but are less successful than local

whites in the search for work. The frustrations of all young people in high
unemployment areas are especially acute among the ethnic minorities.

Unemployment and mobility

It is not difficult to translate this evidence into a case for positive action,
but ensuring that the action does not backfire may prove more difficult.
Young blacks are *not* demanding equal opportunities with the disadvantaged whites who share so many of their problems. Local whites' jobs and
unemployment rates will not satisfy the black communities' aspirations.
Why should the latter rest content with the quàlity of education and
employment considered adequate only for the most disadvantaged whites?
Britain's ethnic minorities are not prepared to wait generations while the
prevailing rate of social mobility, reduced in their case by racial disadvantage, distributes their people throughout the social structure. It would
obviously be inflammatory and politically inexpedient to attempt to
promote inner city blacks at the expense of their white neighbours. This is
why assaults on racial disadvantage are likely to succeed only in the context
of wider policies to improve the prospects of *all* young people in the inner
cities, which means removing class barriers and unequal opportunities.

Many unemployed young people, black and white, would be entirely
willing to 'get on their bikes' if there were jobs to cycle to. Few demand that
any job they will consider must be local. Of course, it all depends on the job.
University teachers, senior police officers and social workers often move
across the country, sometimes across oceans, to advance their careers, but
how many would move for £30–£40 per week? Young people cannot always
afford to travel each day, even to their city centres. The only genuine
opportunity for the majority of 16-year-old school-leavers to migrate is to
join the armed forces. Where else would they live? Given the types of jobs
and levels of pay they are offered, the majority cannot afford to work
anywhere other than locally. If sufficiently attractive jobs were available,
many young people, black and white, would travel, and if necessary leave
their families and friends to live in other parts of the country. At the same
time, some young blacks are apprehensive when faced with the prospect of
leaving known people and places, given the existing social climate. Would
they be accepted elsewhere?

It is often difficult for the white majority to even grasp, let alone respond
to, certain features of the ambitions being nurtured among Britain's ethnic
minorities. It has been taken for granted that aspiring working class parents
and children want to leave our inner cities, to move to better homes and
neighbourhoods. Blacks are equally, if not more, attracted by the prospect
of better housing, education and job opportunities. But many hope to
progress while remaining in their present neighbourhoods. Within Britain's

ethnic minority communities, there is plentiful interest in moving out and up, geographically and socially. But there is also a demand for better opportunities and life-chances to be created *within* Brixton, *within* Moss Side and *within* Toxteth. This type of ambition is far less familiar within the white working class. It is doubtful whether the public in general even understands the ethnic minorities' ambitions, which adds another twist to the latter's frustration.

A final ethnic difference is that black youth have an obvious explanation for all their difficulties—racial disadvantage. All inner city youth, black and white, are arrested by social class barriers, but however strongly sociologists argue their case, class divisions remain invisible. It is much easier to see skin pigmentation (see Scarman, 2.21–2.22, and 6.35). Young people suffering involuntary unemployment may not regard themselves as victims of an unjust society. There are many different ways in which individuals who face intractable difficulties can interpret their predicaments. Some regard themselves as just plain unlucky, victims of fate, the wheel of fortune determining who gets a job. Others treat unemployment and limited opportunities as facts of life, like the geographical terrain, to be accepted and lived with, rather than questioned and challenged. These attitudes occur among blacks and whites, but the former are far the more likely, and have more cause, to regard themselves as victims of an unjust society. This was part of the background, the setting, within which the 1981 riots erupted.

Unemployment, crime and policing

No-one pretends that a solution to unemployment would automatically eradicate crime, or even improve police–community relationships. But while high levels of unemployment persist, it is difficult to envisage any measures making a substantial and lasting impression on these problems (Scarman, 6.1, and 8.43–8.48). Recorded crime has risen, between several plateaux, since the 1950s. Unemployment has not been persistently in the background, operating as the main underlying source. There has been a long-term weakening, or at least a decisive change in the character of local community and family controls. Crime rates can escalate without there being any unemployment problem, but where delinquency has already become a common part of young people's life styles, high levels of joblessness can hardly avoid accentuating criminogenic pressures.[11] Young people are on the streets, at risk, during daytimes, as well as evenings and weekends. Whether or not they are otherwise involved in crime, they are at risk of contact and friction with the police. Many young people in high unemployment areas are chronically short of money. This must increase criminal temptations. Perhaps most insidiously of all, high levels of unemployment provide local communities with a vocabulary of motive.

Teachers, youth and community workers explain how, in the absence of legal means of support, crime is too tempting to be resisted. Young people and their parents adopt this justification. It helps young people to condone each other's delinquency, and enables parents to disclaim responsibility for their children's offences. It is difficult to establish a statistically incontrovertible link between youth unemployment and crime. At the same time, it is impossible to ignore the evidence of probation officers who explain how 80 or 90 per cent of their clients were unemployed at the time of their offences. It is also impossible to ignore the implications of how it becomes not just difficult, but often impossible for young people with 'records' to obtain any employment in labour markets where employers have scope for choice.

High and rising levels of crime bring pressures on police forces to 'do something', and the measures available to the police are often experienced as harassment by local youth. Those who already feel victimised by an unjust society are easily persuaded that the police are a front-line force, agents from a hostile society, that is intent on keeping them down and holding them back.

Prophecies of youth unemployment breeding political extremism, propelling young people into the British Movement, the National Front or the far left, are being confounded. The overwhelming majority of the young unemployed remain apolitical. Some express their disinterest with considerable passion, insisting that all politicians are 'on the make' for themselves, and that, at the grassroots, it make little difference whoever 'gets in'. The young unemployeds' coping strategies are more likely to involve criminal enterprise than political activity, conventionally defined. Rather than being channelled into party politics, their discontents are more likely to be expressed on the streets.[12]

When the chance to vent their feelings arose—when urban disorder spread in the summer of 1981—many young people in Britain's high unemployment areas, blacks and whites, but particularly the former, were predisposed to grasp the opportunity. Unless the underlying socioeconomic conditions are changed, can attempts to improve police–community relationships amount to anything more than managing discontent? Are the underlying conditions being changed? Since 1981 unemployment has risen to new record levels. From the streets of Brixton and Toxteth, the new initiatives look like old wine in new bottles—more 'rubbish jobs', and schemes offering training that leads nowhere in particular. The wider society is still debating the merits of early retirement and married women working—transferring unemployment to other disadvantaged sections of the population.

Are sexism and ageism more acceptable than racism? On the other hand, we have more and better-equipped police. Strengthening control apparatuses may keep the streets clear and the young people quiet. These strategies may suppress, but they will never *solve* the young people's problems.

Notes

1. K. Roberts, J. Duggan and M. Noble, *Unregistered Youth Unemployment and Outreach Careers Work, Part I, Non-Registration*, Research Paper 31, Department of Employment, 1981.
2. K. Roberts, M. Noble and J. Duggan, *Unregistered Youth Unemployment and Outreach Careers Work, Part II, Outreach Careers Work*, Research Paper 32, Department of Employment, 1982.
3. M. Colledge, C. Llewellyn and V. Ward, *Young People at Work*, Manpower Services Commission, 1977.
4. K. Roberts *et al.*, 1981, *op. cit.*
5. N. Morley-Bunker, 'Perceptions of unemployment', Paper presented to the British Psychological Society, Sussex, 1982.
6. S. Allen and C. R. Smith, 'Minority group experience of the transition from school to work', in P. Brannen (Ed.), *Entering the World of Work*, HMSO, 1975; B. Fowler, B. Littlewood and R. Madigan, 'Immigrant school leavers and the search for work', *Sociology*, **11**, 1977, pp. 65–85; D. Brooks and R. Singh, *Aspirations Versus Opportunities*, Commission for Racial Equality, 1978; Commission for Racial Equality, *Looking for Work*, 1978.
7. G. Driver, 'How West Indians do better at school (especially the girls)', *New Society*, 17 January 1980; M. Fuller, 'Black girls in a London comprehensive school', in R. Deem (Ed.), *Schooling for Women's Work*, Routledge & Kegan Paul, 1980.
8. *West Indian Children in our Schools*, the Interim Report of the Committee of Inquiry into the Education of Children from Ethnic Minority Groups (Chairman: Mr Anthony Rampton, OBE) (Cmnd 8273), HMSO, 1981.
9. J. Rex and S. Tomlinson, *Colonial Immigrants in a British City*, Routledge & Kegan Paul, 1979.
10. See M. Sonte, *The Education of the Black Child in Britain*, Fontana, 1981.
11. See T. Crick, 'Black youth, crime and related problems', *Youth in Society*, **40**, 1980, pp. 20–22.
12. See K. Pryce, *Endless Pressure*, Penguin, 1979.

CHAPTER 16

Black initiatives in Brixton

DEVON THOMAS

I am a black person, of Afro-Caribbean origin. I have spent the major part of my life in this society, so I feel I know it well. While having spent my early formative years in Jamaica, most of my education both formal and informal took place in England. My parents came to this country in the early 1950s when they themselves were relatively young people. They did not come because they saw Britain as the promised land, or because they thought the streets of London were paved with gold. In fact they had quite a lot of information about the reality of life for blacks in this society. Members of my family and community in Jamaica had served in the armed forces during the war and had reported what it was like to those back home. In their letters they talked of meeting some nice people and seeing some interesting sights, but they also talked about cold weather, fog, and racism.

The early years

My parents were not amongst the very first who came in the late 1940s and early 1950s, so they read the reports that came back about trying to find somewhere to live, finding work, keeping the job and putting up with 'the so-and-so foreman'. Therefore, the decision to come was not made on the basis of pure adventure. The reality of life for them—like so many others of that generation—was grinding economic hardship. In the rural areas of the Caribbean, life consisted of hard work on the land for very little return. In the urban areas, if you were lucky enough to have a job at a time when real unemployment was 30–35 per cent of the working population, your wages were very low.

After thirty or more years of struggle to establish institutions to represent their economic, social and political interests, many Afro-Caribbean people could see no great change, and insufficient opportunities for themselves and their children were being created. The collective fruits of our labour had been redirected and dissipated by the colonial authorities in this country. It was therefore logical for them to come to this country to reclaim some of this

184

wealth, for although things were not as they would ideally like, economic, social and educational opportunities existed in greater abundance than at home.

The social scientists and researchers who have examined the black community mercilessly over the past few years are fond of saying that the first generation of immigrants who came after the war were unskilled. From my personal experience I know this to be a fallacy. Many members of my family had formal qualifications in academic and vocational areas on their arrival, but were told—in spite of the fact that our home territories were the responsibility of this country at the time—that these qualifications were 'colonial' ones, and no good. Other members of the community who did not have formal qualifications had long years of experience in many different areas, including agriculture, construction, dock work and other fields, but the role this society had for them was unskilled labour at the bottom of the pile, so any experience or qualifications were irrelevant.

The other qualities and skills that these people had were ones of resilience, fortitude and determination to see things through in spite of difficult circumstances. These are the qualities that had brought us through three hundred years of grinding colonial existence, and it is the same experience that we have had to draw on to survive the last thirty years inside this society.

The second generation

The relevance of the facts outlined above is to show that the problems that black people face today are not a recent phenomenon, but the continuing story of an ongoing process. The second chapter of the story was that of my generation. The years from the late 1950s to the late 1970s were characterised by increasingly frantic attempts to prevent black people coming to this country using legislation and any other means available. There was miseducation of those young blacks going through school, and a systematic attempt to blame blacks for the increasing economic problems of the country by fringe racist groups and then by the 'respectable' political organs of this society. This was the background against which I grew up and went to school. Black people stoutly resisted the pressures they were being put under by the various sections of this society. They came together to form organisations to defend themselves and to campaign against racists in their communities who were trying to brutalise them. They formed groups that provided support in dealing with the complex institutions of this society such as social services departments, educational institutions, unions and work places. Anywhere that we were put under pressure, we responded.

In this regard the police were one of the first institutions that blacks had to organise and campaign about, due to their partial and unfair modes of operation. It is important to stress this activity, as the impression that some would like to put about is that blacks are helpless people who do not organise, and respond only in their own interests; if they do respond it is in a mindless and destructive manner. I would suggest that this is yet another fallacy to be laid to rest.

It is now clear to me, reviewing my own personal history and that of the black community generally, that this society has attempted to reproduce in my generation, and those that have followed, a similar role for us as for my parents' generation—that of unskilled labourers at the bottom of the labour pile.

One of the highest priorities on the list of objectives so far as my parents were concerned was the need to provide their children with the best education possible. They saw this as the means of helping us escape the fate they had experienced. This was not a straightforward or easy task. The school system did not regard myself or most of my other contemporaries as worthy of much attention or encouragement. My experience was that black students succeeded in spite of the education system, and not because of it. An example here would illustrate this point.

In the early 1960s on reaching the age of 11 I took and passed my '11 plus' examination. This opened up the opportunity for me to attend grammar school, which pleased my parents greatly. I applied and was offered an interview to the local grammar school. This pleased me, as one of my best friends, a white boy, had also passed the exam. He had an interview at the same school the week after my own. I attended the interview along with my father where I answered all the questions asked by the headmaster, apparently to his satisfaction. At the end of the interview the head said: 'It is very interesting, we don't get many of you people coming here. Your son seems to be a very bright chap. We've only ever had one chap like him attend this school, but he was rather naughty and we had to expel him.' He turned to me and said, 'I hope you're not like that.' This was typical of the kind of attitude that many teachers had towards their black pupils. Needless to say, my friend attended his interview the next week, and was offered a place. However, my father received a letter shortly afterwards informing us that the school was full and they therefore could not take me. I consequently attended the local comprehensive school which catered largely for the locality of Brixton.

The black students had to fight individually and collectively to progress. Most of the blacks were confined to the bottom few forms in the school and while I was one of only three blacks in the top form, I associated mostly with the black students, as our experiences were more common than those of most of our white classmates. These black students were concentrated at the bottom of the school not because their abilities, academic and otherwise, were low, but because the school and education authorities *felt* their ability level was low. In later years most of them acquired qualifications of the highest order outside that institution through individual determination and collective encouragement.

The other disadvantage that we suffered, and that young blacks still suffer, was that of lack of information on and access to opportunities on leaving school. The middle class white students at the school knew that they were going to take and pass their 'O' and 'A' levels, whereupon they would apply to this university or that college or the other company for career training. The white working class student knew that his father was in the print or had a fruit shop in the market, or that some other related route would take him into working life. Although some of this has changed due to the rise in youth unemployment, the reality is that black young people have no such routes laid out for them in this society, and all I had was the encouragement of my parents and peers and a determined belief in my own abilities.

The post-school years

I left school with some academic qualifications. I searched for employment in career fields which I felt were commensurate with my ability and qualifications, but I remained unemployed for over six months. The theme of recurring unemployment and underemployment is one that has followed black people for some time and is a factor, I would contend, that with others has led to the civil unrest now common in inner city areas. It is not simply a question of qualifications. I searched diligently for employment during that period, attending interview after interview. The usual excuse from personnel officers for not appointing me would be: 'If we give you the job, you will have responsibility. Some of the people you have to work with are very touchy and might not be willing to take orders from a person like you. I wouldn't like to expose you to that kind of thing, so I think perhaps it might be better if I didn't offer you the job.' This put me in a situation where they were trying to get me to collude with the racism implicit in the situation and literally agree to exclude myself. This I would not do—but I still did not get the jobs. There would be several degrees of this kind of approach right down to the other extreme where my compatriots with less qualifications than I would be told at interviews that they had insufficient qualifications and experience. In the end most of us had to start off in jobs far below our ability and aspiration.

These are very important reasons why many Afro-Caribbean people are now seeking to establish their own independent economic enterprises.

The need for more self-generated economic activity

Because of these historical factors, Afro-Caribbean people are under-represented in the field of self-generated economic activity. In the general community approximately 10 per cent of whites and a similar percentage of Asians are involved in their own self-employment, small business or co-operative enterprise. There are only 3 per cent of Afro-Caribbean people so engaged. This is not because black people lack the desire, motivation or skills to be successful in this field, it is more to do with the structure of this society and its view of our role within it. This can be borne out by examining the situation in the United States, a place no less racist than here but where Afro-Caribbean people have developed their own enterprises and independent employment-creating activities to a much larger degree.

The lack of this activity in the Afro-Caribbean community here seriously constrains our ability to mobilise influence and power and independent political and social activity.

In areas such as Brixton, with large Afro-Caribbean communities, effort and attention is now being focused on this issue. The Brixton community is and always has been very active and dynamic, and it has been active in creating structures and institutions to cope with its members' needs. This is a very different picture to the superficial one usually presented: of dereliction, despair and apathy. I have been involved in this activity in many different capacities over the years and it has shaped my experience.

Effort is increasingly being expended in creating a support framework for the development of business enterprise. Resource pools of skilled and experienced people are coming together to provide assistance to those who are attempting to get started. Many community organisations and self-help groups are looking at how their activities can become more independently self-sustaining, and they are trying to apply their previous experience in other fields to that of the world of business.

In spite of the hostile economic climate many opportunities exist for the development of these kinds of activities among blacks. In the inner city areas of this country, where most Afro-Caribbean people live, many gaps now exist where previous businesses have left or closed down. Many buildings are now empty and unused. Our task is to mobilise the resources to put these redundant facilities into use for our own purposes and to improve our communities and the environment. This process has to be, however, more than just individual entrepreneurial activity: the black community does not need a handful of whizz-kid business people who exploit it as it has been exploited in the past. This community needs a .process that improves the collective position of blacks and one that provides the opportunity for greater influence over its activities than previously.

The wider context

In order for this to become a reality, effort is required on many levels. The public and private institutions in this society that possess the bulk of our wealth have to be made to understand what our priorities are and where we want to see resources directed. This is a relatively straightforward process in the case of the public sector and as outlined above the black community has evolved a whole range of strategies to redirect local and central government finance. This has to be intensified in order to move the approach to the needs of black people from being a token one, as is the case presently, to something more substantial. The most difficult task, however, is influencing those in this society who control the *private* sector. This is essentially the greatest task facing us. These institutions, such as banks, insurance companies, pension funds and the like, now control the bulk of the wealth of this society. It is not enough to have influence on the structures that have political accountability: it is equally if not more important to develop a strategy for gaining more influence over the private sector, which has no such accountability. The people who decide what happens to the wealth that we have created in these institutions have to be shown their responsibilities and the fact that they have to play a role in the development of our communities. An example of this is the very politically emotive issue surrounding organisations such as Barclays Bank.

For most Afro-Caribbean people Barclays was the only bank in their countries of origin. Even now many of the banks operating in these territories are Barclays, but are now called by another name and have a certain amount of local participation. It is therefore no accident that Barclays is heavily involved in South Africa, as it is the original colonial bank. So for black people it is not a simple issue of whether to deal with Barclays or not, for this institution has come to its pre-eminent position through our efforts and still retains a good portion of our wealth, and we have to find ways of making it disgorge it for us to use in our endeavours.

The political tasks

The central issue is therefore one of power and how we are to organise and mobilise ourselves for the acquisition of more power. The leaders of this society are putting heavier pressure on black people and trying to take away the little gains that we have made over the years. They are promulgating more racist and restrictive nationality and immigration laws, instigating heavier and more oppressive policing in our communities, and moving in similar ways in a whole host of areas. 1981 signalled the intention of black people, young people, poor people and many others living in the inner city to resist this trend by force if necessary. Many other levels of response are now emerging.

The relevance of Scarman

I have resisted the temptation to discuss the issues outlined above within the context of Lord Scarman and his work. I have done so because I believe that Scarman has been the most successful diversionary mechanism that the state could have constructed. It created a false sense of hope for many who thought that the Inquiry would investigate the *real* causes of the 1981 uprisings and make recommendations accordingly. It fooled many into thinking that the Government would then take substantive action. In reality the way the Scarman Inquiry was constituted made it highly unlikely that it could get at the facts of the events of spring and summer.

Lord Scarman himself had to admit that the crucial people who should have given evidence came nowhere near his deliberations. The description of events therefore lacks that vital perspective. In addition, Lord Scarman had insufficient resources and inclination to research the background to the events adequately, and so his recommendations are also inadequate. Where he has made progressive suggestions, whether by design or accident, these have largely been ignored and the law and order aspects have been accentuated and implemented. It would be foolhardy, therefore, for black people in particular to be sucked into the trap of discussing their needs in terms of Scarman.

The next step

In the period since summer 1981 nothing fundamentally has changed. Using Brixton as an example, unemployment has risen and most social and economic indicators have worsened. The response by central and local government has been superficial at best. Anything that does not move gets painted, and every available vacant space gets landscaped and tree-planted. While not decrying these efforts, they do not go to the *heart* of the matter. When resources are directed to the area, they do not reach those that most need them. Increasing numbers of people are engaged in making cases for grants, administering grants, writing reports and the like, but much of this activity does not address itself to the people it is supposed to. The people with the needs have to start determining the programmes that meet their needs, and the achievement of this is the task in hand.

CHAPTER 17

Disadvantage and discrimination in cities
JOHN REX

There is some misunderstanding of the significance to be attributed to the Scarman Report. It is widely thought to be a definitive statement on race relations: a guide to policy in that area for the 1980s. Actually it is nothing of the sort. Lord Scarman, a widely respected judge and one generally regarded for his liberal views, was appointed to conduct an inquiry under the Police Act into the disturbances in Brixton. For this purpose he had obvious competence; but he is no social scientist. When, therefore, at the last moment it was suggested that he should also consider all the other disturbances which occurred later in 1981, he was forced to take on a task for which he and his advisers were totally unequipped.

Scarman and the social causes

It is interesting to compare the sequence of events surrounding the Kerner inquiry[1]* into the disturbances of 1967 in the United States. There a state governor carried out an extensive inquiry and, in reaching his conclusions, took account of a vast amount of social science evidence. By comparison the Scarman tribunal's quest for social science evidence was both random and trivial. Anyone who wished to submit evidence did so,[2] but there are few signs that what emerged as an account of the 'social causes' rested on any foundation in social science research. What did emerge was pretty well the received wisdom of the civil service on these matters.

The recommendations of the tribunal were inevitably affected by this. On the one hand there were a series of recommendations on policing which are discussed in other contributions to this book. But the social policy recommendations, on the other hand, suggested little more than an extension of government policies already in hand. These included an extension of the Youth Opportunities Programme to meet the needs of increasing numbers of young unemployed blacks and to keep them off the streets, and a renewed

* Superscript numbers refer to Notes at end of chapter.

sense of urgency about the Inner City Programme. It is with this latter aspect of the policy that this chapter is concerned.

The question of the inner city

The arrival of the Conservative Government in 1979 did not bode well for the inner cities. At an early stage of her administration, Mrs Thatcher had indicated that she saw inner city expenditure as part of a general socialist tendency to solve social problems by 'throwing money' at them. The resources available to the programme, already thought to be meagre by the programme's supporters, were cut even further as a part of the general Conservative assault on public spending.

But the question of the inner city is not simply a question of resources. Resources would be useful if the policy itself[3] was well conceived as a means of dealing with problems of racial discrimination and conflict. It is my contention, however, that far from dealing with these problems it at best ignored them and at worst exacerbated them. What I want to do, therefore, is to consider the evolution of the Inner City Policy and to argue that, in the wake of Brixton and the other disturbances of 1981, it has to be totally rewritten.

What do we mean by the 'inner city'? The answer is 'almost anything'. In fact the term is one of a whole set of ideological words, together with others like 'multi-cultural society', 'multi-cultural education' and 'community policing', through which those who use them claim to be good men. But all sorts of people use the terms and use them in many different ways.

In fact the term 'inner city' has a statutory definition which has very little relation to the social problems with which Scarman was concerned. The areas affected by Inner City Policy are the so-called 'Partnership' areas which cover rather peculiarly defined areas. In Birmingham, for example, most of the wards of the city are in the partnership areas and they include areas which differ sharply from one another. They include about six wards in which more than 50 per cent of the population are living in households with a New Commonwealth head and where most of the property is in General Improvement or Housing Action Areas. But they also include large areas of semi-detached mortgaged property and council houses, and with New Commonwealth populations as low as 2 per cent. When we talk about giving money to the inner city, we are talking about a very diverse area, not all of it by any means beset by the problems of Brixton.

Within this, however, there is a special type of area which we should think of as the 'inner city's inner city'. This is the area of poor housing and high immigrant density. Such areas may not be geographically in the inner ring at all, but rather in the surrounding area which has not benefited from urban redevelopment. In Birmingham such an area is Handsworth, which is actually on the north-west border of the city.

What has happened is that the term inner city has come to be used to misdirect our attention. We use it to mystify and cover up ugly problems which we do not like to talk about. If, however, we do want to look at the real problems of the inner city's inner city, we should recognise that there are actually five sets of problems.

The inner city's real problems

First of all there is the environmental problem, particularly a problem of housing. Secondly, there is a jobs problem which results from the fact of industrial dispersal. Thirdly, there is a further jobs problem which results from the general economic recession and from economic restructuring. Fourthly, there is the whole question of trying to develop social services through voluntary action when the Government has ceased to have a clear idea of what services are necessary. Finally, there is the problem of the segregation and integration of minorities in our society. My belief is that the Inner City Policy deals with the environmental problem and with the part of the jobs problem which results from industrial dispersal and it also does something to sustain voluntary social work organisations. So far as the general problem of the economic recession is concerned, policy development in the inner city simply whistles in the dark, as do policies in other areas, although it pretends that this kind of unemployment is largely due to dispersal. But so far as the ethnic minorities are concerned what this Inner Cities Policy Statement proposes is likely to do the minorities more harm than good.

The environmental problem

So far as the environmental problem is concerned, the inner city is something which was brought into being in the late 1960s when the Government published a report called *Our Older Homes*[4] and then a subsequent White Paper called *Old Houses into New Homes*.[5] This was a deicision not to have a further slum clearance programme, but rather to look at the next worst houses after slums had been cleared and to give improvement grants to try to keep them alive, and then, at a later stage, a policy of housing action arose in which some houses were declared due for demolition and replacement and others for improvement. These policies divided the city into different kinds of area with very different kinds of look and very different kinds of smell.

Most people when they discuss this problem use the word 'intractable'. It seems a Canute-like problem in which the tide of urban decay cannot be turned back. Yet in my own experience I think some progress *is* being made on the environmental front. If one goes round Birmingham on a Sunday morning in the improved areas one sees scaffolding and one sees jobbing builders' vans and something is clearly going on. Unfortunately the process is desperately slow and it is slow through want of money. Not least among the problems of an area like Sparkbrook, where I have worked, is that although there has been an enormous amount of improvement, there are many houses bought by the council for renovation which stay for months, if not years, with their bay windows covered by corrugated iron sheeting. And there are many sites which remain undeveloped as deserts of ash and rubble. It may be that in thirty years time this will be a good area, but if ever there were an area of policy in which Lord Keynes' famous comment 'in the long run we are all dead' was true, this is it.

Yet, for our children at least, there will be progress and it must be asked whether the anxieties which people feel are solely due to the slowness of the renewal process. The feelings of despair which they express may not be understandable in fact under this heading at all. They have to do with an entirely different question, namely that of race.

The jobs problem and dispersal

Secondly, I turn to the jobs problem. One of the things which the Inner Cities White Paper did address itself to, and for which it was applauded, was that it related the question of the inner city to that of jobs by bringing together the Departments of the Environment and of Trade and Industry with local government in a new way. The theory behind this was that with the process of suburbanisation, both residental and industrial, jobs had moved from the inner city, and that it had indeed been government policy to encourage such dispersal. More and more jobs were leaving the inner city and it was said that the people who still lived there no longer had access to jobs.

The new policy was to give inducements which had until recently been given for location in the New Towns to those who now wished to locate industries in the inner city. Such a decision should, however, be considered more critically than it has been. One does not hear of the citizens of Sutton Coldfield in suburban Birmingham complaining that there is no industry on their doorsteps. What they have done is to get a fast new railway line to take them to the city centre. Why should not the citizens of the inner city respond in a similar way?

I would think that there is a case for bringing industry back to the city, but not necessarily to the residential inner city. It could be brought to specialised industrial suburbs. What the inner city residents would then need most would be efficient and cheap transport to give them access to labour markets. Unfortunately the Inner Cities Policy says little about this and in the cheap fares row in London and elsewhere the demand of the urban poor for cheap transport was rejected. Instead the residential inner city suburbs are being planned as places for industrial development, in which the residential environment is likely to be polluted further, even if more jobs become available.

Jobs and the recession

The third problem to which the 1977 White Paper did not actually address itself is the problem of job loss due to the recession and economic restructuring. This, of course, has created a whole new ball game, because it is one thing arguing about the location of jobs, quite another if there are no jobs to be relocated.

This is no place to speculate about the general economic and industrial future. But it does seem from current forecasts that we are likely to see a wholly new pattern of industrial employment with high technology on the one hand and the growth of small business and self-employment on the other. The danger is that high technology will go elsewhere and that the inner city may become the site for the older type of factory and the small business, as well as the home of the majority of the unemployed. Clearly what is needed is that inner city people should have equal access to the better parts of the job market and that is, I suppose, the reason for the emphasis upon bringing new industries there. Unfortunately the Policy is ambivalent on this. It does want to bring jobs to these areas, but actually proposes encouraging the movement of people away from them. This is a point to which I return under 'Ethnic minorities in the inner city' below.

Inner city policy and the urban programme

The fourth matter dealt with by the White Paper is that of the Partnerships taking over the so-called Urban Programme giving grants to local groups and, included in that, giving grants to ethnic minority projects. As far as I understand it the ethnic minority groups have had a rather raw deal in this matter. They have not had their appropriate share of money provided in this way.[6] Unfortunately, however, the debate about ethnic minorities in the inner city has been conducted almost wholly under this head. They are forced into competing with other groups like old age pensioners for a share in the charitable soup kitchen and their attention is diverted away from the question of their share of the benefit which comes from the main programmes.

Ethnic minorities in the inner city

As background to the way in which Inner City Policy treats the question of minorities, I should like to review briefly our own experience of this problem in Birmingham.[7]

In the first place when West Indian and Asian immigrants arrived in the 1950s and 1960s the normal housing channels were closed to them. Normal channels for British people are through mortgaged private housing or through council tenancies. Before the passing of the 1968 Race Relations Act building societies and estate agents were able to and did discriminate freely against black people. At the same time the councils in London and the West Midlands abandoned the policy adopted after the war of setting aside such housing for key workers and, so far as West Indian and Asian immigrants were concerned, threw up barriers to their being housed in council housing for a very long period. In Birmingham a newcomer had to wait five years to go on the list, had to compete unequally with the native-born for residential points under the points scheme and then, even if he or she qualified despite these obstacles, was likely to be put, not into a council house, but into a slum awaiting demolition.

During this period there was no serious policy for housing immigrants. They did the best they could: they bought houses, they converted them, they let them in lodgings, and, incidentally provided for all the other people, like single people and people with family problems who were debarred by various rules from council housing. In effect they provided the net beneath the net of the Welfare State. The so-called 'twilight zone' as that term then came to be used provided a last-ditch alternative housing system.

Despite all the obstacles, however, some did eventually qualify for council housing. At first they were simply put in council-owned slums awaiting demolition. Then as the slums were finally cleared, policies of dispersal were adopted, meaning that, in Birmingham at least, a black man was not allowed to have a black neighbour within five houses. Finally when this policy was shown to be illegal under the 1968 Race Relations Act their right to ordinary council housing was admitted, although the evidence suggests that on the whole immigrants got the worst council houses.

When the housing panel of the National Committee for Commonwealth Immigrants discussed the whole question of immigrant housing with a junior minister in 1966, he suggested informally that what he would be looking for in his constituency were 'some terraces of old houses where we can put these people where no-one would see them'. That was an immediate, and, one must say, prejudiced reaction of one individual. It could be argued, however, that this was the basis of the new housing policy for immigrants in general.

As immigrants began to qualify in larger numbers the new policy was to offer them another option, namely that of buying old property in the improvement areas with council mortgages. The result was that the improvement areas became quasi-ghettoes. The frustrated black council house tenants were joined there by Asians who in any case wanted to buy houses, but could not do so in the better areas because of discrimination, and by the tenants of Housing Associations, which took advantage of the improvement policy to convert houses. The result is that today, according to the 1981 census figures one has wards like Soho in Birmingham with 71 per cent of its population in households with New Commonwealth heads and five other wards with about 50 per cent and above. The new policy was, in effect, a recipe for segregation. Parallel with the immigrant concentrations there were wards just across the inner city boundary line where the New Commonwealth population dropped to less than 5 per cent.

At the very time that this new policy was being developed in 1967, many people became worried about the inner city because of the disturbances in the United States in that year. In 1970 Peter Walker became Secretary of State for the Environment, and he was particularly concerned about the problem and sought to alert his colleagues to the danger, particularly as it became linked with black youth unemployment. He commissioned three major studies of the inner city, and their reports on Lambeth, Small Heath and Liverpool 8 laid the basis of the White Paper eventually published in 1977.

Although the White Paper was widely thought to be an attack *inter alia* on race relations problems and was represented as such by the Labour Government, when one actually turned to it one found that it quite explicitly rejected the notion that it was about racial discrimination as such. That, it suggested, was a matter for the Commission for Racial Equality. The policy was intended to deal with the problems of the disadvantaged inner city poor, and it was only insofar as they were in that category that immigrants were to benefit.

Most disturbing, however, were the sections of the White Paper which dealt with 'Population Movements'.[8] Basing itself on the Lambeth Study entitled 'Dispersal and Balance',[9] it argued that as the inner city revived, the people who lived there would be unsuitable for the new jobs because they were largely unskilled or retired, and that they would do better to move to the periphery. This, of course, within a policy aimed at bringing resources back to the centre.

There are two things wrong with this. First of all it assumes that a person's present occupation is an indication of his or her skill and qualifications which is very far from being the case, particularly in the case of Asian immigrants who are often over-qualified for the jobs which they do. But secondly, and worse than this, it seems to suggest that the characteristic of being unskilled is hereditary, since their children would be required to move as well. It is this that leads me to say that the White Paper rests on racist assumptions. What is interesting is that these assumptions have hardly been questioned by social scientists.

Personally, I think that the White Paper on Inner City Policy now needs to be totally rewritten. What we need is a policy for the *people* of the inner city. And first we must get the facts right. There are a lot of myths about the inner city. When it is said for example that it is full of old people, this is not true. The inner cities have *lower* proportions of old people because the young immigrant families more than outweigh the concentrations of older white people. We need, therefore, to find out who really lives where and to provide services accordingly. Above all we need to look at the question of education, which is strangely neglected in the White Paper. The questions should be 'how can we bring jobs in the necessary numbers to the potentially skilled people growing up in the inner city?' and 'how can we develop the skills of those who are there to man (and woman) the new industries?'

In fact I think that what we have done in developing Inner City Policy is to pander to two subterranean demands. One is to reconquer the inner city for the respectable indigenous working class. The other is simply to get rid of the immigrants, if not by repatriation, then by consigning them to an unknown 'periphery'.

Conservative approaches to the inner city

It is worth noting that whatever changes have been introduced by the Conservatives before and after Scarman are largely irrelevant to the problems I have been discussing. In the main the Conservatives have been slowly converted to the policy of 'throwing money at the cities', which they at first rejected, and they have sought to do so not merely by providing grants, but by reminding private investors of their public responsibilities. All this is fine if it works. But it will do little to ensure that ethnic minorities benefit from the policy except perhaps through an increased share of the Urban Programme. It seems that, whatever the ideology, whether it supports public or private enterprise, there is little understanding of the fact that what we have done so far is to ghettoise and discriminate against black people and that they are angry.

The inner city and Scarman

What has been said here does not immediately answer the question of why young blacks rioted in Brixton and young Asians in Southall. There are many intermediate links in the causal chain, including the roles of the schools, discrimination in the job market and, last but by no means least, the relations between black youth and the police. It should be clear, however, that so long as the Inner City Policy fails to deal with the racial discrimination which is inherent in our housing and planning policies, black youth will live in conditions of hopelessness and despair, and that the ghetto will provide the terrain in which all the problems of our society burst out into violence.

It is possible to envisage an Urban Policy based on quite different assumptions. There could be a Senior Race Relations Officer in all the Inner City Partnerships who would bring a new perspective to all the decisions which are being made. And such Race Relations Officers would work within an overall policy of ensuring that Britain's two million citizens of New Commonwealth ancestry had fair and equal opportunities to obtain work and housing where they chose, rather than being forcibly confined and policed in the worst parts of the city. It is when one considers issues like this that it becomes clear that the Scarman Inquiry into the social causes of the Brixton disturbances hardly began to tackle the problems.

Notes

1. O. Kerner *et al.*, *Report of the National Advisory Commission on Civil Disorders*, US Government Printing Office, 1968.
2. See the Scarman Report: the list of those giving evidence is on pp. 155–163.
3. The Department of the Environment, *Policy for the Inner Cities* (Cmnd 6845), HMSO, 1977.
4. Central Housing Advisory Committee, Ministry of Housing and Local Government, *Our Older Homes: A Call for Action*, Report of the Sub-Committee on Standards of Housing Fitness (the Denington Report), HMSO, 1966.
5. Ministry of Housing and Local Government, *Old Houses into New Homes* (Cmnd 3602), HMSO, April 1968.
6. C. Cross, *Ethnic Minorities in the Inner City*, Commission for Racial Equality, 1978.
7. J. Rex and R. Moore, *Race, Community and Conflict*, Oxford University Press, 1967; J. Rex and S. Tomlinson, *Colonial Immigrants in a British City*, Routledge & Kegan Paul, 1979.
8. *Policy for the Inner Cities*, paras. 66–70.
9. Department of the Environment, *Inner London: Policies for Dispersal and Balance*, Final Report of the Lambeth Inner Area Study, HMSO, 1977.

CHAPTER 18

Equal respect, equal treatment and equal opportunity

RUSSELL PROFITT

This is a black perspective on aspects of the Scarman Report and it needs to be stressed at the outset that to most black people at least three fundamental factors stand out. First, there is the problem of racialism in contemporary Britain; second, much of what Lord Scarman finds has been pointed out many times before, and finally, there are the omissions from the Report, particularly those concerning the obstacles to progress. In my view, these must be borne in mind when one considers the Report.

Racialism in Britain

First, I feel it must be recognised that even if the recommendations of the Scarman Report were implemented *in their entirety* (and this I know is a major assumption) British society would still have a long way to go before any of the forms of racialism which the Report seeks to consider were dealt with in any substantive way.[1]*

The fact is that racialism in Britain is now so deep-seated, and its effects so far reaching on the consciousness of the population, that a great deal more than 'better' policing in the inner city is required if we are ever to begin to deal with this matter as purposefully and effectively as we should. Unfortunately some people, particularly policy-makers, still insist on seeing the Scarman Report as a major social and political benchmark, totally framing their considerations of policy on these issues. But to many, especially to young black people, the Report remains no more than a flawed indication of the direction in which thinking *ought* to be heading, if a clearer understanding of what is at stake is ever to be developed. However, some of the comments made on the Report by one or two of our chief police officers, as well as those from certain representatives of the Police Federation, suggest that the small gains the Report represents now appear to be resting

---

* Superscript numbers refer to Notes at end of chapter.

on precarious foundations, such that at any moment even these could collapse, leaving little, if anything, behind.

Scarman says nothing new

The second point which also needs to be recognised is the fact that to many of us the Scarman Report engenders not only a sure feeling that we have all been here before but, more seriously, it encourages a real sense of seething outrage. Much of what Scarman says, both in his analysis and in his recommendations, has been said before, and it has certainly been said far more strongly and bluntly by representatives of Britain's black communities, time and time again over the last few decades and longer. But it has been to no avail, so surely something is being missed.

Let it not be forgotten that racial disadvantage has been an unfortunate and unacceptable fact of life for black people who, because of discrimination, have been forced to live in Britain's inner city areas for generations. Wherever we have lived, whether in the East End of London, or in parts of Liverpool, or Leeds, or in the central area of London, we have made vociferous and repeated complaints about the poor living conditions to which we have been subjected. Over that time there have been a number of campaigns, all demanding that action of various sorts be taken to transform those bleak, neglected inner city areas. Sadly though such campaigns have, in the main, been largely ignored or 'misunderstood', both by politicians and by public authorities, as a result of which pent-up frustrations have led to anger, and generated a desire to take forms of direct action, as was demonstrated in Brixton.

Clearly, if anything is to be learnt by this society from the Brixton uprisings, it must be that it is now high time that such politicians and administrators show that they recognise the gravity of need, and they must begin to inject the resources, on a massive scale, which those needs demand, so that rapid change can at last take place. Failing this action, the message is clear: *the uprisings will continue.* Public hypocrisy on this issue must be understood and be rapidly brought to an end, for only in this way can real changes be made.

Sadly, perhaps the most significant thing to note about this issue is that it took the explosion of Brixton, together with the almost inevitable appointment of the learned judge (not to mention the production of an expensive report), before notice was at last taken of some of the things black people were saying about everyday life in the inner city areas, and of the need for urgent action to be taken to remedy the appalling social and environmental conditions suffered by Britain's black communities. It may well be, therefore, that direct action bears its own reward.

But what needs to be understood about the Scarman response is that he only recognised and presented as recommendations those ideas for action which were acceptable to his 'white' eyes. The real proof of public concern, and of public desire to correct the wrongs of the past, now rests on the quality and strength of the forms of action, if any, which follow in the wake of the Report. Unfortunately though, on most of these recommendations, two years later, we still await action. Something is clearly missing.

Scarman missed the point

The third factor which needs to be understood—perhaps the most important—helps us, I think, to see what it is that is missing. So far most of the discussion on the need for action to counter British racialism has been conducted inside an almost impenetrable shell of hypocrisy, erected for their own ends by those with power within 'white' society. Time after time, the black perspective, for various reasons, tends to be lost along the way. Young black people, of course, perhaps more than any other group—because of the nature of their everyday lives on the street—can see through this. This no doubt in part explains their direct and sharp reactions to life in Britain today. It is surely right that those responsible for the perpetuation of this hypocrisy should be exposed, particularly if real or lasting progress is to be made. Lord Scarman, of course, did not do this, possibly because such an exposition must begin with politicians, and as is clear from the Report, that was beyond his brief. This matter, however, cannot and *must* not be ignored by those wishing to see real changes made. Three groups of people stand out—politicians, members of the Labour movement, and educationalists, and the roles played by these groups cannot be ignored.

Politicians

Whether they be of the old varieties—Labour or Tory—or of the new—the SDP—in many people's eyes politicians all look the same on this question. It should be noted, for example, that Shirley Williams, now of the SDP, was a leading member of those Labour governments which, during times when action should have been taken, did so little (apart from issuing White Papers) towards improving the quality of life in inner city areas. So too were some of her colleagues, now masquerading as some new 'improved' variety of politician. The individuals, it seems, and their reactions, remain the same—only the names are changed, possibly to dupe the innocent. Young black people—and some not so young—see this. This is why unless and until black people actually see the 'goods' being delivered, in terms of improved employment opportunities, living conditions, and better social and recreational facilities, all politicians will continue to be seen as no more than hypocrites.

The Labour movement

Politicians apart, a number of other obstacles to clear thinking and action remain, all untouched by the Scarman Report. An example is the Labour movement. And writing now as someone directly involved, not everyone has been as positive on the issue of racialism as they like to believe. The trade unions are of course important members of the Labour movement. In my experience as a member of Lewisham Borough Council, where a number of attempts have been made over several years to try to devise acceptable equal opportunity policies, it must be recorded that the unions, at the local level, have proved to be the major stumbling block to progress. They have not even been as forthcoming on this issue as their counterparts at a national level like to pretend to be. Locally, we have seen the need for clear equal opportunity policy statements and, more to the point, we accept the need for such statements to be properly 'monitored' so that, where necessary, 'positive action' can be taken to try to create equal opportunities. Unfortunately, no action can be taken on this simply because as councillors we find it impossible to gain the support we require for the statement, let alone its implementation, from our local trade union colleagues. This farcical situation must now change. It is quite useless for those in the Labour movement to continue to make pious statements, particularly about brotherly love, but when action is required to seek convenient bolt-holes to hide in. Trade unionists[2] like every section of our society must now stand up and be counted on this issue.

The educationalists

Another group whose activities should, I feel, be commented upon are the educationalists. I would, incidentally, like to include the media in this category, but that unfortunately does not seem possible: the activities of some of the members of *this* group, particularly on the race issue, leave so much to be desired that one suspects them of being far more interested in sensationalism and miseducation than in elucidation, or in presenting balanced information which could take the debate further on towards understanding, and away from the usual prejudiced types of responses.

As someone who has spent some time in schools working on, or trying to work towards, the removal of prejudice, I feel I must express my own general disappointment over the way the race issue has been dealt with by the teaching profession. A great deal has been said, and continues to be said, by the unions about the need for rapid change, particularly in terms of what is actually being taught at classroom level, if lasting progress is to be made. However, as the Rampton Report[3] showed, so far very little real change in policy or practice has actually taken place.

Racial prejudice against black pupils and black teachers remains rampant, and both groups continue to fail to make progress in schools. In desperation, black parents, more and more frustrated and angry over the astounding indifference currently demonstrated by most members of the teaching profession about these highly disturbing matters, are now taking increasingly to the idea of some separate educational facilities for their children. Sadly, largely due to indifference, I suspect, rather than principle, few records are kept of the progress, if any, of pupils of ethnic backgrounds, or of the career prospects of black members of the teaching profession. In my view, the monitoring of such matters is needed if we are ever to either understand the racist experiences faced by black pupils and black teachers in British schools, or take action to change these experiences in a positive way.

In summary, it seems to me that whether in politics, the unions or in education, black people are not only excluded from debate, but white people show little desire or will to understand their prejudice, or to include us, as equals, in the debate. This state of affairs, of course, holds tremendous implications for the future. Lord Scarman missed this and, I am bound to say, as long as Scarman-type approaches are adopted, these issues will continue to be missed. In which case, sadly, the debate will continue to be a rather one-sided affair which in time is bound to generate a great deal more than anger on the other side.

What the Report does say

In his Report, Lord Scarman looked first at what he saw as the immediate causes of the disturbances in Brixton, then went on to look at what (again to him) were the wider issues. He heard evidence, made a number of visits, studied a number of documents, and of course produced a Report. In that, he mainly concentrated on matters to do with policing and, although it was no Kerner Commission Report (indeed it was far short of that), to be fair, a few of the recommendations he makes, if implemented, may well prove helpful. But to be honest, this would certainly not get us to the position I would like to see us reach if we are to see *real* improvements made.

Generally, it is unfortunate that the social and economic factors were not made more central in the Report. One of the real problems with the Report arises from the way Scarman looked at the issues in terms of policing, rather than in terms of social and political needs. Such needs are, of course, mentioned (Scarman, 6.1–6.34), but only in passing. Tragically, therefore, in my view, the Report ends up merely dealing with the out-turns of disadvantage rather than with its true causes.

To be specific, when Scarman looked at life in inner city areas (Scarman, 2.1–2.38), he was fairly forthright in his condemnation of some aspects of government policy (Scarman, 6.1–6.35 and 8.43–8.51). For instance, he made it absolutely clear that there is a need for greater direction from central government on this issue (Scarman, 6.6 and 6.31), and he criticised the fact that there is no effective co-ordination centrally to deal with inner city problems. He pinpointed something with which as a local councillor I am bound to agree, and that is the conflict which often exists between the policies of local governments and those of central government (Scarman, 6.5–6.7). Such conflicts of course often exist between one government department and another.

Then again, he commented on the need for a clear commitment towards the elimination of discrimination in housing (Scarman, 6.15) and on the need for equal opportunity policies and services to be monitored (Scarman, 6.30–6.35). But I am bound to stress that while these things *must* be done— and *ought* by now to have been done—they are *not*, and therein lies the problem. Unfortunately, some still seem only prepared to become involved in discussions and debate over these sorts of issues when, to many of us, the implications of leaving things as they are are truly horrendous. The urgency of the situation, therefore, is not recognised. And that is part of the institutional racism which Lord Scarman fails to recognise.

Lord Scarman, of course, comments on the breakdown in relations between the police and the community in inner city areas. But even here, I feel, we need to go much further than Scarman suggests towards community control of the police. Consultations of the sort proposed would not be adequate, for such forums would merely end up as talking shops—literally.

In the end, Scarman leaves more questions unanswered than answered. And that perhaps explains why, like so many reports, it has been, in the main, left to gather dust, and has been seen as irrelevant by most black people.

Other questions which were either not understood or were simply brushed over include:
—the causes and consequences of the *social and political inertia* which supports racial disadvantage;
—the fundamentally *unbalanced power relationships* which exist in British society;
—the true nature and the operation of *institutional racism* in Britain.
But then, this was only to be expected, given the nature of present considerations on these issues.

What now needs to be done

More analysis is certainly required, but more commitment to taking *action* to bring about change would not go amiss. First of all, we need a much stronger Race Relations Act. Here we could take a leaf out of the book of some of our European colleagues. Belgian law, for instance, requires that public officials found guilty of discrimination are not only fined, but sent to gaol as well. Perhaps we ought to look at that. And since I suspect that a lot of what is called institutional racism actually does occur in our town halls and in the offices of the Department of Health and Social Security and in the civil service, tougher race relations legislation along such lines may well be a help in forcing some to think more carefully and clearly about the things they do. Institutional racism goes much beyond this, of course, but this would be one way of beginning to deal with these issues.

Secondly, perhaps we need to see the establishment of some agency, along the lines of, say, a Standing Commission on the Inner City, which would have the power to cut through the cant of local government. It could directly finance and support self-help projects and voluntary organisations concerned actually to get things done in our inner city areas. Funds would also be available to other statutory agencies, but clearly unless we get something far more dynamic than that which exists at present, we are simply going to find ourselves in future years repeating this same old debate.

In the end, though, I suspect that the sorts of changes that black people wish to see will only come through a continuation of the political struggle for social and economic justice which, in Britain, is only just beginning to include the race dimension. The riots or uprisings are only a part of that struggle—made far worse by the economic policies of the Government.

Lord Scarman, of course, did not discuss this issue within that context. But black people must, and as the uprisings show, they will continue to do so. Ways of eradicating racism must be found—honestly, and without hypocrisy. It needs to be understood that uprisings such as those seen in Brixton are bound to continue until equal respect, equal treatment and equal opportunities become the way of life. Black people, I feel certain, will continue to struggle in various ways, until that state of affairs is created both here in Britain and elsewhere.

Notes

These notes have been added by the editor.

1. For discussions of racism and racialism in Britain see, for example: D. Hiro, *Black British, White British*, Pelican, 1973; J. Rex and R. Moore, *Race, Community and Conflict*, Oxford University Press, 1967; S. Zubaida (Ed.), *Race and Racialism*, Tavistock, 1970; N. File and C. Power, *Black Settlers in Britain 1555–1958*, Heinemann, 1981; R. Miles and A. Phizacklea, *Racism and Political Action in Britain*, Routledge & Kegan Paul, 1979.

2. For further discussions of trade unions and equal opportunities see for instance: R. Miles and A. Phizacklea, 'The TUC and black workers, 1974–1976', *The British Journal of Industrial Relations*, Vol. xvi, 2, 1978; R. Moore, *Racism and Black Resistance in Britain*, Pluto, 1975; D. Smith, *The Facts of Racial Disadvantage*, PEP, 1976.

3. *West Indian Children in our Schools*, The Interim Report of the Committee of Inquiry into the Education of Children from Ethnic Minority Groups (Chairman: Mr Anthony Rampton, OBE) (Cmnd 8273), HMSO, 1981.

CHAPTER 19

The need for positive action

USHA PRASHAR

The term 'positive action' is often confused with the term 'positive discrimination'—and no single idea arouses greater controversy in the field of race relations than that of positive discrimination. This is often taken to mean 'reverse discrimination', that is, discrimination in favour of blacks such as quotas in employment, Bakke style,[1]* although such 'reverse discrimination' is unlawful under the 1976 Race Relations Act. Confused discussion about these terms has not helped policy development in the field of race relations and it is not a question of mere semantics to insist that the two meanings should be distinguished. Ken Young and Naomi Connelly in their book[2] have clearly illustrated that this single misunderstanding constitutes a barrier to adoption of relevant policies and initiatives. It is therefore crucial that the meaning of positive action is clearly understood.

What is positive action?

Positive action essentially means taking steps to remove barriers which hinder equality of opportunity. Equality of opportunity results from a combination of non-discrimination and active intervention, but even if all discriminatory barriers were removed, there would still not be equality of opportunity. In this ideal situation there would be equal access to jobs, education and services but not an equal *share* of the jobs, educational opportunities and other services. This results from the handicapping effects of past discrimination, historical factors or other social and economic disadvantages. Achievement of equal share of the benefits requires positive intervention, and this positive action can take several forms. It can mean actively preventing or eliminating discrimination or it can mean taking specific steps to remove barriers which obstruct achievement of equality of opportunity—that is, meeting the needs of minority groups and changing unjustifiable policies and practices. Positive action is based on diagnosis of the problems and needs and allocation of appropriate resources.

* Superscript numbers refer to Notes at end of chapter.

Under the Race Relations Act 1976,[3] positive action is permitted under precise circumstances. For example, when racial groups are under-represented in an occupation or skill level specified employment bodies can actively encourage members of that racial group to apply for the jobs in question or to undertake appropriate training. Under similar conditions, specified employment bodies can provide special training for members of under-represented racial groups. The object of such training is to raise the trainees to a point where they can compete more effectively in the open market. An employer or other employment body can provide this form of training but *cannot* systematically give preference to members of a racial group when selecting for employment. This would be 'reverse discrim-ination' and is unlawful. If one accepts that due to racism, discrimination and other social and economic factors minorities face special problems, then it logically follows that positive intervention is necessary to deal with special problems. *Positive action, therefore, is about promoting racial justice and equality of opportunity, and not giving special privileges to minority groups.*

The Scarman Report and positive action

In his Report Lord Scarman made a well-founded case for positive action. He argued strongly for positive action within the context of a realistic strategy 'directed to specific areas of racial disadvantage' (Scarman, 9.4). He provided a strong justification for taking positive measures and he stressed that the sole criterion for taking such measures should be need—'and no other' (Scarman, 6.32). Lord Scarman developed his argument in the following way:

> The evidence which I have received . . . leaves no doubt in my mind that racial disadvantage is a fact of current British life. . . . Urgent action is needed if it is not to become an endemic, ineradicable disease threatening the very survival of our society (Scarman, 9.1).

He argued that although minority communities will benefit from a concerted strategy to regenerate the inner cities, such a strategy will not solve all their problems—hence there should be a recognition of minority need within the more general problems of deprivation, and a clear co-ordinated response to it from government (Scarman, 6.10). He said that there should be greater willingness to tackle related but not identical problems of inner city decline and minority disadvantage. In other words, he was saying that although the outcome of attempts to deal positively with race must ultimately be bound up with the outcome of the uphill struggle to revive the economy, it does not follow that positive initiatives are not required to tackle special problems facing minorities.

The existence of special problems is demonstrated by a range of investigations over the past decade[4] and even if the ultimate danger of civil disorder did not exist, there would be sufficient argument for a programme of positive action. Those who argue against positive action need to demonstrate that no special problems exist.

Having argued the need for positive action Lord Scarman posed the question: how far is it right to go in order to meet special needs? He stated:

> It is clear from the evidence ... that, if the balance of racial disadvantage is to be redressed, as it must be, positive action is required. I mean by this more than the admirable approach adopted by at least some central and local government agencies at present, which is intended chiefly to persuade the ethnic minorities to take up their share of general social provisions. Important though this is, it is not, in my view, a sufficient answer. Given the special problems of the ethnic minorities, exposed in evidence, justice requires that special pro-grammes should be adopted in areas of acute deprivation. ... I recognise the existence of a legitimate and understandable fear on the part of both public and private institutions that programmes which recognise and cater for the special needs of minority groups will stimulate a backlash from the majority. I suspect that this fear, rather than 'institutional racism' is the primary factor inhibiting the necessary development of such programmes. I believe that if the justification for such programmes were fully explained, the backlash threat might prove to be over-rated. Nevertheless, it must not be allowed to prevent necessary action. Certainly special programmes for ethnic minority groups should only be instituted where the need for them is clearly made out. But need must be the criterion, and no other. The principle has already been recognised by Parliament (sections 35, 37, 38 of the Race Relations Act 1976), and must be made effective (Scarman, 6.32).

In this paragraph Scarman underlines the point that the law already provides for such measures. However, he underestimates the impact of 'institutional racism' when he argues that majority backlash rather than institutional racism is inhibiting necessary developments; the so-called white backlash occurs because of racism. The question of catering for special needs by special provisions for particular areas or groups has long been an aspect of British social policy, for example in education and health. These policies have been acceptable both to political parties and the public and have not carried with them the stigma that they are being pursued at the expense of the rest of society. What has been lacking in the field of race relations is the will to adopt and implement positive policies, and successive governments have taken no clear steps to explain what positive action is. Special training, financial aid programmes and community development funds are all acceptable aspects of social policy and in the case of minorities all these can be justified on the grounds of well-demonstrated need. Lord Scarman also ignores the Government's racist immigration laws which have been a major hindrance to the development of positive race policies and have poisoned any attempts to improve race relations.

The important contribution of the Scarman Report is that it sets the debate about positive action within the framework of special needs. However, the importance of this point is lost by the use of the term 'positive discrimination' in the concluding part of the Report (Scarman, 9.4). It would have been more satisfactory if Lord Scarman had confined himself to the well-founded case for positive action, based on an appraisal of the additional resources required for effective intervention. As one might have expected, the call for 'positive discrimination' was widely criticised and misinterpreted, and distracted attention from his main argument in the body of the Report. Newspapers, in particular, focused on this question. The *Daily Mail*,[5] under a banner headline 'THE CASE FOR REVERSE DISCRIMINATION' stated:

> Deprived blacks must get a better deal than whites over the next few years if Britain is to avoid a racial holocaust. . . .
> Giving blacks better opportunities than their fellow citizens has become more important than improving relations between police and ethnic minorities, says the Report. . . .
> The key issues, said Lord Scarman, are education and employment—and local authorities must ensure that funds were [*sic*] made available particularly in these areas.
> But Lord Scarman's proposal of 'positive discrimination' to prevent further rioting drew criticism last night from the Police Federation, representing 120,000 officers up to the rank of chief inspector.
> Chairman James Jardine warned, 'Lord Scarman is taking an awful gamble—as far as we are concerned, there is only one law for everybody.'
> And the CBI, the bosses' organisation, had 'serious reservations'. A spokesman said: 'It is harmful to harmonious working relationships, and we do not believe it will genuinely help the employment prospects of black people.'

In its editorial, *The Times* said:[6]

> He notes that if the balance is to be redressed, 'as it must be', positive discrimination is required. But it is not clear whether he is content that positive discrimination should take the form of spending programmes for identified areas or categories of citizen, which is the form it has taken up to now; or whether he is among those who think it should be

extended to positive discrimination between individuals on the basis of colour, in such matters as recruitment, promotion and educational selection, which is likely to be both more effective and more widely resented.

The Government's record on positive action

Some argue that positive action which is permitted under the Race Relations Act 1976 is limited, but the opportunities for positive action allowed by the 1976 Act are by no means insignificant. Moreover, a great many administrative steps can be taken to ensure equality of opportunity and promotion of racial justice, for example the support government provides through use of its executive powers. The problem is that very little effort has been made to make the maximum use of these provisions. There is little if any significant evidence of active and positive government intervention; the will of central government to adopt positive initiatives appears to be weak. The record of government as an employer, and the use of its powers as a purchaser of goods and services has been far from exemplary.

In the civil service an unequivocal statement of the Government's equal opportunities policy was made known to all government departments, and responsibility for its implementation was placed on the principal establishment officer of each department. The policy stated not only that there would be no discrimination but warned departments of the dangers of unconscious discrimination and advised of the possible need for special training 'to enable staff to realise their full potential'.[7]

In 1978, however, the report of the Tavistock Institute's study of the civil service[8] found that black people were considerably less successful than white people in applying for jobs in the civil service. A sample of 317 applicants for posts in the Department of Health and Social Security in the London North Region showed fully one third coming from black candidates. Yet only 18 per cent of these were offered posts compared to a success rate of 54 per cent for the white applicants.

Following this report, a Joint Working Party was established with representatives from the Civil Service Department, government departments and the national staff side. Its purpose was to consider arrangements for the implementation of the equal opportunity policy. However, in 1981 the Government rejected the idea that there would be systematic monitoring of the ethnic origins of civil servants as a way of detecting and preventing unfair discrimination. This appeared to be the last word on the matter until November 1981 when Lord Scarman's Report recommended that the Government think again about its decision. In December the

Government announced that it was to begin an experimental census of the civil service as the first step towards full monitoring.

If central government has done little to implement equal opportunity as an employer, so too it has done little through 'contract compliance', that is, ensuring that companies given government contracts strictly observe the Race Relations Act. From 1969 all government contracts contained a standard clause requiring contractors to conform to the provisions of the Race Relations Act 1968 and to ensure that sub-contractors and employees did the same. The operation of this clause and its impact were never monitored by the Department of Employment or any other government department.

The private sector and equal opportunities

The 1975 White Paper[9] said that it was the Government's intention to require a similar undertaking in relation to the new law and that 'it should be a standard condition of government contracts that the contractor will provide on request to the Department of Employment such information about its employment policies and practices as the Department may reasonably require'.[10] The Race Relations Bill contained no such provision and attempts to insert a new clause were unsuccessful. In 1978, after the Act had been in force for more than a year, the Home Secretary announced that detailed proposals for the monitoring of contract compliance would be discussed with the CBI and the TUC.

The CBI were, however, indignant at the Government's attempt at monitoring and in a letter to the Home Secretary in 1979, the CBI's director-general, Sir John Methven, said that the inclusion of the clause in contracts seemed to be 'an attempt to impose a more onerous obligation indirectly' rather than directly through legislation. The then Under-Secretary of State for Employment, John Grant, told Parliament, however, that the clause should cause no anxiety 'unless employers are either entrenched in complacency or have something to hide'. The clause, he said, was sensible and proper when there were still 'too many employers . . . who readily subscribe to the concept of equal opportunity but who turn a blind eye to discriminatory practices'.[11]

The evidence very much supports the view that in the private sector there appears to have been little real effort to promote equality of opportunity. A survey by Political and Economic Planning[12] in 1974 of 283 firms at plant level found that only fourteen claimed to have equal opportunity policies. Only 8 per cent had taken concrete steps to implement the policies and only 1 per cent could mention a specific instance where action had been taken. A later study for the Runnymede Trust showed a similarly bleak picture where twenty-seven of the largest forty companies in the country had done nothing or gone no further than discussion.[13] Companies such as Mars Limited and the Ford Motor Company have such policies. Mere adoption of an equal opportunity policy is no guarantee against discrimination. Brook Street Bureau, who have an equal opportunity policy, were found by an industrial tribunal in 1978 to have unlawfully discriminated against a black applicant for a job, and BL Cars, found by a CRE formal investigation to have discriminated in 1981, also have such a policy.

The Trades Union Congress in 1973 approved an equal opportunities clause designed for inclusion in national agreements, concluded by unions and employers. This required employers to develop 'positive policies to promote equal opportunity in employment'.[14] A survey in 1979 showed that only seventeen out of 106 unions had actually adopted the clause. The TUC reissued the model clause as a part of its Black Workers Charter in 1981 which, among other things, calls on unions to remove barriers preventing black workers becoming union officials.

The record of local government

The Government has provided no guidance to local authorities on important ingredients of positive action, such as record-keeping and monitoring. The posture which central government has adopted towards local authorities has been lacking in conviction and its unwillingness to set an example and explain the basis for positive action has been appalling. For instance, the 1981 Report by the Home Affairs Select Committee[15] argued for greater use of the positive action provisions of the Race Relations Act. In response the Government said, 'It is important to emphasise that such declarations (i.e. equal opportunity declarations) do not imply discrimination in favour of ethnic minority workers . . . and that they will not lead to the imposition of racial quotas. The Government would strongly resist any pressure in that direction.'[16] Again the opportunity to explain 'positive action' was missed and this oblique reference to 'quotas' did nothing to clarify the position. Rather than take the opportunity to support positive action and explain what it entails, the Government pandered to the negative and confused views which exist about this issue.

Local authorities have a special duty under section 71 of the Race Relations Act 1976 to eliminate racial discrimination from their various activities, and to promote equality of opportunity and good race relations. This is additional, of course, to the other requirements of the Act for example in relation to an authority's duty as an employer. In 1978, Lord Avebury, the Liberal Party spokesman on race and immigration, said that the Act had had 'a very modest impact' on race relations. An enquiry carried out by the Liberal Party had shown a wide variety of attitudes among local authorities as to their duties, and these ranged from mere awareness of a duty, to systematic review of policy—although these were carried out by only a few authorities. Only one-quarter of the responding authorities appeared to have adopted some form of equal opportunities policy.

More recently, the Standing Conference of Afro-Caribbean and Asian Councillors carried out a survey of London's local authorities. Only fifteen replied and of these only five (Brent, Camden, Lambeth, Lewisham and Wandsworth) had had an equal opportunities policy for some years, while another two (Hackney and Kensington) had recently implemented such a policy.[17] Clive Robinson's study, again of London councils, found that responses of local government had been largely *ad hoc* and unsystematic. Corporate structures were more likely to have been established where the political leadership displayed an unusually high commitment to race relations, or where the role of the community relations council had been significant, or where a corporate and centralist approach already existed within the authority.[18]

A few local authorities have established special 'race units' to implement positive action in all local authority activities and the work of one, in the London Borough of Lambeth, is extensively described in *The System*.[19] It argues that most local authorities take a 'colour blind' approach and are therefore likely to be discriminating, 'whether consciously or otherwise, directly or indirectly'. Others make a formal declaration of intent not to discriminate and to provide equal opportunity. They might well be complacent about what could be achieved without positive action and are likely also to be discriminating. Only those few local authorities embarking on positive action programmes

> ... would be in a strong position to refute all allegations of unfair treatment and to demonstrate to black people that their different and special needs would be identified, adequately considered and provided for.[20]

In housing some local authorities have taken steps to monitor their housing allocation policies and change or adjust their policies where necessary, while a number of 'special access' courses have been introduced with the encouragement of the Department of Education and Science in colleges of further education and polytechnics.[21] However, as this brief overview of the initiatives which have been taken illustrates, progress is slow and most of these initiatives are in early stages of development.

The attack on racial disadvantage

The White Paper on *Policy for the Inner Cities* in 1977[22] stated that the needs of black people would be 'fully taken into account in the planning and implementation of policies . . . and in the allocation of resources'. At the same time, however, it said that 'the attack on the specific problems of discrimination would have to be through the new law and work of the Commission for Racial Equality (CRE)'. These were no more than mere statements of intent. The stated aims and commitments have not been carried out in practice. The striking conclusion from the Runnymede Trust workshops, which were run in conjunction with the National Council for Voluntary Organisations (NCVO), was the absence of any real aim or policy in relation to race and equal opportunity as a dimension of all policies in the inner city.[23] We formed the view that the Government failed to use the vehicle of the inner cities programme, and the close relationship it brings with authorities, to take a lead in establishing a more effective framework for improving the prospects of black groups. Lord Scarman also argued for a more direct attack on racial disadvantage. He said:

> The attack on racial disadvantage must be more direct than it has been. It must be co-ordinated by central government, who with local authorities must ensure that the funds made available are directed to specific areas of racial disadvantage (Scarman, 9.4).

Within the approach adopted by the 1977 White Paper there is a need for mechanisms to ensure that resources reach those who lack equality of opportunity. A strategy for positive action in this context has been suggested by Naomi Connelly and Ken Young.[24] They argue that:

> There is an overall need for an authoritative clarification of policy in relation to discrimination, disadvantage and diversity. Local authorities cannot be asked to play a leading role in promoting racial equality until there is a far better understanding among them of the basic premises of a multi-racial society; nor can they develop policies to achieve it without grasping the need to be explicit about issues of race.

They recommended:

> A ministerial initiative to clarify and reaffirm the basis of law and policy on race relations; better communication of priorities; establishment of an action group or task force chaired by a Department of the Environment (DOE) minister, including local political leaders and officials supported by the regional offices at the DOE, to promote developments; transferring responsibility for securing change from central to local government by encouraging the adoption of such corporate, consultative and employment practices as will make for self sustained development; sharing of experiences and dissemination of good practice.

The Government has to some extent moved in this direction with the appointment of Sir George Young as junior minister at the Department of the Environment with special responsibilities for race.

Attempts are being made to develop a new role with an emphasis on facilitating action and to ensure a more efficient functioning of the existing machinery of government. Such positive action is indeed necessary but it has to be said that while it is right to think of administrative reforms to ensure relevant changes, such administrative reforms alone are not enough. These should be seen as complementary and not as a substitute for prudent public investment. By the same token investment by the Government or the private sector will continue to have a marginal impact on black communities if certain specific steps are not taken to ensure that they benefit from new initiatives. A systematic programme of positive action is needed but within the context of effective public investment: positive action mechanisms without resources are just as ineffective as resources without positive action. Effective initiatives to deal with the problems of discrimination, deprivation and social and economic disadvantages must of necessity attend both to the scale of the resources required to implement positive action and to the effective allocation of the resources. This demands mechanisms for correcting the maldistribution of resources and where necessary injection of resources.

The broader context within which positive action takes place is equally important. For instance, Lord Scarman argued for more black policemen (Scarman, 5.6–5.15). He said that despite advertising campaigns few blacks have applied to join the police and he pointed to the strong undercurrent of hostility towards the police. He argued for vigorous action, for instance: special training; recruiting black police officers to suitable civilian jobs in the police force when tuition could be provided by adapting some of the Manpower Services Commission (MSC) schemes to achieve this special end; getting more members of the ethnic minorities recruited through personal contacts at schools, youth clubs and unemployment offices; using the cadet scheme; recruiting black youths in auxiliary capacities in various aspects of the police force. He said 'the object of policy must be that the composition of the police fully reflects that of the society the police serve' (Scarman, 5.13). Some police forces have made such attempts, but these formal attempts will not be sufficient. A negative view of the police results from negative policing. Any positive attempts by the police to recruit blacks will not succeed if insensitive policing continues.

Publication of the crime statistics in 1982 and 1983 which projected a section of the community either as criminal or supporting criminals did untold harm to the relationships between the police and the black community.[25] Therefore the broader context within which such attempts are made is extremely important.

The need for positive action

The few initiatives which have been taken following the Scarman Report are piecemeal and *ad hoc*. Race as a social policy issue has always been a marginal issue—it has never been on the main agenda and is usually excluded from the mainstream policy debate. It forces itself on to the agenda at a time of crisis when there is a desperate search for solutions and so, inevitably, the remedies which are pursued at such times are patchy and do not deal with the fundamental flaws in the policy.

Following the 1981 disorders there was a frantic search for solutions. In February 1982, Sir George Young became the minister designated to act at the Department of the Environment as the focal point for action on race. Some more local authorities have started to adopt equal opportunity policies, and have set up race relations units. The creation of such units may indicate that the significance of race has been recognised, but in practice the existence of such arrangements may in itself signify very little. All kinds of marginal adaptations have been made by local authorities, departments and individual practitioners to provide services more appropriate to the needs of blacks. Some authorities have made minor adjustments to the allocation of funds to ensure that black groups have access to resources. The Home Office set up two working parties, one to consider police recruitment and the other to consider police training. Without minimising the significance or the importance of the above developments, it has to be said that these initiatives are only peripheral. *What is required is systematic effort to implement positive policies at all levels and in all areas.* The Government should also create a climate where such reforms can be implemented without difficulty. Positive action planning does not mean taking isolated and *ad hoc* steps; it means adopting a deliberate strategy designed to ensure racial justice and equality of opportunity. The Government should ensure that adequate resources are allocated no matter what the current economic circumstances; it should create a framework within government to ensure that the race dimension is taken into account in all policy developments. There is a great need for better co-ordination between different government departments. This was strongly argued for by the Home Affairs Committee:

> Some provisions must be made at official level for inter-departmental co-ordination of government policies for combating racial disadvantage.[26]

Apart from making adequate resources available and creating a suitable framework for consideration of race policies, it is important that the Government takes a positive lead on issues such as government contracts, equal opportunity within the civil service, record-keeping and monitoring, and it must also take a lead in stating what positive action is and why it is needed, thus creating a public climate where such policies are acceptable. The Government should encourage more effective partnerships between itself, local government and the private sector to ensure explicit consideration of race in all policy initiatives.

Local authorities on the other hand should vigorously pursue equal opportunity policies both in the fields of employment and the delivery of services. They should also review all other areas of their activity, for example the local economy. In the field of employment, both in the private and public sector, concerted efforts should be made to dismantle both direct and indirect discrimination.

An effective positive action plan to achieve equality of opportunity means diagnosing those aspects which erect discriminatory barriers for minorities. It means examining the numerical employment profile and those policies and practices which produce that numerical profile. It requires an understanding of the subtle and covert forms of discrimination. These initiatives require continuous demonstration of commitment and allocation of adequate resources. An effective positive action programme is that which aims to identify and change those practices and conditions which produce inequality. Unless such comprehensive initiatives are taken with conviction the problem of racial injustice and lack of equality of opportunity will become even more intractable than it is at the moment.

The case for positive action is difficult to refute. If the Government fails to act now it will be difficult to disagree with those who believe that the entire Scarman operation was a cynical substitute for positive government action.

Notes

1. Although Alan Bakke, an applicant for a medical school place in the United States, won his particular challenge, the case validated properly constituted 'affirmative action' based on giving preference to quotas from ethnic minorities. See 438 US 265 (1978); J. Dreyfuss and C. Lawrence, *The Bakke Case—The Politics of Inequality*, Harcourt Brace Jovanovitch, 1979; T. Eastland and W. J. Bennet, *Counting by Race*, Basic Books, 1979.
2. K. Young and N. Connelly, *Policy and Practice in a Multi-racial City*, Policy Studies Institute, 1981.
3. Sections 35, 37 and 38 of the Race Relations Act 1976.
4. See, for example, S. Field, G. Mair, T. Rees and P. Stevens, *Ethnic Minorities in Britain: a Study of Trends in Their Position since 1961*, Home Office Research Study. No. 68; House of Commons, *Racial Disadvantage: Fifth Report from the Home Affairs Committee, Session 1980–1981*, HC 424–I, HMSO, 1981.
5. *Daily Mail*, 26 November 1981, pp. 1–2.
6. 'Lord Scarman's Report', *The Times*, 26 November 1981, p. 15.
7. *Racial Discrimination* (Cmnd 6234), HMSO, September 1975, para. 17.
8. Tavistock Institute of Human Relations, *The Application of Race Relations Policy in the Civil Service*, HMSO, 1978.
9. *Racial Discrimination*, *supra*, note 7.
10. *Ibid.*, para. 20.
11. *Hansard*, 6 March 1979.

12. D. J. Smith, *Racial Disadvantage in Employment*, Broadsheet 544, Political and Economic Planning, June 1974.
13. M. A. Pearn, *Beyond Tokenism: Equal Employment Opportunity Policies*, Runnymede Trust, 1978.
14. For an interesting discussion of TUC policies see R. Miles and A. Phizacklea, 'The TUC and black workers, 1974–76', *The British Journal of Industrial Relations*, Vol. xvi, No. 2, 1978, pp. 195–207.
15. *Racial Disadvantage: Fifth Report from the Home Affairs Committee, supra*, note 4.
16. *Racial Disadvantage: The Government Reply to the Fifth Report from the Home Affairs Committee* (Cmnd 8476), HMSO, January 1982, p. 26.
17. *No Problems Here*, Briefing Paper, The Black Councillors, 1980.
18. C. Robinson, *The Origins of Corporate Structures for Race Relations Policy in Inner London Borough Councils*, Commission for Racial Equality, 1981.
19. H. Ouseley, D. Silverstone and U. Prashar, *The System*, Runnymede Trust/South London Equal Rights Consultancy, 1981.
20. *Ibid.*, p. 15.
21. The DES announced a scheme intended to encourage minorities to enter teaching and other professions. Avon, Bedfordshire, Birmingham, Haringey, Inner London, Leicestershire and Manchester were asked to set up pilot schemes.
22. *Policy for the Inner Cities* (Cmnd 6845), HMSO, 1977.
23. See the two reports on *Inner Cities and Black Minorities*, Runnymede Trust and National Council for Voluntary Organisations, November 1979 and December 1980.
24. See Young and Connelly, *supra*, note 2.
25. Metropolitan Police, *Criminal Statistics*, March 1982 and March 1983.
26. *Racial Disadvantage: Fifth Report from the Home Affairs Committee, supra*, note 4, para. 40.

CHAPTER 20

The challenge to local government

KEN YOUNG

In the Report on the Brixton disorders, Lord Scarman makes a number of observations concerning social policies and the role of central and local government in identifying and responding to ethnic minority needs. His remarks are a mixture of panacea and challenge and it is regrettable that neither he nor the Home Affairs Committee in their almost contemporaneous report on racial disadvantage took the opportunity to spell out more fully the nature of the challenge to local government.[1]*

Lord Scarman's panaceas

Let us first dispose of Lord Scarman's panaceas. Reviewing the broader context of social policies and problems he implied that, within the constraints of current financial and economic policy, hopes should be pinned on two developments: the better co-ordination of urban policies and programmes (Scarman, 6.6) and the reduction of unemployment through the 'successful outcome of current economic problems' [sic] (Scarman, 6.28).

Better co-ordination and economic revival are, in this context, somewhat specious remedies. The first was all too familiar as a panacea in the 1960s, a decade in which institutional tinkering enjoyed a vogue among many commentators and politicians. What is evidently lacking in the arena of inner cities policies (so well summarised by Lord Scarman) is not the better co-ordination of action, but its prerequisites: a clear conception of the future of cities in a changing economy and a clear expression of policies designed to ease the transition to that future. Urban policy, it has so often been said, is addressed to the consequences and not the causes of change; better co-ordination of action is a pious hope when there is so little agreement—and indeed, surprisingly little debate—on what such action is intended to achieve and what it can achieve.

Lord Scarman's second point, that economic regeneration of the cities

---

* Superscript numbers refer to Notes at end of chapter.

induced either by inner city policies (Scarman, 6.10) or by general economic revival (Scarman, 6.28) will relieve the stresses underlying the disorders is equally ill-founded. There seems to be a widespread belief that if the economy picks up everything will be well with the inner cities. Yet there have been great changes taking place in the economies of cities since the mid-1960s. There has been a progressive flow of wealth-creating potential, of industrial development, of investment—in short of *job generation*—from the inner cities to the outer parts of cities and from the outer parts of cities to non-urban areas and smaller, free-standing towns. Such places as Leicester and Bristol (paradoxically given the disorders in those towns in 1980) have done relatively well out of this restructuring of the British economy; the older cities and the larger metropolitan areas in particular have done badly. The causes of this spatial reallocation of economic opportunity have been discussed in depth elsewhere; perhaps the most dramatic way to make the point is to recall that impoverishment, riots and criticism of the police were intimately associated with the stresses of nineteenth-century urbanisation; we are now experiencing the analogous stresses of twentieth-century *counter-urbanisation*.[2] I do not therefore see any obvious way in which a revival of the national economy is going to solve the problems of the inner city in the older metropolitan areas. Indeed, in so far as economic revival means that industrial restructuring and the opportunities for the relocation of firms pick up, then the inner city problems may well intensify both relatively and absolutely.

The implications of this pessimistic view cast doubt upon another panacea on which Lord Scarman, for understandable reasons, chose not to comment (Scarman, 6.2). It is a widely held view in local government that recent reductions in central government grant and the restrictions on revenue expenditure in particular greatly outweigh any efforts made by local authorities to tackle racial disadvantage, with or without the supplementary funding provided through the urban programme. It is natural enough for such bodies as the Association of Metropolitan Authorities to claim that a restoration of funds will enable their members to get on with the job and that the Secretary of State for the Environment's well-publicised special initiatives on Merseyside and elsewhere merely distract their attention from the serious drain on local resources. Increased revenue spending is a favoured panacea and one which provides for the convenient evasion of the basic challenge to local government: the transformation of policies, programmes and procedures better to meet the largely neglected needs of Britain's black populations.

The role of the local authority

In considering the role of local government in multi-racial Britain and under the Race Relations Act 1976 in particular, it is important to keep in mind the tendency to overestimate the significance of local authorities to the everyday lives of black and white people. Government bears upon the ordinary citizen in various ways, but so too do many other phenomena which are either less directly under the control of government or are entirely beyond it. Most black people in most cities are not public sector tenants; most blacks are not clients of the social service departments; most are in employment. Their economic fortunes are not determined by the policies of local authorities; dissatisfaction with the delivery of public services is not unique to any one ethnic or social group but is common to most. People live their lives in many distinct if overlapping 'domains'. Local government impinges on but a few of them; how critically we cannot tell—unless we pause to ask and to listen.

Those who choose to listen will find at least three areas in respect of which ethnic minority groups voice a sense of grievance. The first concerns the barriers to local authority employment, barriers which may be unfair in themselves and constricting of the authorities' own effectiveness in relating to the black communities. The second concerns the provision of local authority services, including those services of support which directly distribute benefits and those services of opportunity—principally education—where skills can be acquired, abilities extended and life-chances improved. The third concerns access to decision-making, an area where a sense of grievance may be exacerbated by insensitive or heavy handed official action. In considering each in turn it must be stressed that while black people voice many specific grievances on each of these issues, the benefits of review and adjustment will not necessarily accrue to blacks alone but may enhance the lives of those white people who are systematically disadvantaged by current patterns of provision and procedure.[3]

Taking employment first, local authorities occupy a strategic position as large employers; in many areas they are the *largest* employer. Their recruitment policies, often with undue reliance on formal qualification unrelated to job performance and with decentralised manual labour recruitment, may encompass a wide range of hazards to fairness. In adopting and enforcing equal opportunity practices local authorities may—even with the reduced recruitment of the current financial regime—have substantial effects on the local labour market and on the perception of opportunity. It is also open to them to try to influence the decisions of large private sector employers by exemplary action or by attaching conditions to contracts.[4]

The problems which arise in respect of service provision are too various to do them justice here. The problems of the under-achievement of children from ethnic minority groups have been fully discussed, if less satisfactorily measured.[5] The apparent reluctance of social service department (SSDs) to adapt to the different needs of clients from diverse ethnic and religious backgrounds is emerging as a particularly intractable problem; few SSDs have the black social workers they need to cope more effectively with social work in multi-racial areas.[6] The problems of achieving fairness in housing allocations have long been recognised. Many of the more blantantly discriminatory practices have been abandoned; yet it is clear that there are many points in the process of allocating housing benefits of all sorts where stereotyping can lead to discriminatory judgements.[7] There is of course more to local service provision than these issues; planning controls and environmental health are among the other sensitive areas. But these are particularly significant, housing and education being singled out by Lord Scarman for special comment (Scarman, 6.12–6.15 and 6.16–6.25 respectively).

The third area concerns access to decision-making. The entry barriers to full participation (and especially candidacy) in the political parties are of obvious significance. Yet it is particularly necessary for local authorities as service providers in multi-racial areas to find ways of enabling the feelings of the ethnic minority communities to be made known to departmental managers. More important still are the channels of access to the higher levels of the policy process, channels which, it may be argued, must be established if a local authority is to carry out its obligation to review its operations under section 71 of the Race Relations Act 1976.

Tackling racial discrimination and disadvantage

Section 71 puts a very clear statutory responsibility upon local government to tackle racial discrimination and disadvantage. It specifically requires all local authorities to make appropriate arrangements for the review of their procedures and their operations and to take effective steps towards eradicating racial discrimination and providing equality of opportunity. It is worth considering how local authorities have responded to this now several-years-old statutory obligation.[8]

The implication of section 71 is that local authorities have to start by creating mechanisms for policy review, and by asking themselves how far, in what ways, and with what consequences, do the decisions that they take and the procedures that they operate, impinge upon the well-being of people from the ethnic minority communities. Any policy review in this particular area, if it is to be effective, must in my view conform to four requirements.[9]

First it should involve the elected members—the senior politicians—at the highest level, and should express their real political commitment. Those policy reviews in local government that do not involve the political leadership in a very real sense are likely to be ineffective. Second, any mechanism of policy review has to involve the top administrators, the heads of departments and their staff, because those reviews that do not bring the officials at an early stage into the business of asking questions about the impact of local decisions on the black communities, tend to be ineffective simply because any decisions have little official support and may be evaded or not followed through: they fail at the implementation stage. The third requirement is that any policy review has to make a direct provision for the expression of the viewpoints of the people from the black communities, in whatever forum or working party or sub-committee is established for that purpose. Without this input on behalf of the people on whom the decisions impinge, there is a high probability that any such review that a local authority will carry out will tend towards the self-congratulatory endorsement of existing patterns of provision.

The fourth requirement is to provide for some kind of continuity of policy review. Local authorities are not fulfilling their responsibilities if they merely pause to question how the black population are faring from the provision of services, before passing on to the next *ad hoc* issue. Rather, there is a responsibility for them to consider making a major and *continuing* contribution to the enhancement of opportunities for the people of the black communities; this will entail the long-term monitoring of the effects of policy change. Such continuity is only achieved when—whatever the set-up under section 71 of the 1976 Act—it involves the opposition parties, and thereby provides for the possibility of maintaining the continuity of effort through changes in political control.

If those are 'appropriate arrangements' for local authorities, they are obviously only just the beginning of the attack on racial discrimination and disadvantage that is being mounted by local authorities in some of our major cities.[10] It is only the beginning because the implications of such a policy review within individual service departments are quite profound. There are major areas of operation where local authorities need to reconsider and reshape what they are doing, to think about the use of specialist staff, and in some cases to consider the appointment of race relations units and advisers. They will need to think hard about the ways in which they spend the existing grants that come from central government, in particular those provided under section 11 of the Local Government Act 1966; section 11 is still described as our major financial programme for tackling racial disadvantage, although I am convinced that the major proportion of it is not used in that way. They will need to think about the ways in which they use their urban programme funds, the extent to which the black communities are involved in urban programme bids, and the actual distribution of benefits that follow from this joint local and central government funding arrangement. Overall, local authorities must consider equal opportunity in employment, as well as in service delivery; they will need to consider the operation of a system of ethnic record keeping for the assessment of who gets what—and who gets *where* and *when*—for these are the basic questions about equal opportunity in its broadest sense.[11]

Nor is this all. There is much that local authorities can do in the absence of a lead from central government to initiate and innovate, not just in developing their own programmes and policies (in respect of which they have a very considerable amount of autonomy), but also by influencing public opinion, by publicising the equal opportunity issues locally; and by representing the claims of their black populations to ministers and to other national bodies and inquiries. They can take the lead, and be seen to be doing so, thereby establishing it as a norm of political debate that we live in a multi-racial society.

The 'colour-blind' approach

If we ask how many local authorities actually do all these things, a rough judgement would be something like one in ten of those major authorities whose areas include substantial black populations.[12] Clearly something has intervened between the intentions (weak and half-hearted as they were) in section 71 of the Race Relations Act 1976, and current practice. Although practice is changing, it is changing very slowly; probably, given the critical state of race relations, too slowly.

Looking at the general picture, there are four distinct groups of local authorities within the fifty or sixty in whose decisions we should be interested.[13] First, there are the pacesetters; they are very few but surely include such places as Lambeth, Bradford and Brent. The pacesetters are in genuine dialogue with their local communities and are reviewing in a fundamental sense the impact of their decisions on the well-being of the local black population. They are each involved in trying to adapt their provision and their decisions to their particular local circumstances. As pioneers, they are necessarily learning not from others' but from their own mistakes; there are few such authorities, and doubtless those I have mentioned are only at the beginning of a long and difficult process.

There are three other major groups of authorities. There are those local authorities where politicians and officials are concerned and aware at some level that something is wrong, that they need to make some more appropriate provision, but they are not quite sure what they should be doing, or how they should be doing it. Below them is a group of others who have a dim awareness that something *might* be wrong, but who are unwilling to make any kinds of change, partly because of fear of what is sometimes described as 'a white backlash' (see Scarman, 6.32). Below them again is the fourth group, of those local authorities whose response to raising such questions tends to be 'there are no problems here'. 'We have a small "coloured" population', they are likely to say, 'and they are very well integrated and there is nothing we need to do.'

I want to consider the factors which seem to bear upon the two middle groups; those that are concerned but are not sure what they should be doing, and those that are vaguely aware but basically unwilling to do anything. The decisions that the policy-makers in these two groups of authorities take over the next few years will have major implications for the prospects of tackling the roots of the grievances that people in the black communities feel. Moreover, they will have major implications for the prospects for public order in the cities over the next decade.

The major areas of confusion within these local authorities who, at the present time, are not doing very much, relate to two particular issues. The first is what can be called the facts of racial disadvantage: the varieties of deprivation and disadvantage that people in the black communities experience disproportionately.[14] Such disadvantage is to be found in employment, in the allocation of benefits, in income, in education and in many other aspects of life-chances and welfare generally. Many of these disadvantages arise from being members of unskilled groups in the population. Some arise from newness to the country. Some are specific to people for whom English is not their first language.

Many of these aspects of disadvantage also arise from past discriminatory decisions or are compounded by present discrimination, direct or indirect, intended or unintended. It is important to keep the facts of *discrimination* in mind, for one of the obstacles to tackling what is often called 'racial disadvantage' is the tendency to reduce it to some other 'deracialised' aspect of disadvantage, and to claim that there is no essential basis for differentiation between the black and the white populations as such.[15] One version reduces racial disadvantage to disadvantage in a *locational* sense; some people happen to be concentrated in the inner cities. Another reduces it to disadvantage in a *linguistic* sense; people have not managed to learn English fast enough or, having learned it, fail to teach it to their children. Another variant focuses on *occupational* disadvantage, claiming that people from the black communities simply happen to be in certain occupational groups, and that these occupational groups are the ones that are suffering most from unemployment. Yet another leads people to say, 'we should not be talking about *race*, we should be talking about *class*'.

The point about this tendency among local councillors and officials is that it leads them to believe that the attack on racial disadvantage can be led by policies that are not race-specific. They claim that if they manage to solve the housing problems, or employment problems, then they will have solved the problem of being black in the inner city. Thus the preponderant tendency in British public policy is to maintain a colour-blind posture and to move readily from talking about race to talking about other—more familiar, or more apparently manageable—aspects of disadvantage. The assumption of this position is that if we suddenly came across the crock of gold and solved the housing problem overnight, or if the economy picked up and unemployment fell, then there would be nothing distinctive about being black in a white society. This I find implausible.

Confusion about the law

The second major area of colour-blindness within local government arises from a confusion about the law, particularly as it relates to discrimination and disadvantage. There is a great deal of confusion about the meaning of 'positive discrimination'. It is a confusion that Lord Scarman has done little to clarify (see Scarman, 6.30–6.32 and 9.4). There is a need for a major promotional and educative campaign among and within the local authorities themselves, for 'positive discrimination' tends to be used as a catch-all label to be attached to any lawful attempts towards positive action of the sort advocated by the Commission for Racial Equality. In particular, ethnic record keeping, that vital tool for the monitoring of public policy (see Scarman, 6.30), is dismissed in some local authorities as discriminatory and improper.

The Race Relations Act's major innovation was to outlaw *indirect* discrimination, under section 1(b) of the Act, and this is a fertile source of confusion. Indeed, I recently addressed a meeting of local authority chief executives, and had hardly begun to speak when one of them stopped me to ask the meaning of the term indirect discrimination. The fact that, despite his being interested enough to come to a meeting to discuss race relations, he did not know of the existence of this prohibition struck me as a very alarming comment on local government today.

The importance of indirect discrimination is that, for the greater part, it is the outcome of well intentioned, colour-blind actions. It is found as an unintended consequence of practices which seem on paper to be fair as between individuals from different ethnic groups, but in their outcomes are not fair, and are systematically unfair. Effect, and not intention, is what indirect discrimination is all about, and there is a sense in which the Race Relations Act, in embodying the concept of indirect discrimination, is probably ten years or so ahead of current practice in the public sector.

The problem about such confusion is that, within the public sector alone, decisions with possible discriminatory outcomes are taken by tens of thousands of individuals at all levels, down to low-level supervisors. If such decision-makers are maintained in a fog of confusion about positive discrimination and about indirect discrimination, then there is very little hope of the Race Relations Act having any bite whatsoever.

The resistance to examining the possibilities of indirect discrimination occurring is underpinned by the cultural convention of colour-blindness, of not differentiating the circumstances of people from the black and white communities. There is certainly a widespread sense that to differentiate between ethnic groups, in terms of their circumstances and their needs and their strengths and their contributions and so on, is itself discriminatory and possibly unlawful; that misunderstanding is a major barrier to any useful and progressive dialogue within local authorities. This resistance to differentiation is maintained by many Labour councillors, who have got a long record of opposing racism, who remember the anti-semitism of the 1930s, who are above all extremely reluctant to engage in any open and meaningful discussion of race and racial disadvantage. They have in a sense fallen into the racist trap of their own anti-racism.

It is this colour-blindness more than any other single factor which in my view sustains the greater proportion of our local authorities in practices which risk the maintenance of indirect discrimination. In so far as indirect discrimination is the heart of the Race Relations Act, colour-blindness subverts its intentions and thereby puts law enforcement on the defensive. As Lord Scarman said (Scarman, 6.35), 'What is required is a clear determination to enforce the existing law and a positive effort by all in responsible positions to give a lead on the matter'. That, precisely, is the challenge to local government.

Notes

In revising these remarks for publication I have tried to incorporate a number of useful points made at the Leicester Conference, in particular those by Councillors Stewart Lansley (Lambeth) and Phil Sealy (Brent) and by a number of other speakers.

1. *The Brixton Disorders, 10–12 April 1981: A Report by The Rt. Hon. The Lord Scarman, OBE*, HMSO, 1981; House of Commons, *Racial Disadvantage: Fifth Report from the Home Affairs Committee, Session 1980–1981*, HC 424–1, HMSO, 1981.
2. For changes in the spatial distribution of manufacturing industry see S. Fothergill and G. Gudgin, *Unequal Growth*, Heinemann, 1982; a more general review is given in K. Young and L. Mills, *Managing the Post-Industrial City*, Heinemann, 1983.
3. For an important account of these issues in one authority see H. Ouseley, *The System*, Runnymede Trust, 1981.
4. See S. Ollerearnshaw, 'The promotion of employment opportunity', in N. Glazer and K. Young (Eds.), *Ethnic Pluralism and Public Policy: Achieving Equality in the United States and Britain*, Heinemann, 1983.
5. Committee of Inquiry into the Education of Children from Ethnic Minority Groups, *West Indian Children in Our Schools*, HMSO, 1981.
6. See N. Connelly, *Social Services Provision in Multi-racial Areas*, Policy Studies Institute, 1981; J. Cheetham, *Social Work Services for Ethnic Minorities in Britain and the USA*, Oxford, Department of Social and Administrative Studies, 1981.
7. For an up-to-date review of the evidence see V. Karn, 'Race and housing in Britain; the role of the major institutions', in Glazer and Young, *Ethnic Pluralism and Public Policy*, *op. cit.*
8. See Commission for Racial Equality, *Local Government and Racial Equality*, London, The Commission, 1982; K. Young and N. Connelly, *Policy and Practice in the Multi-racial City*, London, Policy Studies Institute, 1981.

9. The following discussion draws upon research conducted with support from the Social Science Research Council. For further discussion see K. Young and N. Connelly, *After the Act: Policy Review for Local Authorities in Multi-racial Areas*, London, Policy Studies Institute, forthcoming.

10. For which see Ouseley, *The System*.

11. Commission for Racial Equality, *Why Keep Ethnic Records?*, London, The Commission, 1980; K. Young and N. Connelly, *Ethnic Record Keeping in Local Authorities: A Discussion Paper*, London, Policy Studies Institute, 1981.

12. This judgement is based on the collection, by PSI, of information from some fifty-nine local authorities selected according to demographic indicators of multi-ethnicity. The information was given in confidence in connection with the Institute's ongoing research in this field, and we do not identify particular authorities. Moreoever, this is a field in which change is rapid, if uneven. Accordingly, it is dangerous to take too static a view or to categorise any one authority too rigidly. It nonetheless remains my impression that real changes in local authority practice will take some years to implement.

13. Further discussion is given in K. Young, 'An agenda for Sir George: local authorities and the pursuit of racial equality', *Policy Studies*, 3(1), 1982.

14. See D. J. Smith, *Racial Disadvantage in Britain*, Penguin Books, 1977.

15. Although the concept of racial disadvantage incorporates the effects of past and present discrimination, it is sometimes used as if 'discrimination' and 'disadvantage' were quite independent aspects of black people's lives. Moreover, the term may, in loose usage, carry the connotation that 'disadvantage' is inherent in particular ethnic categories, rather than arising from the ways in which ethnic and 'racial' differences are construed in society.

PART 5

Scarman and After

CHAPTER 21

Scarman and after

JOHN BENYON

The authors of the essays in this book represent a wide variety of groups and opinions, and in each approach one or more the political perspectives outlined in Chapter 2 can be discerned. As Stan Taylor points out in that chapter, the Scarman Report can be criticised from each of these perspectives and indeed all the foregoing contributions have found faults, to a greater or lesser extent, in Lord Scarman's findings and recommendations.

Perhaps it can be taken as a measure of Lord Scarman's success that he is criticised by such a diverse group of people as journalists, police officers, community leaders, politicians, pressure group officials and academics. Perhaps also this variety of opinions illustrates the difficulties of reaching agreement on the ways of solving the problems highlighted by the riots and Lord Scarman's Report.

The Report itemised and stressed particular issues which arose from the disorders, and while the writers in this book do not necessarily agree with his emphases or with his particular recommendations, there does seem to be general agreement on the broad topics which require attention. The contributors appear to believe that a more reponsible attitude is needed by the news media and there also seems to be agreement, although with considerable differences of emphasis, that the police service should review its relations with the public. There is consensus that inner city problems and unemployment must be ameliorated, for 'good policing will be of no avail, unless we also tackle and eliminate basic flaws in our society' (Scarman, 9.4). And there seems to be a common concern that racial disadvantage and discrimination must be fought and eliminated.

'Urgent action is required'

But above all the Scarman Report was a call for action—a call echoed by the contributors to this book. 'Racial disadvantage is a fact of current British life', wrote Lord Scarman, and 'a significant factor in the causation' of the riots (Scarman, 9.1).

> *Urgent action* is required if the social conditions which underlay the disorders in Brixton and elsewhere are to be corrected (Scarman, 6.42, *emphasis added*).

Unfortunately, two years after this call was made there is little evidence of any such 'urgent action' to improve the problems of the inner cities, particularly unemployment and poor housing, or to lessen racial disadvantage and discrimination. The police service has taken action to implement some of Lord Scarman's proposals and greater stress has been laid on home beat policing in areas such as Brixton and Liverpool 8. However, complaints are still made in some places about bad police behaviour and the Police and Criminal Evidence Bill seemed only to stir further contention.

Throughout this book references have been made to various changes which have been brought in. In the next chapter, the ex-Minister of State at the Home Office, Timothy Raison, gives a positive account of action which the Government has taken or is considering. But despite these encouraging developments, there still appears to be a lack of co-ordinated and concerted action such as that taken in the United States from 1967 onwards. Disadvantage and racial discrimination will remain prevalent in our cities unless the Government initiates a far more purposeful and committed programme than it has so far. Cosmetic changes and 'tinkering' with police–community relations or the inner city policies are unlikely to eradicate the feelings of injustice and frustration which seem to have been instrumental in causing the riots.

Doubtless a number of those who participated in the 1981 riots did so because they enjoyed the 'fun' and excitement, and three of the contributions to Part 2 make this point. Running on the rampage in a riot appeals to some young people, as evinced by the occasional problems on Saturday afternoons after football matches. This does not appear to be a new phenomenon: in the 1960s, for example, the 'mods and rockers' outraged many people by rampaging through seaside resorts. Some commentators appeared to believe that the 1981 riots were simply a more serious manifestation of the football hooliganism syndrome. But this was not Lord Scarman's finding:

> The disorders were communal disturbances arising from a complex political, social and economic situation, which is not special to Brixton. There was a strong racial element in the disorders; but they were not a race riot. *The riots were essentially an outburst of anger and resentment by young black people against the police* (Scarman, 8.12; *emphasis added*).

In short, the message which comes out of the Scarman Report and several of the essays in this book is that if people are pushed too much and too often they will push back. Anger, resentment, bitterness and frustration can lie smouldering until a final indignity causes an eruption of rage and vengeance. It is clear that the police were the target of this rage, and if further riots are to be avoided, this build-up of anger and resentment must be prevented.

It is equally clear though that the complex social problems which Lord Scarman found must be improved. There is a great danger that many people in Brixton, Liverpool 8, Moss Side and elsewhere are becoming extremely disillusioned with the whole basis of government. The neglect of these areas, the high levels of unemployment and deprivation and the gulf between some members of the community and the police are likely to have serious repercussions for the government of such districts.

> Where any social group perceives government institutions as being indifferent to its needs, the authority and legitimacy of social controls ultimately promulgated by those same institutions will be increasingly questioned.[1]*

Youth demoralisation and estrangement

In the last decade or so a great deal has been said and written about the increasing problems of governing Britain. Richard Rose has pointed out that 'Britain enjoys, if that is the word, the ripest variety of prognoses of doom'[2] and in 1977 the median Briton was found to believe that there was almost a fifty–fifty chance of civil war in the years ahead.[3]

A number of different reasons have been offered for the perceived increasing difficulties of government. Among these, some have suggested that there is too much asked of government, which has become 'over-loaded',[4] while others have claimed that the rise of groups prepared to pursue ruthlessly their self-interest jeopardises democratic government.[5] This argument was developed by Brittan, alongside the view that the British system of political competition has led to the generation of excessive expectations among the population. As these expectations are unrealistically high, they cannot be met and consequently many people have become disenchanted with the political processes and institutions. However, says Brittan, we should also note that 'differences in status, because they lie in the eyes of the beholder, are potentially both more disruptive and more emollient than material differences'.[6]

This theme is developed by G. L. Field and J. Higley.[7] They claim that there is 'a serious weakening of western social orders' primarily because

---

* Superscript numbers refer to Notes at end of chapter.

young people 'see few opportunities for improving their status'. These writers take the view that a social order consists essentially of occupational and associated statuses, and when it fails to provide opportunities for people to improve their status the result is likely to be widespread alienation and rebellion by those affected. Field and Higley argue that many young people have quite high aspirations, but see their hopes dashed by unemployment. This social rejection leads to demoralisation which means that the young unemployed, and indeed those in employment who have dull and unsatisfying jobs, are likely to feel estranged from society and its predominant values. According to this view:

> The demoralised segments of western populations cannot be charmed into less angry, more allegiant postures by government programmes that merely seek to alleviate their material conditions. Many young people who belong to ethnic minorities and other disadvantaged groups, and who bitterly resent their exclusion from the workforce . . . now treat the dominant culture of the country in which they live as that of an enemy. . . . The bulk of the young people who hold this view will not train diligently for what they regard as menial, unworthy, make-work jobs. . . .[8]

Field and Higley conclude their rather depressing analysis by calling for a substantial reduction of western populations, through extensive encouragement of birth control, the creation of new and reasonably attractive jobs in areas such as environmental and 'human services' and 'a clearer recognition of the need for political élites to manage tensions and conflicts which can only be contained, not resolved'.

While this analysis seems unnecessarily pessimistic, and some of the prescriptions are both contentious and of doubtful practicality, the essential argument of youth demoralisation and alienation in inner city areas appears convincing. Lea and Young have identified a growing 'political marginalisation', characterised by 'powerlessness, alienation and deprivation to which the vicious circle of rising crime rates and violence, and the militarisation of policing, is a tragic response'.[9] It certainly seems reasonable to suggest that many of those who took part in the disorders were bitter and angry at what they saw as their rejection by society. The police were the targets because they were seen as a hostile force which was guilty of harassment and bullying behaviour, and also because they were representative of the established order—an order which the rioters considered offered them little hope or status. Perhaps this was the explanation being offered by Kenneth Oxford, Chief Constable of Merseyside, when he pointed out: 'I have no doubt that we are the readily identifiable symbols of authority and discipline which are anathema to these people.'[10]

As Basil Griffiths points out in Chapter 10, it is important to remember that some people will inevitably oppose representatives of authority, such as the police, preferring instead to lead a life of crime and violence, and the majority of people look to the police as their means of protection. However, it is clear that the most effective form of policing is when a close relationship based on trust exists between this majority and their police officers. Without this support and co-operation from the community the police find it increasingly difficult to operate effectively, for the information upon which they depend to solve most crimes ceases to be forthcoming.[11]

The most worrying development, then, is not that *some* young people display animosity towards the police but that *significant sections* of certain communities appear to lack confidence in them, leading to 'a serious breakdown in relations' (Scarman, 4.1–4.2). Incidents such as those described by George Greaves in Chapter 6 lead to a loss of faith by people in the operation of the political system in general, and the police service in particular. The police complaints system is one example of an institutional structure which leads people to question the effectiveness and fairness of government. In the triennial review report published in April 1983, the chairman of the Police Complaints Board, Sir Cyril Philips, seemed to suggest that the present procedures are not satisfactory. *The Observer* detailed a case where 'an innocent Nigerian student . . . was dragged from a car in London and assaulted by police so badly that one of his testicles was removed. The fourteen-month "investigation" has failed to identify the man's police assailants and has concluded that no further action is necessary.'[12] Despite the failure to discipline or charge any officers, the student was paid compensation of £4000 for his injuries by the Metropolitan Police.

Cases such as this must exacerbate the feelings of injustice and frustration already held by many people who have experienced unemployment and inner city neglect. For black people, these perceptions of oppression and rejection, and their consequent anger, must be heightened by encounters with racial abuse and harassment, and possibly actual assault, as well as the images peddled by the 'popular' press of black crime and violence.

Ineffectiveness and repudiation of political authority

Two essential elements of political authority are effectiveness and consent.[13] To be effective, a government must be able to take positive action to tackle problems, and needs to manage the increasingly complex set of arrangements that constitute the political system. Clearly a regime can be effective in that it is able to accomplish a cogent programme, without popular consent, depending instead on coercion, but it seems likely that effective and efficient action will be facilitated if the citizenry accept it voluntarily. Hence, 'the ideal government is a fully legitimate authority, enjoying both the consent of citizens and effectiveness in action'.[14]

If political institutions and processes fall into discredit some of the public are likely to withdraw their consent. Cumulative disappointment at policy failures and broken political promises, and increasing resentment at perceived injustices, may lead to disenchantment with the established procedures. This can result in the repudiation of political authority manifest as civic indifference, a refusal to comply with laws and directives or as open conflict and violence. The extent to which this has occurred in Britain is a matter of speculation, but it does seem that significant numbers of people in some city areas are increasingly disillusioned with the existing regime. The repercussions of a growing repudiation of the established system could obviously be very serious. Samuel Brittan, whose brother Leon in June 1983 became Home Secretary in Mrs Thatcher's Government, considered that there were two endemic threats to liberal representative democracy—the generation of excessive expectations, and the disruptive effects of the pursuit of group self-interest in the market place.[15] In a particularly sombre prognosis Brittan wrote:

> There could be a gradual process of disintegration of traditional political authority and the growth of new sources of power. Indeed, a continuation of present trends might lead to a situation where nothing remained of liberal democracy but its label. Nor need we assume that a new system will be repressive but efficient. It is just as easy to imagine a combination of pockets of anarchy combined with petty despotism, in which many of the amenities of life and the rule of law are absent, but in which there are many things which we will be prevented from doing or saying.[16]

This daunting prospect was outlined several years before the 1981 disorders, events which appeared to give testimony to the 'gradual process of disintegration of traditional political authority' of which Brittan warned. And some claimed that the Police and Criminal Evidence Bill, which failed to reach the statute book in 1983, illustrated the kind of repressive measure likely to erode liberal democracy; Lord Salmon, for example, stated:

> I think that there is a danger that the Bill brings Britain closer to being a police state.[17]

And a *Daily Mail* editorial considered it was:

> . . . more likely to threaten traditional liberties than to protect society against the evil doer . . . let us not clamp upon ourselves the apparatus of an authoritarian state.[18]

As a result of government ineffectiveness in dealing with problems such as inner city deprivation, youth unemployment, racial discrimination and police–community relations, the political regime appears to be increasingly questioned by significant sections of the urban population. The resultant alienation[19] of some of these people is aggravated by perceptions of injustice leading to diminishing political consent. This repudiation of political authority can be seen in what Peter Hall has described as 'the increasing political polarisation of British society'.[20] Only vigorous and committed action by government agencies will begin to reverse this trend: but so far this had not occurred.

Issues, action and good intentions

It was pointed out in Chapter 1 that even when a problem has gained attention, and been recognised as a legitimate matter for government involvement, there is no guarantee that a serious attempt will be made to solve it. Political and economic resources are limited and there are many demands for them. The proponents of a particular issue are competing with those in favour of different concerns and their success in ensuring action depends upon their political power. There are many power resources, such as money, knowledge, skills, status, possessions, access to the media, and these are obviously unequally distributed in society. Clearly, people living in British inner urban areas are likely to have less power resources than those in more affluent areas.

The exercise of political power is sometimes quite visible, such as, for example, a pressure group successfully campaigning on a particular issue. However, there is also another 'hidden face' of power, which is less overt and which involves 'creating or enforcing social and political values and institutional practices that limit the scope of the political process . . .'[21] According to this approach, some problems are prevented from becoming issues at all by the operation of non-decisions: 'the power to prevent issues and conflict from surfacing may be one of the most insidious forms of political power of all'.[22]

Steven Lukes has identified a 'third dimension' of power which may be exercised through the bias in 'the socially structured and culturally patterned behaviour of groups and practices of institutions',[23] and he claims that power is exercised over another person or group when their interests are adversely affected. Perhaps this form of power is illustrated by the figures announced in April 1983 which revealed that only those earning at least £29,567 a year were paying less direct taxes in 1983 than they were in 1979. Married couples with two children, earning the average income of £172 a week, were paying extra tax equivalent to 6.9 pence on the standard rate, while a poorer family on three-quarters of the average earnings had been even worse hit: their tax payments had risen from 1979 to 1983 in real terms by the equivalent of 7.9 pence on the standard rate of income tax.[24] There was little evidence that the wealthy had been actively campaigning for these changes, but nevertheless political power was exercised to further their interests to the detriment of the less well off.

These covert and insidious forms of power can greatly affect the outcomes of issues which appear on the political agenda. As discussed in Chapter 1, frequently the response is one of consensus seeking and cosmetic change, or the management of evidence or delay and emasculation. Even serious attempts to tackle an issue can be thwarted by lack of commitment and inaccurate information. Unless the proponents of an issue have sufficient power to ensure that it continues to receive attention, it may fade from the political agenda.

Attention has been drawn to the difficulty of sustaining interest in an issue by Anthony Downs, who outlined the five-stage 'issue-attention cycle'. Each stage may vary in duration, but the same sequence is usually followed.[25]

1. *The pre-problem stage:* some highly undesirable social condition exists, which may be of concern to experts and groups, but which has received little public attention; for example, racism and poverty in the United States.
2. *Alarmed discovery and euphoric enthusiasm:* the public suddenly becomes aware of and alarmed by the evils of a particular problem, often as the result of dramatic events—such as the American riots in 1967. Invariably there is great enthusiasm about solving the problem within a relatively short time.
3. *Realising the cost of significant progress:* gradually there is a spreading realisation that the cost of solving the problem is very high and may require sacrifices by large numbers of people, as the most pressing social problems often involve either exploitation of one group in society by another, or the prevention of one group from enjoying something that others want to keep for themselves.
4. *Gradual decline of intense public interest:* the public become discouraged, or they feel threatened, or they get bored and their desire to keep attention focused on the issue wanes, particularly if another issue is entering stage two.
5. *The post-problem stage:* the issue moves into a prolonged limbo—a twilight realm of lesser interest or spasmodic recurrences of interest. But the public has become aware of the problem and it may resurface sporadically, and new institutions and policies may have been created which are likely to continue to have some impact on the problem.

The issues raised by the riots seem to have passed some way through the issue-attention cycle. The problems of police relations with the community, and associated questions such as recruitment, discipline, equipment, complaints and accountability, were highlighted by the disorders and passed into stage two of the cycle. There was also 'alarmed discovery' of inner city deprivation, youth unemployment and racial disadvantage. The costs of solving some of these problems have been highlighted and stress has been laid on the claimed growth of crime in the cities. It seems that some of these issues have entered stage four of the cycle, where some people have become discouraged or bored. Yet others may feel threatened either by the financial costs of taking action or by the 'costs' of what has been portrayed as a softly-softly approach to crime.

In his account, Downs stressed the crucial importance of the news media in determining how long attention is focused on a problem. 'As soon as the media realise that their emphasis on this problem is threatening many people and boring even more, they will shift their focus to some "new" problem.'[26] If Downs's account is right, a government can delay action which it dislikes because of cost or ideological aversion until the issue disappears from the public agenda. Of course it is usually necessary for the authorities to do something, particularly if an inquiry has made positive recommendations, and it is possible that unless the root cause of the problems are tackled, the issues may again be thrust on to the agenda by dramatic events. But even such recurrences may fail to revitalise the issues if the news media does not report them, either as a matter of policy or because they believe the public's appetite for those topics has been sated.

A number of reports have indicated that further rioting, on a reduced scale, occurred in some areas in 1982 and 1983. In 1982 the media's attention was riveted on the South Atlantic and very few accounts of any disorders appeared in the press. One researcher reported that

> Many people in Toxteth believe that police and media are in a conspiracy of silence. 'Last summer's riots didn't stop', they say. 'They went on in different forms. It was the reporting that stopped.'

But Neil Lyndon did not feel there was a conspiracy of silence by the media; rather he considered that this failure to mention the events he had witnessed indicated something far worse.

> A 100-strong, stone-throwing mob, fighting riot police around a sealed-off major thoroughfare, has come to be seen as an unexceptional event in a section of a major British city.

> If such a riot goes unreported to society at large once, it can happen again and again. By such means, among many others, is a ghetto created—when the events that occur within it are not judged by the normal standards which pertain without.[27]

It seems then that Britain has a choice. Either we can take vigorous action to cure the problems which the riots and Lord Scarman's Report exposed or we can procrastinate and tinker, hoping that somehow the problems will go away, but more likely creating ghettos, characterised by deprivation and neglect, tough policing and disintegrating political authority.

In the next chapter, Timothy Raison outlines the Government's approach to Lord Scarman's findings and recommendations. He stresses that the challenge extends beyond government and the police, to every citizen and group.

The final word is left to the author of the Report which is the subject of so much scrutiny in this book. Lord Scarman's inquiry will long rank as one of the most important post-war investigations, but, as this chapter has iterated, his report is above all a call for action.

Well-meaning sentiments are no substitute for the resources and the action which are needed, for as G. B. Shaw pointed out, the road to hell is paved with good intentions. The riots may have had a cathartic effect on many of those involved, but violent outbursts are bound to recur unless the underlying problems are conquered. The war against deprivation and injustice in the cities and against unemployment, crime and undisciplined policing is a daunting one which requires unflinching determination. Such a crusade will entail some material sacrifices by the more affluent members of the population, and will threaten certain entrenched interests. But if urban violence is not to become endemic, and if British society is to profess liberty, compassion and civilised values, there is no alternative.

Notes

1. S. Field, 'Urban disorders in Britain and America', in S. Field and P. Southgate, *Public Disorder*, HMSO, 1982 (Home Office Research Study No. 72). p. 33.
2. R. Rose, 'Ungovernability: Is there fire behind the smoke?', *Political Studies*, Vol. 27, No. 3, September 1979, p. 352.
3. See *Euro-Barometre* (Commission of the European Communities, 1978), No. 8, pp. 28–35, quoted by Rose, *op. cit.*
4. See, for example, J. Douglas, 'The overloaded crown', *British Journal of Political Science*, **6**, (1976), and A. King, (Ed.), *Why is Britain becoming Harder to Govern?*, BBC Publications, 1976.
5. See, for example, S. Brittan, 'The economic contradictions of democracy', *British Journal of Political Science*, **5**, 1975, and R. Clutterbuck, *Britain in Agony*, Penguin, 1980.
6. Brittan, *op. cit.*, p. 157.
7. G. L. Field and J. Higley, 'The population surplus', *The Times Higher Education Supplement*, 15 October 1982, pp. 13–14.
8. *Ibid.*, p. 14.
9. J. Lea and J. Young, 'The riots in Britain 1981: urban violence and political marginalisation', in D. Cowell, T. Jones and J. Young, *Policing the Riots*, Junction Books, 1982, p. 20.
10. Quoted in M. Kettle, 'The Toxteth troubles', *New Society*, 9 July 1981, p. 60.
11. This argument is further discussed by Lea and Young, *op. cit.*

12. D. Leigh, 'Why police are not so good at helping their own inquiries', *The Observer*, 17 April 1983.
13. For full discussions of these aspects of political authority see R. Rose, 'Dynamic tendencies in the authority of regimes', *World Politics*, 1969, Vol. 21, and R. Rose, 'Ungovernability: Is there fire behind the smoke?', *op. cit.* Some of what follows is drawn from Rose's account.
14. R. Rose, 'Ungovernability: Is there fire behind the smoke?' p. 354.
15. Brittan, *op. cit.*
16. *Ibid.*, p. 155.
17. *The Standard*, 14 March 1983.
18. *Daily Mail* leader, 15 March 1983.
19. George Gaskell and Patten Smith were critical of the alienation argument and could find little evidence of alienation among the 240 young black and white Londoners who they interviewed. They found that the young blacks had positive attitudes towards training, the media and British people; see G. Gaskell and P. Smith, 'Are young blacks really alienated?', *New Society*, 14 May 1981. Lord Scarman drew attention to these findings and commented:

    > But it would be surprising if they did not feel a sense of frustration and deprivation. And living much of their lives on the streets, they are brought into contact with the police who appear to them as the visible symbols of the authority of a society which has failed to bring them its benefits or do them justice (Scarman, 2.23).

20. See P. Hall, 'Intervention in the new Britain', *The Geographical Magazine*, January 1982, Vol. 54, No. 1, p. 19.
21. P. Bachrach and M. Baratz, 'The two faces of power', *American Political Science Review*, Vol. 56, 1962, p. 948.
22. T. Benton, ' "Objective" interests and the sociology of power', *Sociology*, Vol. 15, No. 2, May 1981, p. 163. Benton offers a different view of power based on achievement of objectives.
23. S. Lukes, *Power: A Radical View*, Macmillan, 1974, p. 22.
24. 'Treasury admits 7p rise in average tax rate', *The Guardian*, 20 April 1983.
25. A. Downs, 'Up and down with ecology—the "issue-attention cycle" ', *The Public Interest*, No. 28, Summer 1972, pp. 38–50. The following account of the 'issue-attention cycle' is closely drawn from that given on pages 39–41.
26. *Ibid.*, p. 42.
27. N. Lyndon, 'Inside the ghetto', *The Sunday Times*, 4 July 1982, p. 17.

CHAPTER 22

The view from the Government

TIMOTHY RAISON[1]*

Both within the Home Office and in the Government as a whole, we recognise the need to see Lord Scarman's Report in the round, and to relate the parts to the whole. As the title of this piece implies, I shall focus on areas of government responsibility and action, but the responsibilities we face are not for the Government alone or indeed for the police alone. They are for society as a whole and for the attitudes and approach of us all. The need is for a community view, and to avoid selective or partial perception.

It was the Home Secretary who appointed Lord Scarman to conduct his Inquiry, the day following the serious disorders in Brixton in April 1981.[2] Deliberately his terms of reference extended beyond the events of the disorders and their immediate causes to the *underlying* causes.[3] This registered that we saw immediately both the gravity of the disorders and the complexity of the issues which were raised and needed to be tackled.

The Government responded immediately to the publication of Lord Scarman's Report. Consultation and discussion are among its central themes. Many of his recommendations and observations are deliberately expressed as principles and objectives. They are aims to which he invites all concerned to work constructively. For example, he hoped that his recommendations on policing would, in the words of the Report:

> help to provide an agenda for a continuing dialogue between the police and the public about the nature of policing in today's society (Scarman, 5.77).

But this does not mean that the Government has responded merely by promoting discussion of the Report. The Home Secretary made a statement to Parliament on the day of publication.[4] In that statement he accepted the general principles which the Report set out for policing policy; he accepted the need to develop formal arrangements in every police force area for consultation between the police and the community at different levels; he accepted the need for more effort to be put into training; and he accepted

---

* Superscript numbers refer to Notes at end of chapter.

that the procedure for handling complaints against the police must be substantially reformed. In the compass of a short initial statement on publication of a major report, none could have looked for firmer guidance of intent.

Of course, neither the Report itself nor the Government's response to it has been confined to issues of policing. In debates in Parliament,[5] and in action outside, we have addressed other issues, both in the light of the Report and in the context of general social policy. These include, for example, racial disadvantage and discrimination and the particular problems of the inner cities, and I shall refer to these later in my discussion. But I shall follow the order of Lord Scarman's Report by first considering policing issues.

Recruitment to the police service

The issue of police recruitment raises the related questions of whom we recruit, and how and for what they are trained. Lord Scarman said that vigorous action would be required to recruit more members of the ethnic minorities into the police, if the police service was to become more representative of the community it serves (Scarman, 5.6–5.13). I am sure we would all agree with this, but he also recognised that there were no easy options, such as the introduction of quota systems or a lowering of standards (Scarman, 5.7–5.8). Such devices might well provide more black policemen, but by dividing recruits into two categories—those who meet the normal entry requirements and those who do not—they could lead to all black officers being regarded as second-class policemen. That would not be in the interests of the ethnic minorities, the police service, or society as a whole.

So we are looking for substantial numbers of black candidates who meet the normal standards for appointment as a police officer. This will not be easy, for the screening procedures for candidates for the police service are rigorous and rightly so. A candidate who meets the minimum height requirements and satisfies the force medical officer that he is physically fit has to pass the standard educational test, unless he is exempt by virtue of his educational qualifications. He then has to satisfy a selection board that he has the right character for the job. If he passes the interview, detailed inquiries are made into his background. It is only when candidates get over all these hurdles that they are offered appointment as a constable.

The Edmund-Davies Report on police pay, published in July 1978,[6] revealed that nearly one-third of the candidates taking the standard entrance test were eliminated by it and that one-third of those who went on to appear before a selection board were rejected. After allowing for those rejected at other stages of the selection procedure, only 20 per cent of all applicants were accepted. At that time, nearly all police forces were desperate for recruits. Now, most forces outside London are up to strength and many have waiting lists. Even the Metropolitan Police are getting as many applications as they can handle. For some years now, the physical, educational and character standards demanded of recruits to the police service have been high. As the number of vacancies has fallen and the standard of applicants improved, they have become higher still. It is now very difficult to get into the police service. It is against this background that recruitment of members of the ethnic minorities must be considered.

Over the past ten years there has been a slow but steady growth in the number of black police officers. At the end of 1971 there were only 47. At the end of 1981 there were 339, including 138 in the Metropolitan Police.[7] But we still have a situation in which only one police officer in 400 is a member of the ethnic minorities. This is a matter of concern both to me and to the police service. We genuinely want more recruits from the ethnic minorities—not as a token gesture towards the improvement of race relations, but because the police service believes, as I believe, that the service should be truly representative of our multi-racial society.

Considerable efforts have been made both locally and nationally to attract more black recruits. For example, special national advertising campaigns were held over a period of three months in 1979 and six months during the winter of 1980–1, in which advertisements in the appropriate languages were published in the ethnic minority press. A similar three-month's campaign was conducted in mid-1982, but our efforts have not been as successful as we would have wished: more clearly needs to be done. We have therefore set up a special study group, with representatives of the Home Office, the local authority associations, the police staff associations, the Metropolitan Police and the ethnic minorities, to examine the steps which have already been taken to increase recruitment from the ethnic minorities and to consider what more might be done. The group began work in March 1982 and one of the ethnic minority representatives told us, for example, that advertising is likely to attract little response from the Asian communities: what they respond to is the personal approach. We must clearly learn from such advice: our efforts to attract ethnic minority recruits must be channelled in the right direction.

We need to look closely at the reasons why so many candidates from the ethnic minorities have difficulty with the standard entrance test. For one thing, we need to be sure that these tests are free from cultural bias. Arrangements have therefore been made for new tests to be scrutinised by independent experts before they are introduced.

We also need to establish whether there are any other respects in which candidates from the ethnic minorities start off at a disadvantage. With some, their limited knowledge of English may be a handicap, and we need to explore the best means of helping otherwise suitable applicants who find the written English tests an insurmountable obstacle. As I pointed out earlier, there can be no question of lowering standards. We could not accept candidates whose English is sub-standard, because they would not be able to cope with their initial training and they could certainly not cope with their subsequent duties. But we can see whether arrangements could be made to overcome this handicap.

We also want to ensure that good quality candidates are not rejected because of an over-rigid application of the minimum height requirements. Chief police officers have discretion to accept candidates of less than minimum height if they appear to possess other qualities and I hope that they will use this discretion in appropriate cases.[8] I must stress again that I am not advocating a lowering of standards. But I should certainly be concerned if an otherwise suitable candidate who was, for example, fluent in a language used by the Asian communities, were rejected because he was half an inch under the minimum height limit.

I recognise, as did Lord Scarman (Scarman, 5.6), that there is underlying hostility to the police, which is probably the major reason for our failure to attract more West Indian recruits. We shall do everything we can to overcome the problem but it would be unrealistic to think that there is any short-term solution. It is likely to be removed only when the present suspicions and misunderstandings have been removed and the ethnic minorities have achieved a better understanding of the role of the police service in this country and the opportunities offered by a police career.

Police training

As regards training, the Goverment fully accepts the importance Lord Scarman attaches to it, and the need for further improvements on the basis of Lord Scarman's recommendations are being examined in detail (Scarman, 5.16–5.32). This is being undertaken by the Police Training Council[9] which advises the Home Secretary on all major training matters.

We share Lord Scarman's particular concern about the need for adequate probationer training and aim to extend the present initial course at police training centres and improve the quality of the subsequent probationer training in individual forces.[10] Lord Scarman recommends that a recruit should receive at least six months of initial training at a training school and the remaining eighteen months of the probationary period largely on supervised practical experience of police duties (Scarman, 5.19 and 5.24). It would be unrealistic, however, to accept a target of six months without first knowing what the six months will contain, and it will be for the Police Training Council to advise on the length of initial training and on the best balance between central and in-force training, and between classroom training and practical training on the beat.

Lord Scarman points to three other areas where training needs to be increased and improved—race relations, public order and supervision and management (Scarman, 5.28, 5.29 and 5.33–5.37). Here too with the assistance of the Police Training Council we are looking again at existing arrangements and will take into account the need for common programmes and minimum standards.

Whilst accepting that general and specific improvements are needed, we must not lose sight of the fact that much excellent training is already given to police officers at all levels and that in some of the areas mentioned by Lord Scarman improvements have recently been made or are under way.

For instance, in the Metropolitan Police all ranks up to and including that of chief superintendent are given instruction in community and race relations, and 'street duty' courses have been introduced to instruct young constables in how best to deal with the public, including ethnic minorities, and to carry out these practical aspects of policing. The Metropolitan Police are also carrying out a thorough examination of the race relations content of their initial recruit training course, which was extended from fifteen to sixteen weeks in early 1982 and is now twenty weeks. The Metropolitan Police Force is being assisted in this by members of the ethnic minority communities. Initial courses for recruits to provincial forces also contain sessions on community and race relations and the nature and understanding of prejudice. These have also been recently revised with advice and assistance from ethnic minority representatives. Further training is given to recruits locally to meet local needs which, of course, can vary considerably from area to area.

We also accept the need for additional emphasis on the training of those with more police experience—especially in the area of supervision and management. This is essential and affects all ranks in the police service from chief officer to constable. Again there is already a considerable management and supervision input into existing police training. Improvements in the structure and content of 'command courses' at the Police Staff College, Bramshill, have already been made following a review by the Police Training Council. Following a further review it is intended to introduce a standard form of development course for inspectors throughout England and Wales.

Much valuable police training is therefore already taking place, but further major improvements will be introduced when the Police Training Council brings forward recommendations and as circumstances change.

The police and the community

I will now turn to a number of recommendations in the Report concerned with contact between the police and the public—the reinforcement and, where necessary, restoration of good relations between the two.

Firstly, Lord Scarman registered the importance of achieving a fair and effective police complaints procedure. In his response to the Scarman Report the Home Secretary immediately endorsed Lord Scarman's assessment that the machinery for dealing with complaints against the police was in need of reform if it is to command public confidence, and he announced his intention to bring forward proposals as soon as possible.[11] Very soon afterwards the Select Committee on Home Affairs announced that they were to conduct an enquiry into police complaints and related matters.[12] This was a welcome development because it gave all those concerned, not just those having statutory responsibilities, an opportunity to put forward their views for consideration. This enabled the difficult issues involved to be examined in the light of all the interests that have to be taken into account. Our own evidence to the Committee included proposals for introducing a new independent element at the *investigation* stage in relation to serious complaints. This would take the form of an assessor, entirely unconnected with the police, whose main function would be to ensure that the investigation is done expeditiously, thoroughly and impartially. We also put forward outline arrangements by which less serious complaints could be made subject to a new informal procedure, including an element of conciliation, on the lines recommended by Lord Scarman (Scarman, 7.24–7.26). Changes will require legislation and a Bill was put before Parliament late in 1982.[13]

Consultation and accountability

A second and important action we have taken is to seek to dispel a misconception about the philosophy of policing stated in the Report and which the Government endorses. The misconception is that the philosophy invites the police, in order to preserve the peace, to turn a blind eye to crime or to enforce the law differently for different sections of the community. To counter this, it has been right for us to emphasise Lord Scarman's strictures on law-breaking and the historical basis of his argument. He found the disorders inexcusable. In his words, the police officers who had to confront that fearful violence 'all deserve, and must receive, the praise and thanks of all sections of the community' (Scarman, 4.98). Similarly, it has been right to point out that the approach to policing in the Report does not excuse street crime and mugging. Lord Scarman's conclusion that there will be circumstances requiring saturation policing is, I am sure, correct (Scarman, 5.46). There is no question of impeding the police in their task of dealing with crime, and the Government is committed to helping to improve their effectiveness. There has been much progress in terms of pay, conditions, numbers of men and training, which combine to enhance efficiency. We have emphasised that consultation is not merely consistent with the primary task of increasing police effectiveness—it is an essential part of it.

We have, therefore, made clear our view that Lord Scarman's recommendations that there should be consultative machinery between the police and the community at different levels is crucial (Scarman, 5.69–5.71). It is a challenge not only to the Home Office and to the police service, but to the community at large. General policing policy is already a matter for discussion between chief constable and police authorities, but Lord Scarman's recommendation goes much wider than that. He reminded us that the essence of effective policing in a free society is full community support for the police, and a police service which is in tune with the needs and wishes of the community it serves (Scarman, 4.60).

Lord Scarman set his recommendation against a background of two traditional principles of policing in a free society (Scarman, 4.55–4.60). The first is consent and balance. He reminded us that, to secure the full consent of the community which is essential to effective policing, the police must strike a balance between the three elements of their work: preventing crime, protecting life and property, and maintaining a peaceful community (Scarman, 4.57 and 4.58). The first priority of the police is to preserve the peace. That does not mean turning a blind eye to crime. Lord Scarman made clear that the law must be firmly and fairly applied. But it does mean keeping in touch with the needs and wishes of all law abiding members of the community. That is no more than common sense.

The second principle is independence and accountability. The police must be independent in the decisions they make about tackling a particular type of crime, or enforcing the law in a particular case. No politician, no pressure group can—or should—direct the police (Scarman, 4.59). But the police must act within the law and they must remain accountable to the public they serve (Scarman, 4.60). Because the police are part of the community—not apart from it—they must be sensitive to the needs and wishes of that community.

The mechanisms for ensuring that policing policies reflect the needs and wishes of the community are accountability and consultation. Under the Police Act 1964 chief constables are accountable to their police authorities for the policing of their area. It may be that some authorities need to take a wider view of this aspect of their responsibilities than they have in the past (Scarman, 5.64–5.66). The Home Secretary has consistently encouraged this. It may also be that some chief constables should be readier than they have been to discuss their policies with their police authorities.

In London the constitutional position is different. The arrangement under which the Home Secretary is police authority for the Metropolis is of long standing.[14] Successive governments and the Royal Commission on the

Police in 1962[15] have consistently taken the view that the exceptional arrangement in London is justified by the nature of the problems of policing the capital city and seat of government; and also by the fact that the force provides a number of services on a national basis. And Lord Scarman recognised that there are good reasons for the 'national accountability' (Scarman, 5.68) of the Metropolitan Police. He added that he did not believe that Parliament would wish to see the ultimate responsibility for policing the nation's capital transferred from a senior cabinet minister accountable to Parliament and put in the hands of a local body, however important (Scarman, 5.68–5.69). That is also the Government's view. We nevertheless recognise that there is a local element in the accountability chain which may not always be adequately represented. That is why we are seeking to encourage the setting up of local consultation groups in London, and throughout the country, to extend and improve the links between the police and the communities they serve.

Local consultation can promote better understanding between police and public. The police can explain what they are doing, what the problems are, and how they are tackling them. And in turn they can learn about the local community's perceptions of the problems and their expectations of the police.

Lord Scarman said that consultation arrangements should be backed by legislation, but no law made by Parliament can compel people to talk to each other, and to listen to each other's problems. Equally the efforts made by chief police officers and police authorities will be in vain if they meet with apathy or half-hearted public support. Consultation arrangements must reflect the needs and wishes of the community and be able to work in practice. For this reason we consulted widely with chief constables and police authorities, and Home Office officials visited a number of police areas to find out about the various arrangements—some formal, many informal—that already existed for consultation between the police and the community. From this work we have drawn up guidelines on procedure and best practice for consultation which will form a framework for national policy adaptable to local needs.[16]

One point that has come across very clearly is that the guidelines should be flexible. They must complement, and not cut across, the good work that is already being done. And they have to be adaptable to local needs because in Leicestershire, for example, the sort of consultation arrangements that might fit the centre of the city could well not be suited to the more rural parts of the county.

Consultation must be a two-way process. It will not work if minds are closed to the difficulties of the police. There is often great misunderstanding about what the police and the law can do. Consultation meetings can provide a forum for the police to explain how they carry out their work and how the law operates. With greater understanding and mutual support the police will be able to serve a community more effectively.

Racial disadvantage and inner cities

I have considered at some length the re-examination and, where necessary, the adaptation, of aspects of policing because we share Lord Scarman's view that the police have a critical role in maintaining the stability of our society. But the social problems of the community, and not least those of the ethnic minorities and of the inner cities, go far beyond the matter of policing alone.

As Lord Scarman made clear in his Report, social conditions cannot be ignored in assessing the causes of the riots and drawing lessons for the future from them (Scarman, 6.1–6.4). Lord Scarman identified the problems facing the inner cities as being of special relevance, and he referred particularly to the disadvantage experienced by many members of the ethnic minority communities (Scarman, 6.5–6.11). A disproportionately large number of the ethnic minorities live in the run-down inner areas of our major cities and they are thus disproportionately victims of urban decay, economic decline, an unattractive environment, poor housing, poor employment and employment prospects, and low levels of educational attainment. For the ethnic minorities these problems are compounded by factors that apply uniquely to them—newness to British society, cultural differences, language difficulties, and, regrettably, racial discrimination.

As a government, we know how important it is to tackle the problems of the run-down inner cities and especially racial disadvantage. Immediately after the 1981 disorders Michael Heseltine and I spent two weeks in Merseyside, the scene of some of the worst troubles, where there are areas of substantial deprivation. We visited these areas; we spoke to many of the people who live there and are victims of the deprivation; we learnt of the problems at first hand. Ours was a relatively brief visit but following upon it the *Merseyside Task Force* was set up under Michael Heseltine's direction to seek new ways of tackling the inner city problems in the area. The *Task Force* has a wide remit but it will be taking particular account of the need to tackle disadvantage among the ethnic minority groups. This is an important initiative and I am sure that the conclusions of the *Task Force* will be relevant to areas besides Merseyside which experience similar problems.

Identification of the problem is, of course, essential before solutions can be applied. In the field of racial disadvantage it is necessary to have factual information about how ethnic minorities fare compared with the rest of the population, for otherwise we have no basis for assessing what remedial action may be appropriate. It is clearly necessary, therefore, to have available relevant data. I can well understand that some people may be concerned about the possible misuse of this information, but it is a vital element in the attack on racial disadvantage. That is why the Government decided to conduct an experimental survey of the ethnic origins of certain grades of its own staff in the civil service, and this survey was carried out in Leeds in mid-1982. We hope that this example will dispel any remaining fears there may be among the ethnic minorities about the need for monitoring of this kind. We also hope that it will establish the relevance of ethnic monitoring to programmes for combating racial disadvantage, and serve as an example to other large employers in both the public and private sectors.[17]

Resources are, of course, an important factor and much money is already being made available, for example by means of the grants under section 11 of the Local Government Act of 1966. The level of grant to local authorities is currently running at more than £70 million a year. This is a substantial sum and it is important to ensure that the money is properly used. The arrangements for the grant have been criticised in the past, notably in the Home Affairs Committee's findings.[18] The Government agreed that the arrangements can be improved. Our proposals for change were outlined in the recent White Paper.[19]

We have abolished the 'ten year rule': the definition of 'Commonwealth immigrant' has been extended to include all first generation immigrants to this country, no matter how long they have lived here. The 'two per cent rule' has also been abolished, in order to encourage local authorities with smaller proportions of Commonwealth immigrants to apply for grant. Local authorities have been asked to consult their local Commonwealth immigrant community about any post before applying for grant. This will ensure that new posts are designed to meet local needs. The present formula arrangements for calculating eligibility for generalist posts has been dropped, and replaced by more workable procedures. We are conducting a review of existing posts—some of which have been in existence for twelve years or more—to see if they still meet the needs of the Commonwealth immigrant community and local authorities will be asked to show that any new post meets the criteria for the payment of grant, every three years from the creation of the post.

These arrangements will, therefore, be better attuned to meeting present-day needs and to directing the grant more effectively in fighting racial disadvantage.[20]

Substantial resources are also available under the Urban Programme, which has a vital part to play in tackling the problems of the inner cities. In recognition of this the Government has increased very significantly the sums available to inner city areas under the Urban Programme: in the year 1982–3 this was a total of £270 million—an increase of £60 million.

But it is not of itself sufficient to provide the resources; Lord Scarman laid stress on the need to ensure that they are properly directed, and that local communities are involved fully and effectively in discussions about the use to which they are put (Scarman, 6.5–6.9). Local authorities are responsible for providing many of the services relevant to the alleviation of disadvantage. The Government has written to the leaders of Partnership and Programme authorities and to the chairmen of the local authority associations about the importance of taking particular account of ethnic minority needs. Arrangements are also being made for representatives of government departments and the local authorities to meet to discuss ways of improving the effort against racial disadvantage. Many local authorities have developed good practice in a whole range of aspects of this problem, but it is important that other authorities get to hear of what can be done.

The appointment of Sir George Young as Minister with special responsibility for race matters in areas falling within the ambit of the Department of the Environment (which includes the inner cities) is a further significant example of the Government's commitment to tackling the problems of racial disadvantage.

As Lord Scarman recognised, it is not for the Government alone to find solutions to these problems (Scarman, 6.8–6.9). The private sector also has a contribution to make to the regeneration of the inner cities, and I am glad to say that it recognises this. A number of leading financial institutions have seconded some of their best managers to work with the Government to help find ways of improving co-operation with the private sector on inner city problems. Other initiatives are under way with the private sector in an attempt to improve facilities for encouraging and helping black businessmen. These positive developments are very much to be welcomed, but they represent only a beginning; I am confident we shall see a greater involvement of the private sector in these areas in the future.

Local people also have a key role to play. Some local authorities already make serious efforts to involve local people, not just from the ethnic minorities but from community and voluntary organisations at large, in planning and in the provision of amenities and projects. Lord Scarman has pointed to the wealth of voluntary effort and goodwill which is to be found in the inner city areas (Scarman, 6.7). It is important to harness these valuable resources in ways which can most benefit the local community. Again, the dissemination of good practice is vital.

In discussing racial disadvantage Lord Scarman referred to the need for 'positive action' to help the ethnic minorities (Scarman, 6.32). This is a difficult and highly controversial area, and it is important to be clear about what is meant by the term 'positive action'. Some interpret it as meaning 'positive discrimination' or 'reverse discrimination' which would involve giving conscious advantages to members of the ethnic minorities in, for example, employment. This might involve such measures as ethnic quotas for workforces, lower standards for certain occupations and similar measures. Neither Lord Scarman nor the Government has suggested that such measures should be introduced.

In the Government's view, the needs of the ethnic minorities should be met, as far as possible, in the same way, through the same spending programmes, as the needs of the rest of the community. It is of course important that the provision of the services should take full account of the particular needs of the ethnic minorities, and that the delivery of these services should be matched, wherever possible, to those needs. However, as I have already explained, it is clear that the needs of the ethnic minorities will sometimes be greater than or, indeed, different in kind from those of the rest of the population. They are not alone in this: there are other groups in our society with exceptional needs. Where this is the case and where these groups are as a result placed at a disadvantage the Government believes that it is right to make special provision to redress the imbalances and to enable them to stand four-square with the rest of the community. This is the Government's understanding of 'positive action'. It is not to give certain groups an unfair advantage, which could lead to resentment on the part of others. *It is to bring the disadvantaged minority up to the level of the majority.*

Conclusion—the challenge to us all

I have concentrated on some of the aspects of Lord Scarman's Report and the issues to which it relates in which I have a particular interest as a Home Office minister. I should like to conclude by summarising the Government's approach to Lord Scarman's Report. In its welcome of his Report and the action which it has taken in its light, we have made it clear that we regard Lord Scarman's work as having considerable and wide-ranging significance. The theme of the Report is that of the fundamental conditions of a fair and peaceful society, with the freedom for ordinary men and women to move safely about their business and to be treated justly under the law.

From the widespread breakdown of order in 1981, the Report takes us forward to an understanding of how these objectives can be achieved in modern conditions. The Report therefore offers broad opportunities. Properly, it also identifies heavy responsibilities. Many rest with the Government, and I have attempted to outline our commitment to discharge them. But as I stressed at the beginning, the challenge extends beyond Government, to every citizen and to the organisations, groups and interests which make up our society. We all share the responsibility to promote the conditions in which violence is rejected and to develop the peaceful resolution of the difficulties of a complex, multi-racial late-twentieth-century industrial democracy.

Notes

1. This is an edited version of the speech made by Timothy Raison at the Leicester Conference; these footnotes have been added by the editor. Mr Raison was then Minister of State at the Home Office and among the subjects for which he had responsibility were immigration and nationality, human rights and race relations. In January 1983 he became Minister for Overseas Development, a post he retained in the Government formed by Mrs Thatcher in June 1983.
2. In the Warrant of Appointment the Home Secretary, William Whitelaw, stated: 'In pursuance of the powers vested in me by section 32 of the Police Act 1964, I . . . hereby appoint the Right Honourable Lord Scarman to inquire urgently into the serious disorder in Brixton on 10 to 12 April 1981 and to report, with the power to make recommendations.'
3. The Home Secretary elaborated on the Inquiry's terms of reference in a statement to the House of Commons; see the House of Commons Official Report (*Hansard*), 13 April 1981, cols. 21–31.
4. *Hansard*, 25 November 1981, cols. 891–900.
5. The first debate in the House of Commons took place on 10 December 1981; see *Hansard*, 10 December 1981, cols. 1001–1080.
6. Committee of Inquiry on the Police (Chairman: Lord Edmund-Davies), *Reports on Negotiating Machinery and Pay* (Cmnd 7283), HMSO, 1978.
7. By late 1982 the figures had risen further: 175 black and brown officers in London (out of some 26,000 officers) and 414 in the whole of England and Wales, out of over 120,000. The target for London was 200 by the beginning of 1983. (See *The Observer*, 7 November 1982.)
8. One authority has put the following view: 'The minimum height requirement effectively rules out most Asians from enrolling: Gujuratis, for instance, have an average height of only 5 ft 5 in, while Gurkhas—not noticeably refused entry to the British Army—have an average of 5 ft 4 in. The Police Federation defend the height rule with the somewhat sweeping assertion that "there is a tendency for small men to make up by truculence what they lack in authority"'; see B. Whitaker, *The Police in Society*, Sinclair Browne, 1982, p. 119.
9. The Police Training Council is composed of representatives of the local authority associations, the Home Office, and the three police associations—Chief Police Officers, Police Superintendents and the Police Federation.
10. The length of initial training for recruits to the Metropolitan Police was increased to twenty weeks from January 1983. Continuing supervision for the recruits after they begin active police work has been introduced and other innovations—such as 'human awareness' training—have been brought in.
11. See *Hansard*, 25 November 1981, cols. 891–900.
12. *Police Complaints Procedures: Fourth Report from the Home Affairs Committee, Session 1981–82*, HC98–I, HMSO, 1982; see also *Police Complaints Procedures: The Government's Reply to the Fourth Report from the Home Affairs Committee, Session 1981–82*, HC98–I (Cmnd 8681), HMSO, October 1982.
13. The Police and Criminal Evidence Bill (1982–83, HCB 16) received its first reading on 17 November 1982, and during its passage through Standing Committee several amendments were incorporated. The Bill failed when Parliament was dissolved on 13 May 1983, but further legislation is expected from the new Government.
14. See section 62 and schedule 8 of the 1964 Police Act and sections 1, 4 and 5 of the Metropolitan Police Act 1829 (as later amended).
15. Royal Commission on the Police, *Interim Report* (Cmnd 1222), HMSO, 1960; *Final Report* (Cmnd 1728), HMSO, 1962.
16. The Police and Criminal Evidence Bill (1982–83, HCB 16) contained provisions for statutory consultation in England and Wales, including London. Two Lambeth MPs—Mr John Fraser and Mr John Tilley—tried to strengthen the provisions while the Bill was in committee, in February 1983. They sought to define membership and to oblige police to consult the committees about local operations, but their amendments were not accepted.
17. Home Affairs Committee, *Ethnic and Racial Questions in the Census, Session 1982–83*, HC33, HMSO, 1983.

18. Home Affairs Committee, *Racial Disadvantage: Fifth Report from the Home Affairs Committee, Session 1980–81*, HC424–I, HMSO, 1981, paras. 10–11.

19. *Racial Disadvantage: The Government Reply to the Fifth Report from the Home Affairs Committee, Session 1980–81*, HC424 (Cmnd 8476), HMSO, January 1982, pp. 10–11.

20. The new guidelines were introduced in November 1982 but were criticised for being too timid; see *The Guardian*, 18 November 1982.

An epilogue

LORD SCARMAN

One contributor contrasts the brevity of the Scarman Report with the length of the United States' *Report of the National Advisory Commission on Civil Disorders*, 1968 (the Kerner Report)—to the disadvantage, as I read the comment, of the Scarman Report. The contrast does, indeed, exist. The Scarman Report was the work of one inquirer assisted by two able and dedicated secretaries; and the inquiry and the drafting of the Report were completed within six months of the disorders. The size of the team and the speed of the work should be contrasted with Kerner's: and the value of a report available to all before public memories had grown dim was, I believe, substantial.

Be that as it may be, what has happened to the Report and its recommendations? Have they been remaindered to a footnote in the history books? Have they made any impact? Has society reacted? Are things better, or worse, as a result of the Report? Or have we moved on our way to whatever may be our journey's end, uninfluenced by it?

The story of the disorders themselves has proved to be itself a therapy. Although the Inquiry and Report are criticised by some for not inquiring in depth into specific incidents of alleged police misconduct, the story has been accepted as a faithful account of the course of events. The conclusion that the disorders were 'communal disturbances arising from a complex political, social and economic situation . . . not special to Brixton' and that they were 'an outburst of anger and resentment by young black people against the police' is now beyond challenge and has become one of the unspoken assumptions upon which social and police reforms are discussed and promoted.

Policing

When one turns to the finding that neither the police nor the local bodies can escape responsibility for the breakdown of relationships between the police and the community, a similar observation may be made. The police have learnt the lesson: and their efforts to mend fences—particular in Lambeth and Liverpool—are notably significant. The police are trying to recruit members of the ethnic minorities: they are already tackling the problems of training, supervision, and monitoring so as to eliminate, or at the very least to diminish, racial prejudice within the force; and the philosophy of the Home Beat Officer has been accepted and is being put into practice. A sad omission, however, is the lack of will to include in the Discipline Code a specific offence of racially prejudiced conduct.

The Report has helped to bring to public attention the vexed and controversial questions of police consultation and accountability. The need for consultation at local level is now fully accepted. The controversy over accountability is not yet solved. On neither question has the Report been ignored. Its recommendation for a statutory solution has been accepted, though opinions differ as to the nature of the solution. But two vitally important recommendations relating to the police are, I fear, very much more doubtful of implementation, namely:

> lay police station visitors; and
> reform of the police complaints procedure.

Both go to the root of the problem of public confidence in policing methods, attitudes, and conduct. One can only hope that there will be legislation on these two matters as well as on consultation and accountability when the new Parliament assembles.

Law reform

The Report has had, I believe, a negative success. It has killed stone dead the proposal for a new Riot Act. It has persuaded the authorities that there is no need to amend the law in order to impose a 'selective' ban on processions and street demonstrations. Panic legislation against the emergence of further disorder has been avoided. On the positive side, it will be necessary to maintain pressure for the implementation by statute of the police reforms I have mentioned and to ensure that any new statutory 'stop and search' power is subject to effective safeguards.

Social policy

There are still no signs of 'an effective co-ordinated approach to tackling inner city problems'. But government at all levels has reacted favourably, and in some respects strongly, to three particular needs exposed by the Report:

> housing,
> education,
> employment.

It is not possible even to hazard a guess as to the extent to which Parliament or government will be prepared to develop the Report's recommendation for positive discrimination in these areas. But, as the Report indicates, a start is possible on the basis of sections 35 to 38 of the Race Relations Act 1976. The principle is already in our law.

Conclusion

The Report has not been shelved. It is having a continuing influence on all concerned with community–police relations. Much remains to be done: but much has already been done. We are now, as a society, aware of the racial disadvantage under which many of the ethnic minorities labour, of their frustrations, and of the risk of alienation. We know that we are a multi-racial society and we are beginning to tackle the problems. Even if the Report had achieved no more than an awakening, it would have served a useful purpose. But it has, in truth, done much more, as is evident from the distinguished contributions to which these few words of mine are an epilogue.

25 May 1983   *Scarman*

Select bibliography

There is a large and growing literature on the topics covered in this volume, and a comprehensive bibliography would probably merit a book of its own. The follow ing selection of books and articles is grouped under five broad headings nd the attention of readers is also drawn to sources referenced at the end of many of the chapters.

Accounts and explanations of civil disorders

Allen, V. L., 'Toward understanding riots: some perspectives', *Journal of Social Issues*, **26**, 1 (1970).
Anning, N., 'How the police swamped Brixton', *The Leveller*, **63** (August 1981).
Bedford, C., *Weep for the City*, Tring: Lion, 1982.
Benewick, R. and Smith, T. (Eds.), *Direct Action and Democratic Politics*, London: Allen & Unwin, 1973.
Betz, M., 'Riots and welfare: are they related?', *Social Problems*, **21**, 3 (1974).
Bristol TUC, *Slumbering Volcano? Report of an Enquiry into the Origins of the Eruption in St. Paul's, Bristol on 2 April 1980*, Bristol, 1981.
Brooke, R., *Liverpool as it was During the Last Quarter of the Eighteenth Century*, Liverpool: Mawdesley, 1853.
Bunyan, T., 'The police against the people', *Race and Class*, Autumn 1981–Winter 1982.
Canetti, E., *Crowds and Power*, Harmondsworth: Penguin, 1981.
Caplan, N. S. and Paige, J. M., 'A study of ghetto rioters', *Scientific American*, **219**, 2 (1968).
Cashmore, E. and Troyna, B. (Eds.), *Black Youth in Crisis*, London: Allen & Unwin, 1982.
Charlesworth, A., *An Atlas of Rural Protest in Britain, 1548–1900*, London: Croom Helm, 1982.
Chetwin, R., 'Brixton and after—discussion', *Marxism Today*, September, 1981.
Cloward, R. A. and Piven, F. F., *The Politics of Turmoil: Essays on Poverty, Race and the Urban Crisis*, New York: Pantheon, 1974.
Clutterbuck, R., *Britain in Agony*, Harmondsworth: Penguin, 1980.
Cohen, N. E. (Ed.), *The Los Angeles Riots: a Socio-psychological Study*, New York: Praeger, 1970.
Cohen, S., *Folk Devils and Moral Panics*, St. Albans: Paladin, 1973.
Cole, G. D. H. and Postgate, R., *The Common People, 1746–1946*, London: Methuen, 1961.
Commission for Racial Equality, *Youth in a Multiracial Society: The Fire Next Time*, London: CRE, 1980.
Critchley, T. A., *The Conquest of Violence*, London: Constable, 1970.
Cronin, J. E. and Schneer, J. (Eds.), *Social Conflict and the Political Order in Modern Britain*, London: Croom Helm, 1982.
Dahrendorf, R., *Class and Class Conflict in Industrial Society*, London: Routledge & Kegan Paul, 1959.
Deakin, N. D., 'Lord Scarman's "Bran-tub" ', *The London Journal*, **8**, 1 (1982).
Donajgrodzki, A. P. (Ed.), *Social Control in Nineteenth Century Britain*, London: Croom Helm, 1977.

Douglas, J. D., *American Social Order*, New York: Free Press, 1971.
Dunbabin, J. P., *Rural Discontent in Nineteenth Century Britain*, London: Faber, 1974.
Elmes, F., 'Mods and Rockers', *Police Review*, **22** (June 1964).
Endelman, S. (Ed.), *Violence in the Streets*, London: Duckworth, 1969.
Farman, C., *The General Strike*, London: Panther, 1974.
Field, S. and Southgate, P., *Public Disorder*, Home Office Research Study No. 72, London: HMSO, 1982.
Fogelson, R. M., *Violence as Protest: a Study of Riots and Ghettos*, New York: Doubleday, 1971.
Fogelson, R. M. and Hill, R. B., *Who Riots? A Study of Participation in the 1967 Riots*, Supplementary Studies for the Kerner Commission, Washington: US Government Printing Office, 1968.
Foster, J., *Class Struggle and the Industrial Revolution*, London: Oxford University Press, 1973.
Fowler, N., *After the Riots*, London: Davis-Poynter, 1979.
Freedman, J., *Crowding and Behaviour*, New York: Viking, 1975.
Gaskell, G. and Smith, P., 'Are young blacks really alienated?', *New Society*, 14 May 1981.
Gattrell, V. A. C. *et al.* (Eds.), *Crime and Law*, London: Europa, 1980.
Glazer, N., 'The Scarman Report: an American view', *The Political Quarterly*, **53**, 2 (April–June 1982).
Graham, H. D. and Gurr, T. R. (Eds.), *Violence in America: Historical and Comparative Perspectives*, London: Sage, 1979.
Grew, R. (Ed.), *Crises of Political Development in Europe and the United States*, Princeton: University Press, 1978.
Gurr, T. R., 'A causal model of civil strife', *American Political Science Review*, **62** (1968).
Gurr, T. R., *Rogues, Rebels and Reformers*, Berkeley: Sage, 1976.
Hall, S., 'Summer in the city', *New Socialist*, September–October 1981.
Havighurst, A. F., *Britain in Transition*, Chicago: University of Chicago Press, 1962.
Hibbert, C., *King Mob*, London: Longmans, 1958.
Hobsbawn, E. J., *Primitive Rebels*, Manchester: University Press, 1959.
Humphries, S., *Hooligans or Rebels?*, Oxford: Blackwell, 1983.
Hytner, B. *et al.*, *Report of the Moss Side Enquiry Panel to the Leader of the Greater Manchester Council*, Manchester, 30 September 1981.
James, C. L. R., 'An accumulation of blunders', *New Society*, 3 December 1981.
Jardine, J., 'Chairman's conference address to the Home Secretary', *Police*, **13**, 10 (June 1981).
Joyce, P., *Work, Society and Politics*, London: Methuen, 1982.
Kamm, J., *Rapiers and Battleaxes*, London: Allen & Unwin, 1966.
Katanka, M. (Ed.), *Writers and Rebels*, London: Charles Knight, 1976.
Kerner, O. *et al.*, *Report of the National Advisory Commission on Civil Disorders*, Washington: US Government Printing Office, 1968; reprinted as *Report*, New York: Bantam Books, 1968.
Kettle, M., 'The evolution of an official explanation', *New Society*, 3 December 1981.
Kettle, M. and Hodges, L., *Uprising! The Police, the People and the Riots in Britain's Cities*, London: Pan, 1982.
Le Bon, G., *The Crowd: A Study of the Popular Mind*, New York: Viking, 1960.
Leech, K., *After Scarman?*, Leicester: Diocese of Leicester Board for Social Responsibility, 1982.
McCone, J. A. *et al.*, *Governor's Commission on the Los Angeles Riots*, Los Angeles: State of California, 1965.
Mackenzie, W. J. M., *Power, Violence, Decision*, Harmondsworth: Penguin, 1975.
McPhail, C., 'Civil disorder participation: a critical examination of recent research', *American Sociological Review*, **36** (1971).
Manning, M., 'At the roots of a black riot', *Community Care*, 13 October 1976.
Marcuse, H., *Eros and Civilisation*, London: Sphere, 1969.
Mark, Sir R., 'The Metropolitan Police and political demonstrations', *Police Journal*, July–September 1975.
Marlow, J., *The Peterloo Massacre*, London: Panther, 1971.

Marsden, D., *Workless*, London: Croom Helm, 1982.

Marx, G. T., *Protest and Prejudice: a Study of Belief in the Black Community*, New York: Harper & Row, 1967.

Masotti, L. and Bowen, D. (Eds.), *Riots and Rebellion*, California: Sage, 1968.

Mather, F. L., *Public Order in the Age of the Chartists*, Manchester: University Press, 1959.

Merseyside Police Authority, *The Merseyside Disturbances: the Role and Responsibility of the Police Authority*, Liverpool: Merseyside Police Authority, December 1981.

Momboisse, R. M., *Community Relations and Riot Prevention*, Springfield, Illinois: Charles Thomas, 1967.

Moonman, E., *Copycat Hooligans*, London: Centre for Contemporary Studies, 1981.

Morris, M., *The General Strike*, Harmondsworth: Penguin, 1977.

Mowat, C. L., *Britain Between the Wars*, London: Methuen, 1956.

Musgrove, F., *Youth and the Social Order*, London: Routledge & Kegan Paul, 1964.

National Advisory Committee on Criminal Justice Standards and Goals, *Disorders and Terrorism: Report of the Task Force*, Washington: US Government Printing Office, 1976.

New Community, **9**, 2 (Autumn 1981), 'Inner City Blues'.

Oberschall, A., *Social Conflict and Social Movements*, Englewood Cliffs: Prentice-Hall, 1973.

Pearce, E., 'Copping out—in malign neglect', *Police*, **14**, 4 (December 1981).

Phillips, D., *Crime and Authority in Victorian England*, London: Croom Helm, 1974.

Pryce, K., *Endless Pressure*, Harmondsworth: Penguin, 1979.

Quinault, R. and Stevenson, J. (Eds.), *Popular Protest and Public Order*, London: Allen & Unwin, 1978.

Roberts, R., *The Classic Slum*, Harmondsworth: Penguin, 1973.

Rock, P., 'Rioting', *London Review of Books*, 17–30 September 1981.

Rudé, G., *The Crowd in History*, New York: Wiley, 1967.

Scarman, Lord, *The Red Lion Square Disorders of 15 June 1974* (Cmnd 5919), London: HMSO, 1975.

Scarman, Lord, *Report of Inquiry into Dispute between Grunwick Processing Laboratories and Members of APEX* (Cmnd 6922), London: HMSO, 1977.

Scarman, Lord, *The Brixton Disorders, 10–12 April 1982* (Cmnd 8427), London: HMSO, November 1981.

Sears, D. O. and McConahay, J. B., *The Politics of Violence: the New Urban Blacks and the Watts Riot*, Boston: Houghton Miflin, 1973.

Sennett, R. (Ed.), *The Psychology of Society*, New York: Vintage, 1977.

Shipley, P., *Revolutionaries in Modern Britain*, London: The Bodley Head, 1976.

Silver, M., 'Political revolutions and repression', *Public Choice*, **17** (1974).

Smelser, N. J., *Theory of Collective Behaviour*, London: Routledge & Kegan Paul, 1962.

Spilerman, S., 'The causes of racial disturbances: a comparison of alternative explanations', *American Sociological Review*, **35** (1970).

Taylor, S., *Social Science and Revolutions*, London: Macmillan, 1983.

Thompson, E. P., *The Making of the English Working Class*, Harmondsworth: Penguin, 1968.

Thompson, E. P., *Writing by Candlelight*, London: Merlin, 1980.

Thurston, G., *The Clerkenwell Riot*, London: Allen & Unwin, 1972.

Turner, R. H. and Killian, L. M., *Collective Behaviour*, Englewood Cliffs: Prentice-Hall, 1957.

United States Department of Justice, *Prevention and Control of Urban Disorders: Issues for the 1980s*, Washington: US Government Printing Office, 1980.

Waller, P. J., *Democracy and Sectarianism: A Political and Social History of Liverpool, 1868–1939*, Liverpool: University Press, 1981.

Waller, P. J., 'The riots in Toxteth, Liverpool: a survey', *New Community*, **9**, 3 (Winter 1981/Spring 1982).

Walsh, S., 'The manufacture of excitement in police–juvenile encounters', *British Journal of Criminology*, **21**, 3 (1981).

Watson, D., *Political Violence and Liberty*, Brighton: Wheatsheaf, 1984.

White, J., 'The summer riots of 1919', *New Society*, 13 August 1981.

Whyte, W. H., *Street Corner Society*, Chicago: University of Chicago Press, 1943.

Williams, D. G. T., 'Protest and public order', *Criminal Law Journal*, 1970.

Wilson, J. G. (Ed.), *The Metropolitan Enigma*, Cambridge, Massachusetts: Harvard University Press, 1968.
Wirth, L., *On Cities and Social Life* (Ed. Reiss, A. J.), Chicago: University Press, 1964.

The media

Belson, W., *Television Violence and Adolescent Boys*, Farnborough: Saxon House, 1978.
Blumler, J. and McQuail, D., *Television in Politics*, London: Faber, 1968.
Boston, R. (Ed.), *The Press We Deserve*, London: Routledge & Kegan Paul, 1970.
Broadcasting, London: HMSO, 1978 (Cmnd 7294).
Chibnall, S., *Law and Order News*, London: Tavistock, 1977.
Clark, M. J. (Ed.), *Politics and the Media*, Oxford: Pergamon, 1979.
Clutterbuck, R., *The Media and Political Violence*, London: Macmillan, 1983.
Cohen, S. and Young, J., *The Manufacture of News*, London: Constable, 1973.
Cranfield, G. A., *The Press and Society*, London: Longman, 1978.
Curran, J. and Seaton, J., *Power Without Responsibility*, London: Fontana, 1981.
Curran, J., Gurevitch, M. and Woollacot, J. (Eds.), *Mass Communication and Society*, London: Edward Arnold, 1977.
Day, R., *Day by Day*, London: William Kimber, 1975.
Eysenck, H. J. and Nias, D. K., *Sex, Violence and the Media*, London: Temple Smith, 1978.
Francis, R., *Broadcasting to a Community in Conflict*, London: BBC, 1977.
Glasgow University Media Group, *Bad News*, London: Routledge & Kegan Paul, 1976.
Glasgow University Media Group, *Really Bad News*, London: Writers & Readers, 1982.
Golding, P. and Elliott, P., *Making the News*, London: Longman, 1979.
Golding, P. (Ed.), *Mass Media and Social Policy*, Oxford: Martin Robertson, 1984.
Halloran, J. (Ed.), *The Effects of Television*, London: Panther, 1970.
Halloran, J., Elliott, P. and Murdock, G., *Demonstrations and Communication*, Harmondsworth: Penguin, 1970.
Hartmann, P. and Husband, C., *Racism and the Mass Media*, London: Davis-Poynter, 1974.
Hood, S., *The Mass Media*, London: Macmillan, 1972.
Husband, C. (Ed.), *White Media and Black Britain*, London: Arrow, 1975.
Jenkins, S., *Newspapers: the Power and the Money*, London: Faber, 1979.
MacKuen, M. B. and Coombs, S. L., *More Than News*, London: Sage, 1981.
McQuail, D., *Sociology of Mass Communications*, Harmondsworth: Penguin, 1972.
Marcuse, H., *One Dimensional Man*, London: Routledge & Kegan Paul, 1974.
Report of the Committee on the Future of Broadcasting (The Annan Report), London: HMSO, 1977 (Cmnd 6753).
Royal Commission on the Press, 1974–77, *Final Report*, London: HMSO, 1977, (Cmnd 6810).
Schlesinger, P., *Putting 'Reality' Together: BBC News*, London: Constable, 1978.
Seymour-Ure, C., *The Political Impact of Mass Media*, London: Constable, 1974.
Smith, A. (Ed.), *British Broadcasting*, Newton Abbot: David & Charles, 1974.
Smith, A. (Ed.), *The British Press Since the War*, Newton Abbot: David & Charles, 1974.
Sumner, C. (Ed.), *Crime, Justice and the Mass Media*, Cambridge: Institute of Criminology, 1982.
Traini, R., 'Police and the press', *Police Review*, 15 June 1979.
Troyna, B., *Public Awareness and the Media: A Study of Reporting on Race*, London: Commission for Racial Equality, 1981.
Tumber, H., *Television and Riots*, London: British Film Institute, 1982.
Whale, J., *The Politics of the Media*, London: Fontana, 1977.
Wintour, C., *Pressures on the Press*, London: Andre Deutsch, 1972.

Policing issues

Ackroyd, C., Margolis, K., Rosenhead, J. and Shallice, T., *The Technology of Political Control*, Harmondsworth: Penguin, 1977.

Adorno, T. W. *et al.*, *The Authoritarian Personality*, New York: Harper & Row, 1950.
Alderson, J. and Stead, P., *The Police We Deserve*, London: Wolf, 1973.
Alderson, J., *Policing Freedom*, Plymouth: Macdonald & Evans, 1979.
Alderson, J., 'Police leadership in times of social, economic turbulence', *Police Journal*, **49**, 2 (1976).
Anderton, J., 'Accountable to whom?', *Police*, **13**, 6 (February 1981).
Ascoli, D., *The Queen's Peace*, London: Hamilton, 1979.
Association of Metropolitan Authorities, *Policies for the Police Service*, London: AMA, 1982.
Baldwin, R. and Kinsey, R., *Police Powers and Politics*, London: Quartet, 1982.
Banton, M., *The Policeman in the Community*, London: Tavistock, 1964.
Banton, M., *Police–Community Relations*, London: Collins, 1973.
Banton, M., 'Police', *The New Encyclopaedia Britannica: Macropaedia*, 14, London: Encyclopaedia Britannica, 1974.
Bayley, D. H., *Forces of Order*, Berkeley: University of California, 1976.
Bean, R., 'Police unrest, unionisation and the 1919 strike in Liverpool', *Journal of Contemporary History*, **15**, 4 (1980).
Belson, W., *The Police and the Public*, London: Harper & Row, 1975.
Blaber, A., *The Exeter Community Policing Consultative Group*, London: NACRO, 1979.
Black, D. and Reiss, A., 'Police control of juveniles', *American Sociological Review*, **35** (February 1970).
Bordua, D. (Ed.), *The Police: Six Sociological Essays*, New York: John Wiley, 1967.
Bowden, T., *Beyond the Limits of the Law*, Harmondsworth: Penguin, 1978.
Bowes, S., *The Police and Civil Liberties*, London: Lawrence & Wishart, 1966.
Brogden, A., '"Sus" is dead but what about "Sas"?', *New Community*, **9**, 1 (Summer 1981).
Brogden, M., 'A police authority—the denial of conflict', *Sociological Review*, **25**, 2 (1977).
Brogden, M., *The Police: Autonomy and Consent*, London: Academic Press, 1982.
Brown, J., *Shades of Grey*, Cranfield: Cranfield Police Studies, 1977.
Brown, J. and Howes, G. (Eds.), *The Police and the Community*, Farnborough: Saxon House, 1975.
Brown, J. and Howes, G. (Eds.), *The Cranfield Papers*, London: Peel Press, 1979.
Browne, D. G., *The Rise of New Scotland Yard*, London: Harrap, 1956.
Bunyan, T., *The Political Police in Britain*, London: Julian Friedman, 1976.
Bunyard, R. S., *Police: Organisation and Command*, Plymouth: Macdonald & Evans, 1978.
Byford, L., 'Hands off the police authorities', *Police*, **16** (March 1975).
Cain, M., *Society and the Policeman's Role*, London: Routledge & Kegan Paul, 1973.
Clarke, R. V. G. and Hough, J. M., *The Effectiveness of Policing*, London: Gower, 1980.
Coatman, J., *Police*, London: Oxford University Press, 1959.
Cobb, R., *The Police and the People*, London: Oxford University Press, 1970.
Cohen, S. (Ed.), *Images of Deviance*, Harmondsworth: Penguin, 1971.
Colman, A. N. and Gorman, L. P., 'Conservatism, dogmatism and authoritarianism in British police officers', *Sociology* (1982).
Committee of Inquiry on the Police (Chairman: Lord Edmund-Davies), *Reports on Negotiating Machinery and Pay*, London: HMSO, 1978 (Cmnd 7283).
Committee of Inquiry on the Police (Chairman: Lord Edmund-Davies), *Report III*, London: HMSO, 1979 (Cmnd 7633).
Cowell, D., Jones, T. and Young, J. (Eds.), *Policing the Riots*, London: Junction, 1982.
Cox, B., Shirley, J. and Short, M., *The Fall of Scotland Yard*, Harmondsworth: Penguin, 1977.
Critchley, T. A., *A History of Police in England and Wales*, London: Constable, 1978.
Deane-Drummond, A., *Riot Control*, London: Royal United Services Institute, 1973.
Demuth, C., *'Sus'—A Report on the Vagrancy Act, 1824*, London: Runnymede Trust, 1978.
Douglas, J. (Ed.), *Crime and Justice in American Society*, New York: Bobbs Merrill, 1971.
Evans, P., *The Police Revolution*, London: Allen & Unwin, 1974.
Fine, R., Hunt, A., McBarnet, D., and Moorhouse, B. (Eds.), *Law, State and Society*, London: Croom Helm, 1981.
Fine, R., Kinsey, R., Lea, J., Picciotto, S. and Young, J. (Eds.), *Capitalism and the Rule of Law*, London: Hutchinson, 1979.
Fox, I., 'Is there a need for a Third Force?' *Police Journal*, 1978.

Goldstein, H., *Policing a Free Society*, Cambridge, Massachusetts: Ballinger, 1977.

Hain, P. (Ed.), *Policing the Police*, volume 1, London: John Calder, 1979.

Hain, P. (Ed.), *Policing the Police*, volume 2, London: John Calder, 1980.

Hall, S., Critcher, C., Jefferson, A., Clarke, J. and Roberts, B., *Policing the Crisis: Mugging, the State and Law and Order*, London: Macmillan, 1978.

Hall, S., *Drifting into a Law and Order Society*, London: Macmillan, 1980.

Hart, J. M., *The British Police*, London: Allen & Unwin, 1951.

Heal, K. and Morris, P., *Crime Control and the Police*, Home Office Research Study, 67, London: HMSO, 1981.

Holdaway, S., 'Changes in urban policing', *British Journal of Sociology*, **28**, 2 (1977).

Holdaway, S. (Ed.), *The British Police*, London: Edward Arnold, 1979.

Home Office, *Criminal Statistics (England and Wales)*, London: HMSO, published annually by Command.

Home Office, *Research Bulletin* (published twice a year).

Hough, J. M., *Uniformed Police Work and Management Technology*, Research Unit Paper, 1, London: Home Office, 1980.

House of Commons, *Police Complaints Procedures: Fourth Report from the Home Affairs Committee, Session 1981–82*, HC 98, London: HMSO, 1982.

Howard, G., *Guardians of the Queen's Peace*, London: Odhams, 1957.

Humphry, D., *Police Power and Black People*, London: Panther, 1972.

Institute of Race Relations, *Police Against Black People*, London: IRR, 1979.

Jones, J. M., *Organisational Aspects of Police Behaviour*, London: Gower, 1980.

Judge, A., *A Man Apart*, London: Arthur Baker, 1972.

Judge, A., 'The police and the coloured communities: a police view', *New Community*, **3**, 3 (Summer 1974).

Judge, A., 'Alderson's Law', *Police* (October 1981).

Judge, A., 'Scarman: Police Responses', *New Community*, **9**, 3 (Winter 1981/Spring 1982).

Judge, A. and Reynolds, G., *The Night the Police Went on Strike*, London: Weidenfeld, 1968.

Keeton, G. W., *Keeping the Peace*, Chichester: Barry Rose, 1975.

Kettle, M., 'The police take a political road', *New Society*, **51** (1980).

King, J. F. S. (Ed.), *Control Without Custody?*, Cambridge: Institute of Criminology, 1976.

Lambert, J. R., *Crime, Police and Race Relations*, London: Oxford University Press, 1970.

Lane, T., 'Liverpool: city in crisis', *Marxism Today*, **22** (1978).

Leigh, L. H., *Police Powers in England and Wales*, London: Butterworth, 1975.

Littlejohn, G. *et al.* (Eds.), *Power and the State*, London: Croom Helm, 1978.

McCabe, S. and Sutcliffe, F., *Defining Crime: a Study of Police Decisions*, Oxford: Blackwell, 1978.

McClure, J., *Spike Island: Portrait of a Police Division*, London: Macmillan, 1980.

Manning, P., *Police Work*, London: M.I.T. Press, 1977.

Mark, R., *Policing a Perplexed Society*, London: Allen & Unwin, 1977.

Mark, R., *In the Office of Constable*, London: Constable, 1978.

Marshall, G., *Police and Government: the Status and Accountability of the English Constable*, London: Methuen, 1965.

Mawby, R., *Policing the City*, Farnborough: Saxon House, 1979.

Miller, W. R., *Cops and Bobbies*, Chicago: University Press, 1977.

Minto, G. A., *Thin Blue Line*, London: Hodder & Stoughton, 1965.

Moore, C. and Brown, J., *Community versus Crime*, London: Bedford Square Press, 1981.

National Advisory Committee on Criminal Justice Standards and Goals, *Police*, Washington: US Government Printing Office, 1973.

National Youth Bureau, *Young People and the Police*, London: NYB, 1979.

Norris, D. F., *Police–Community Relations: a Programme that Failed*, Lexington: Lexington Books, 1973.

Plehwe, R., 'Police and government: the Commissioners of Police for the Metropolis', *Public Law* (1974).

Police Complaints Board, *Triennial Review Report*, London: HMSO, 1980 (Cmnd 7966).

Police Complaints Board, *Triennial Review Report*, London: HMSO, 1983 (Cmnd 8853).

Police Training Council, *Community and Race Relations Training for the Police*, London: Home Office, March 1983.

Pope, D. and Weiner, N. (Eds.), *Modern Policing*, London: Croom Helm, 1981.

Powis, D., *The Signs of Crime: A Field Manual for Police*, London: McGraw Hill, 1977.

Punch, M., *Policing the Inner City*, London: Macmillan, 1979.

Regan, D. E., 'Enhancing the role of police committees', *Public Administration*, **61**, 1 (Spring 1983).

Regan, D. E., *Are the Police under Control?*, Research Paper 1, London: The Social Affairs Unit, 1983.

Reiner, R., *The Blue Coated Worker*, Cambridge: University Press, 1978.

Reiner, R., 'Black and blue: race and the police', *New Society*, 17 September 1981.

Reiner, R., 'Who are the police?', *The Political Quarterly*, **53**, 2 (April–June 1982).

Reith, C., *British Police and the Democratic Ideal*, London: Oxford University Press, 1943.

Reith, C., *A New Study of Police History*, London: Oliver & Boyd, 1956.

Report of Her Majesty's Chief Inspector of Constabulary, London: HMSO, annually.

Report of the Commissioner of Police for the Metropolis, London: HMSO, annually.

Report of the Committee on Police Conditions of Service (The Oaksey Committee), London: HMSO, 1949 (Cmnd 7831).

Rosenhead, J., 'The technology of riot control', *New Scientist*, 23 July 1981.

Royal Commission on Police Powers and Procedure, *Report*, London: HMSO, 1929 (Cmnd 3297).

Royal Commission on the Police, *Interim Report*, London: HMSO, 1960 (Cmnd 1222).

Royal Commission on the Police, *Final Report*, London: HMSO, 1962 (Cmnd 1728).

Royal Commission on Criminal Procedure, *Report*, London: HMSO, 1981 (Cmnd 8092).

Russell, K., *Complaints against the Police*, Leicester: Milltake, 1976.

Schaffer, E. B., *Community Policing*, London: Croom Helm, 1980.

Steer, D., *Police Cautions: A Study in the Exercise of Police Discretion*, Oxford: Blackwell, 1970.

Stevens, P. and Willis, C. F., *Race, Crime and Arrests*, Home Office Research Study, 58, London: HMSO, 1979.

Stevens, P. and Willis, C. F., *Ethnic Minorities and Complaints Against the Police*, Research Unit Paper, 5, London: Home Office, 1982.

Taylor, I., *Law and Order: Arguments for Socialism*, London: Macmillan, 1981.

Tobias, J. J., *Crime and Police in England, 1700–1900*, London: Gill & Macmillan, 1979.

Tuck, M. and Southgate, P., *Ethnic Minorities, Crime and Policing*, Home Office Research Study, 70, London: HMSO, 1981.

Walker, S., *A Critical History of Police Reform*, New York: Lexington, 1977.

Whitaker, B., *The Police*, London: Eyre Methuen, 1964.

Whitaker, B., *The Police in Society*, London: Sinclair Browne, 1982.

Whitelaw, W., 'The police and the public: the James Smart memorial lecture', *Police Review* (26 September 1980).

Wilson, J. Q., *Varieties of Police Behaviour*, Cambridge, Massachusetts: Harvard University Press, 1970.

Zander, M., 'Police powers', *The Political Quarterly*, **53**, 2 (April–June 1982).

Racialism and racial disadvantage

Association of Directors of Social Services, *Multi-Racial Britain: The Social Services Response*, London: Commission for Racial Equality, 1978.

Bagley, C., 'The education of immigrant children', *Journal of Social Policy*, **2**, 4 (1973).

Bagley, C. and Verma, G. K., *Racial Prejudice, the Individual and Society*, Farnborough: Saxon House, 1979.

Banton, M., *The Idea of Race*, London: Tavistock, 1977.

Banton, M., *Racial and Ethnic Competition*, Cambridge: University Press, 1983.

Bethnal Green and Stepney Trades Council, *Blood on the Streets: A Report on Racial Attacks in East London*, London: The Trades Council, 1978.

Billig, M., *Fascists: a Social Psychological View of the National Front*, London: Academic Press, 1978.

Braham, P., *et al.* (Eds.), *Discrimination and Disadvantage in Employment*, London: Harper & Row, 1981.

Brooks, D. and Singh, R., *Aspirations versus Opportunities*, London: Commission for Racial Equality, 1978.

Burney, E., *Housing on Trial*, London: Oxford University Press, 1967.

Carby, K. and Thakur, M., *No Problem Here?*, London: Institute of Personnel Management, 1977.

Cashmore, E., *Rastaman*, London: Allen & Unwin, 1979.

Centre for Contemporary Cultural Studies, *The Empire Strikes Back*, London: Hutchinson, 1982.

Cheetham, J. *et al.* (Eds.), *Social and Community Work in a Multi-racial Society*, London: Harper & Row, 1981.

Cheetham, J. (Ed.), *Ethnicity and Social Work*, London: Allen & Unwin, 1982.

Cohen, A. (Ed.), *Urban Ethnicity*, London: Tavistock, 1974.

Commission for Racial Equality, *Local Government and Racial Equality*, London: CRE, 1982.

Committee of Inquiry into the Education of Children from Ethnic Minority Groups (Chairman: Mr A. Rampton), *Interim Report: West Indian Children in our Schools*, London, HMSO, 1981 (Cmnd 8273).

Connelly, N., *Social Service Provision in Multi-racial Areas*, London: Policy Studies Institute, 1981.

Crick, T., 'Black youth, crime and related problems', *Youth in Society*, **40** (1980).

Cross, C., *Ethnic Minorities in the Inner City*, London: Commission for Racial Equality, 1978.

Daniel, W. W., *Racial Discrimination in England*, Harmondsworth: Penguin, 1968.

Deakin, N., *Colour, Citizenship and British Society*, London: Panther, 1970.

Dummett, A., *A Portrait of English Racism*, Harmondsworth: Penguin, 1973.

Field, S., Mair, G., Rees, T. and Stevens, P., *Ethnic Minorities in Britain*, Home Office Research Study, 68, London: HMSO, 1981.

File, N. and Power, C., *Black Settlers in Britain, 1555–1958*, London: Heinemann, 1981.

Foot, P., *Immigration and Race in British Politics*, Harmondsworth: Penguin, 1965.

Glazer, N. and Young, K. (Eds.), *Ethnic Pluralism and Public Policy*, London: Heinemann, 1983.

Gordon, P., *Passport Raids and Checks*, London: Runnymede Trust, 1981.

Hiro, D., *Black British, White British*, Harmondsworth: Penguin, 1973.

Home Office, *Observations on the Report of the Select Committee on Race Relations and Immigration*, London: HMSO, 1978 (Cmnd 7287).

Home Office, *Racial Attacks*, report of a Home Office study, London: November 1981.

House of Commons, *Race Relations and the 'Sus' Law: Second Report from the Home Affairs Committee, Session 1979–80*, HC 559, London: HMSO, 1980.

House of Commons, *Racial Disadvantage: Fifth Report from the Home Affairs Committee, Session 1980–81*, HC 424, London: HMSO, 1981.

House of Commons, *Commission for Racial Equality: First Report from the Home Affairs Committee, Session 1981–82*, HC 46, London: HMSO, 1981.

House of Commons, *Ethnic and Racial Questions in the Census: Second Report from the Home Affairs Committee, Session 1982–83*, HC 33, London: HMSO, 1983.

Humphry, D. and John, G., *Because They're Black*, Harmondsworth: Penguin, 1971.

Humphry, D. and Ward, M., *Passports and Politics*, Harmondsworth: Penguin, 1974.

Husband, C., *'Race' in Britain*, London: Hutchinson, 1982.

Husbands, C. T., 'Contemporary right-wing extremism in Western European democracies', *European Journal of Political Research*, **9** (1981).

Jones, C., *Immigration and Social Policy in Britain*, London: Tavistock, 1977.

Jones, J. M., *Prejudice and Racism*, Cambridge, Massachusetts: Addison-Wesley, 1972.

Kapo, R., *A Savage Culture: Racism—A Black British View*, London: Quartet, 1981.

Katznelson, I., *Black Men, White Cities*, London: Oxford University Press, 1973.

Lawrence, D., *Black Migrants, White Natives*, Cambridge: University Press, 1974.

Littlewood, R. and Lipsedge, M., *Aliens and Alienists*, Harmondsworth: Penguin, 1982.

Lustgarten, L., *Legal Control of Racial Discrimination*, London: Macmillan, 1981.

Macdonald, I., *Race Relations—the New Law*, London: Butterworth, 1977.

Miles, R. and Phizacklea, A. (Eds.), *Racism and Political Action in Britain*, London: Routledge & Kegan Paul, 1979.

Miles, R. and Phizacklea, A., *Labour and Racism*, London: Routledge & Kegan Paul, 1980.

Moore, R., *Racism and Black Resistance in Britain*, London: Pluto Press, 1975.

Ouseley, H. et al., *The System*, London: Runnymede Trust, 1981.

Patterson, S., *Dark Strangers*, London: Tavistock, 1963.

Peach, C., Robinson, V. and Smith, S. (Eds.), *Ethnic Segregation in Cities*, London: Croom Helm, 1982.

Race Relations, London: HMSO, 1975 (Cmnd 6234).

Race Today (various issues).

Racial Disadvantage: The Government Reply to the Fifth Report from the Home Affairs Committee, Session 1980–81, HC 424, London: HMSO, January 1982 (Cmnd 8476).

Ratcliffe, P., *Racism and Reaction*, London: Routledge & Kegan Paul, 1981.

Rex, J., *Race Relations in Sociological Theory*, London: Weidenfeld & Nicolson, 1970.

Rex, J., *Race, Colonialism and the City*, London: Routledge & Kegan Paul, 1973.

Rex, J. and Moore, R., *Race, Community and Conflict*, London: Oxford University Press, 1967.

Rex, J. and Tomlinson, S., *Colonial Immigrants in a British City*, London: Routledge & Kegan Paul, 1979.

Rose, E. et al., *Colour and Citizenship*, London: Oxford University Press, 1969.

Runnymede Trust, *Beyond Tokenism*, London: The Trust, 1978.

Select Committee on Race Relations and Immigration, *Report on Police/Immigrant Relations*, HC 71, London: HMSO, 1972.

Select Committee on Race Relations and Immigration, *Immigration*, HC 303, London: HMSO, 1978.

Simpson, A., *Stacking the Decks*, Nottingham: Community Relations Council, 1981.

Sivanandan, A., 'Race, class and the state: the black experience in Britain', *Race and Class*, 17, 4 (1979).

Skellington, R., 'How blacks lose out in council housing', *New Society*, 29 January 1981.

Smith, D. J., *The Facts of Racial Disadvantage*, P.E.P. Broadsheet 560, London: Political and Economic Planning, 1976.

Smith, D. J., *Racial Disadvantage in Britain*, Harmondsworth: Penguin, 1977.

Smith, D. J., *Unemployment and Racial Minorities*, London: Policy Studies Institute, 1981.

Sonte, M., *The Education of the Black Child in Britain*, London: Fontana, 1981.

Studlar, D. T., 'Social context and attitudes towards coloured immigrants', *British Journal of Sociology*, 28 (1977).

The Application of Race Relations Policy in the Civil Service, London: Tavistock Institute of Human Relations, 1978.

Taylor, S., *The National Front in English Politics*, London: Macmillan, 1982.

Walker, M., *The National Front*, London: Fontana, 1977.

Wallman, S. (Ed.), *Ethnicity at Work*, London: Macmillan, 1979.

Young, K. and Connelly, N., *Ethnic Record Keeping in Local Authorities: A Discussion Paper*, London: Policy Studies Institute, 1981.

Young, K. and Connelly, N., *Policy and Practice in the Multi-racial City*, London: Policy Studies Institute, 1981.

Young, K. and Connelly, N., *After the Act: Policy Review for Local Authorities in Multi-racial Areas*, London: Policy Studies Institute, 1983.

Zubaida, S. (Ed.), *Race and Racialism*, London: Tavistock, 1970.

Inner city deprivation and urban politics

Abel-Smith, B. and Townsend, P., *The Poor and the Poorest*, London: Bell, 1965.

Agger, R., Goldrich, D. and Swanson, B. E., *The Rulers and the Ruled*, New York: Wiley, 1964.

Ambrose, P. and Colenutt, B., *The Property Machine*, Harmondsworth: Penguin, 1975.

Ashton, D. N., *The Sociology of Unemployment*, Brighton: Wheatsheaf, 1984.

Bachrach, P. and Baratz, M., *Power and Poverty*, New York: Oxford University Press, 1970.
Bailey, R., *The Homeless and the Empty Houses*, Harmondsworth: Penguin, 1977.
Banting, K., *Poverty, Politics and Policy*, London: Macmillan, 1979.
Barnet, R. J., *The Lean Years: Politics in the Age of Scarcity*, London: Abacus, 1980.
Barr, J., *Derelict Britain*, Harmondsworth: Penguin, 1972.
Benington, J., *Local Government becomes Big Business*, London: CDP Intelligence Unit, 1976.
Berry, F., *Housing: The Great British Failure*, London: Charles Knight, 1974.
Boaden, N. T., *Urban Policy Making*, Cambridge: University Press, 1971.
Broadbent, T. A., *Planning and Profit in the Urban Economy*, London: Methuen, 1977.
Burgess, T. and Travers, T., *Ten Billion Pounds*, London: Grant McIntyre, 1980.
Castells, M., *The Urban Question*, London: Edward Arnold, 1977.
Castells, M., *City, Class and Power*, London: Macmillan, 1978.
Central Government Controls over Local Authorities, London: HMSO, 1979 (Cmnd 7634).
Central Office of Information, *Britain 1983: An Official Handbook*, London: HMSO, 1983.
Coates, K. and Silburn, R., *Poverty: The Forgotten Englishmen*, Harmondsworth: Penguin, 1981.
Cobb, R. W. and Elder, C., *Participation in American Politics: The Dynamics of Agenda Building*, Baltimore: Johns Hopkins, 1975.
Cockburn, C., *The Local State*, London: Pluto, 1978.
Committee of Inquiry into Local Government Finance (the Layfield Committee), *Report*, London: HMSO, 1976 (Cmnd 6453).
Community Development Project, *The Poverty of the Improvement Programme*, London: CDP Intelligence Unit, 1975.
Community Development Project, *Gilding the Ghetto; the State and Poverty Experiments*, London: Home Office, 1977.
Cox, W. H., *Cities: The Public Dimension*, Harmondsworth: Penguin, 1976.
Crenson, M., *The Unpolitics of Air Pollution*, Baltimore: Johns Hopkins, 1971.
Crick, B. (Ed.), *Unemployment*, London: Methuen, 1981.
Crouch, C., *British Political Sociology Yearbook, Volume 3: Participation in Politics*, London: Croom Helm, 1977.
Cullingworth, J. B., *Town and Country Planning in Britain*, London: Allen & Unwin, 1979.
Dahl, R. A., *Who Governs? Democracy and Power in an American City*, New Haven: Yale University Press, 1961.
Davies, J. G., *The Evangelistic Bureaucrat*, London: Tavistock, 1972.
Dearlove, J., *The Politics of Policy in Local Government*, London: Cambridge University Press, 1973.
Dennis, N., *Public Participation and Planners Blight*, London: Faber, 1972.
Department of the Environment, *Unequal City: Final Report of the Birmingham Inner Area Study*, London: HMSO, 1977.
Department of the Environment, *Inner London: Policies for Dispersal and Balance; Final Report of the Lambeth Inner Area Study*, London: HMSO, 1977.
Department of the Environment, *Change and Decay: Final Report of the Liverpool Inner Area Study*, London: HMSO, 1977.
Department of the Environment, *Inner Area Studies: Summaries of Consultants' Final Reports*, London: HMSO, 1977.
Department of the Environment, *Factual Background Document to Present Inner City Policy and Urban Programme*, London: Inner Cities Directorate, 1981.
Donnison, D., *The Politics of Poverty*, Oxford: Martin Robertson, 1982.
Donnison, D. and Soto, P., *The Good City*, London: Heinemann, 1980.
Donnison, D. and Ungerson, C., *Housing Policy*, Harmondsworth: Penguin, 1982.
Dror, Y., *Public Policymaking Re-examined*, London: Leonard Hill, 1973.
Duclaud-Williams, R. H., *The Politics of Housing in Britain and France*, London: Heinemann, 1978.
Dunleavy, P., *Urban Political Analysis*, London: Macmillan, 1980.
Dunleavy, P., *The Politics of Mass Housing in Britain, 1945–75*, Oxford: Clarendon, 1982.
Edwards, J., 'Social indicators, urban deprivation and positive discrimination', *Journal of Social Policy*, **4**, 3 (1975).

Edwards, J. and Batley, R., *The Politics of Positive Discrimination*, London: Tavistock, 1978.
Elliott, B. and McCrone, D., *The City*, London: Macmillan, 1982.
English, J., Madigan, R. and Norman, P., *Slum Clearance*, London: Croom Helm, 1976.
Field, F. (Ed.), *Low Pay*, London: Arrow, 1973.
Field, F., *Inequality in Britain*, London: Fontana, 1981.
Friend, A. and Metcalf, A., *Slump City: The Politics of Mass Unemployment*, London: Pluto, 1981.
Gibson, M. and Langstaff, M. J., *An Introduction to Urban Renewal*, London: Hutchinson, 1982.
Goldsmith, M., *Politics, Planning and the City*, London: Hutchinson, 1980.
Goodman, R., *After the Planners*, Harmondsworth: Penguin, 1972.
Gyford, J., *Local Politics in Britain*, London: Croom Helm, 1976.
Hall, P. *et al.*, *Change, Choice and Conflict in Social Policy*, London: Heinemann, 1975.
Hall, P. (Ed.), *The Inner City in Context*, London: Heinemann, 1981.
Hambleton, R., *Policy, Planning and Local Government*, London: Hutchinson, 1978.
Hampton, W., *Democracy and Community*, London: Oxford University Press, 1970.
Harloe, M. (Ed.), *Captive Cities*, London: Wiley, 1977.
Harvey, D., *Social Justice and the City*, London: Arnold, 1973.
Hawkins, K., *Unemployment*, Harmondsworth: Penguin, 1979.
Higgins, J., *The Poverty Business: Britain and America*, Oxford: Blackwell, 1978.
Higgins, J. *et al.*, *Government and Urban Poverty*, Oxford: Blackwell, 1983.
Hindess, B., *The Decline of Working Class Politics*, London: MacGibbon & Kee, 1971.
Hirsch, F., *The Social Limits to Growth*, London: Routledge & Kegan Paul, 1977.
Hirschman, A. D., *Exit, Voice and Loyalty*, Cambridge, Massachusetts: Harvard University Press, 1970.
Hogwood, B. and Peters, B. G., *Policy Dynamics*, Brighton: Wheatsheaf, 1982.
Home, R. K., *Inner City Regeneration*, London: Spon, 1982.
Jackson, P. M., Meadows, J. and Taylor, A. P., 'Urban fiscal decay in UK cities', *Local Government Studies*, 8, 5 (September/October 1982).
Jacobs, J., *The Death and Life of Great American Cities*, Harmondsworth: Penguin, 1965.
Jenkins, W., *Policy Analysis*, Oxford: Martin Robertson, 1978.
Jones, C. (Ed.), *Urban Deprivation and the Inner City*, London: Croom Helm, 1979.
Jordan, W., *Automatic Poverty*, London: Routledge & Kegan Paul, 1981.
Jordan, W., *Mass Unemployment and the Future of Britain*, Oxford: Blackwell, 1982.
Lansley, S., *Housing and Public Policy*, London: Croom Helm, 1979.
Lawless, P., *Urban Deprivation and Government Initiative*, London: Faber, 1979.
Lindblom, C., *The Policy Making Process*, Englewood Cliffs, New Jersey: Prentice Hall, 1968.
Loney, M. and Allen, M. (Eds.), *The Crisis of the Inner City*, London: Macmillan, 1979.
Lukes, S., *Power: A Radical View*, London: Macmillan, 1974.
MacGregor, S., *The Politics of Poverty*, London: Longman, 1981.
McKay, D. and Cox, A., *The Politics of Urban Change*, London: Croom Helm, 1979.
Malpass, P. and Murie, A., *Housing Policy and Practice*, London: Macmillan, 1982.
Marshall, T. H., *Social Policy*, London: Hutchinson, 1975.
Mishra, R., *Society and Social Policy*, London: Macmillan, 1981.
Murie, A., Niner, P. and Watson, C., *Housing Policy and the Housing System*, London: Allen & Unwin, 1976.
Newton, K., *Second City Politics*, London: Oxford University Press, 1976.
O'Connor, J., *The Fiscal Crisis of the State*, London: St. James, 1973.
Offe, C. (edited by Keane, J.), *Dilemmas of the Welfare State*, London: Hutchinson, 1984.
Pahl, R., *Whose City?*, Harmondsworth: Penguin, 1975.
Policy for the Inner Cities, London: HMSO, 1977 (Cmnd 6845).
Polsby, N., *Community Power and Political Theory*, New Haven: Yale University Press, 1963.
Presthus, R., *Men at the Top*, New York: Oxford University Press, 1964.
Ravetz, A., *Remaking Cities*, London: Croom Helm, 1980.
Richardson, J. J. and Jordan, A. G., *Governing under Pressure*, Oxford: Martin Robertson, 1979.
Righter, R., *Save Our Cities*, London: Gulbenkian Trust, 1977.

Roberts, K., Duggan, J. and Noble, M., *Unregistered Youth Unemployment and Outreach Careers Work*, Parts I and II, Research Papers 31 and 32, London: Department of Employment, 1981 and 1982.

Rose, R. (Ed.), *Lessons from America*, London: Macmillan, 1974.

Rose, R., *Politics in England*, London: Faber, 1980.

Rose, R. and Page, E. (Eds.), *Fiscal Stress in the Cities*, Cambridge: University Press, 1981.

Runciman, W. G., *Relative Deprivation and Social Justice*, London: Routledge & Kegan Paul, 1966.

Rutter, M. and Madge, N., *Cycles of Disadvantage*, London: Heinemann, 1976.

Saunders, P., *Urban Politics*, London: Penguin, 1980.

Schattschneider, E. E., *The Semisovereign People*, New York: Holt, Rinehart & Winston, 1961.

Showler, B. and Sinfield, A. (Eds.), *The Workless State*, Oxford: Martin Robertson, 1981.

Simmie, J. M., *Citizens in Conflict*, London: Hutchinson, 1974.

Sinfield, A., *What Unemployment Means*, Oxford: Martin Robertson, 1981.

Smith, M. P., *The City and Social Theory*, Oxford: Blackwell, 1980.

Social Trends, London: HMSO, published annually.

Stewart, J., Spencer, K. and Webster, B., *Local Government and Urban Deprivation*, London: Home Office, 1974.

The Government's Expenditure Plans, 1983–84 to 1985–86, London: HMSO, February 1983 (Cmnd 8789).

Walker, A. (Ed.), *Public Expenditure and Social Policy*, London: Heinemann, 1982.

Webman, J. A., *Reviving the Industrial City*, London: Croom Helm, 1982.

Wedderburn, D. (Ed.), *Poverty, Inequality and Class Structure*, Cambridge: University Press, 1974.

Westergaard, J. and Resler, H., *Class in a Capitalist Society*, Harmondsworth: Penguin, 1976.

Wilding, P., *Professional Power and Social Welfare*, London: Routledge & Kegan Paul, 1982.

Young, K. and Mills, L., *Managing the Post-Industrial City*, London: Heinemann, 1983.

Index

Police—*contd*

tension with youths 6, 7, 28, 38, 46–50, 54–60 *passim*, 63–7, 73–80 *passim*, 82–5, 87–93, 99, 146, 149–50, 175, 199

training 30, 61, 103, 104–5, 110, 111, 116, 121–3, 125, 129, 132–3, 136, 140, 150, 154, 216, 217, 244, 245, 247–8, 250, 256, 260

Watch Committees 108, 136

young officers in 38, 63, 100, 105, 116, 121, 132, 248

see also Brixton, policing in; Crime; Inner cities; Lambeth; Law enforcement; Liverpool 8; London; Metropolitan Police; Racial discrimination; riots; Scarman, Lord

Police 9, 18, 108, 112

Police Act 1964 99, 137, 155, 163, 191, 250, 256

Police Act 1976 109

Police Advisory Board 132, 134

Police and Criminal Evidence Bill 1982–3 15, 19, 72, 101, 107, 110, 146, 149, 151, 155, 157, 234, 238, 249, 256–7, 260

Police Central Planning Unit 150

Police Complaints Board 15, 109–10, 131, 147–9, 237

Police Discipline Code 103, 108, 130, 131, 134, 260

Police Federation of England and Wales 7, 9, 108, 109, 110, 111, 125, 130, 131, 133, 134, 142, 153, 154, 200, 210, 256

Police Magazine 52

Police, Ministry of 100

Police National Computer 119–21

Police Review 9, 18

Police Staff College, Bramshill 122, 133, 248

Police Superintendents Association 134, 142, 256

Police Training Council 104, 112, 133, 134, 247–8, 256

Policies for the Police Service 141

Policy for the Inner Cities 170, 174, 192–9 *passim*, 214–5, 219

Political

agenda 11–17, 24, 73, 88–9, 205, 217, 239–42

demonstrations 3, 28, 29, 70, 144, 260

institutions 21–31 *passim*, 69–71, 81, 185–6, 189, 235, 238

marginalisation 236

parties 12, 16, 31, 81, 85, 108, 118, 137, 182, 202, 209, 223, 224

Political—*contd*

parties—*contd*

see also Conservative Party; Labour Party; Liberal Party; National Front; Social Democratic Party

perspectives on riots 20–34 *passim*

polarisation 111, 239

Political power

and decisions 11–17, 24, 25–7, 31, 88, 136, 222–3, 235–42

ethnic minorities and 10, 22, 28, 30, 32–3, 53, 70, 172, 182, 188, 189–90, 202, 204, 222, 223

in society 12, 21, 24, 26–7, 32–3, 54, 62, 70–1, 202, 205, 206, 235–40

policing and 13, 70–1, 88, 118, 126–8, 136–7, 139, 141–2, 143–4, 152–6 *passim*, 158

Politicians

ethnic minorities and 14, 182, 202–3, 220, 223, 225

police and 4–7, 9–10, 88–9, 127, 130, 131, 136, 139, 143–4, 146

riots and 3–6, 7–9, 12, 13, 78–9, 86, 165

Scarman Report and 8–9, 10–11, 16, 233

see also Councillors; House of Commons; Parliament; *also under individual politicians' names*

The Political Quarterly 112, 113

Political and Economic Planning (PEP) 173, 206, 212, 219

Porter, Bruce 52

Positive action

and employment 14, 29, 103, 167, 180, 199, 203, 207–8, 210–18 *passim*, 222, 226, 234, 253

criticisms of 8, 10, 167, 210–11, 255

in education 29, 168, 180, 203–4, 209, 214

Scarman Report and 8, 10, 29, 30, 103, 166, 167, 168, 173, 204–5, 208–11, 215, 220–1, 223, 225, 227–8, 233–4, 254–5, 261

to combat racial disadvantage 9, 29, 167–8, 173, 180, 199, 202, 205, 207–10, 214–16, 220–9 *passim*, 234, 242, 252–5, 261

see also Deprivation; Education; Employment; Ethnic minorities; Racial disadvantage

Positive discrimination 29, 30, 167, 207, 208, 210, 213, 227–8, 255, 261

Powell, Enoch 6, 18, 52, 169

Power, C. 206

Poverty 5, 27–8, 68, 178, 240

Prashar, Usha xi, 167, 173, 207–19

Pratt, Michael 92, 95